FUNCTIONAL CRITICISM

Essays in British American Commonwealth Literature

C. Vimala Rao

ANMOL PUBLICATIONS PVT. LTD.
NEW DELHI - 110 002 (INDIA)

ANMOL PUBLICATIONS PVT. LTD.
4374/4B, Ansari Road, Daryaganj
New Delhi - 110 002
Ph.: 23261597, 23278000
Visit us at: www.anmolpublications.com

Functional Criticism

First Published, 2004

ISBN 81-261-1799-0

PRINTED IN INDIA

Published by J.L. Kumar for Anmol Publications Pvt. Ltd., New Delhi - 110 002 and Printed at Mehra Offset Press, Delhi.

Contents

Acknowledgement

These articles were written over a period of three decades in my forty-years' experience as a teacher in universities in India and abroad. They are being collected together for the first time, with the hope that they will prove to be popular essays which will interest not only teachers, researchers, and crities but also general readers who are curious about writing and the world of literary work. Literature, after all has the beauty of being ageless, and also being timely, paradoxically enough!

Many of these essays were published individually in academic journals and anthologies. I am grateful to the editors/publishers of the following journals/anthologies for permission in reprint them:

The Indian Journal of American Studies (Hyderabad); *Literary Endeavour* (Hyderabad); *Litterit* (Kerala); *Chandrabhaga* (Orissa); *Comparative Literature Studies* (U.S.A.); *Clues: A Journal of Detection* (U.S.A.); *Commonwealth Quarterly* (Mysore); *The Deccan Herald* (Bangalore); *American Literature Today* (New Delhi); *The Girl-Child in 20th Century Indian Literature* Ed. Viney Kirpal; Sterling Publishers Pvt. Ltd., New Delhi, 1992 for the article "Markandaya's *Two Virgins* and Desai's *Fire on the Mountain*"; *Commonwealth and American Women's Discourse,* ed. A.L. Mcleod/Sterling Publishers Pvt. Ltd., New Delhi, 1996, for article "Asian American Women's fiction and their Ethnic Discourse"; *Commonwealth and American Nobely Laureates in Literature,* ed. A.L. McLeod/

Sterling Publishers Pvt. Ltd., New Delhi, 1998 for article "Theme in Patrick White's *A Fringe of Leaves*"; *Commonwealth Literature: Themes and Techniques*, eds. P.K. Rajan, K.M. George, Jameela Begum, K. Radha/Ajanta Publications (New Delhi), 1993, for article "Parallel Symmetries S. Naipaul's *Adventures of Gurudeva* and V.S. Naipaul's *Miguel Street*"; *Manushi* (New Delhi) ed. Madhu Kishwar for article, "History as Metafiction: The Ayodhya theme in Shashi Deshpande's *Small Remedies*".

C. Vimala Rao

Bangalore

May, 2003

1

The Love Theme in Shakespeare's *King Lear*

If T.S. Eliot felt that Shakespeare's *Hamlet* was intractable, others before him have found *King Lear* even more so. Although stylistically *King Lear* is the simplest of Shakespeare's tragedies, it has intrigued generations of readers and actors by its richness and depth of themes relating to the very meaning of the cosmic existence of man and his universe. The alarming transformation that Nahum Tate gave to the tragedy in order to make it acceptable to his own contemporaries in the 18th century met with unequivocal approval for over a hundred years and his version continued to be more popular than that of Shakespeare. Dr. Johnson, and later Tolstoy, did not help much by their outspoken and vehement comments against Shakespeare's play. It was left for the gentle Charles Lamb to perceive Tate's game when he wrote: "Tate. has put his hook in the nostrils of this Leviathan for Garrick and his followers, the showmen of the scheme, to draw the mighty beast about more easily."[1] By his acute analysis of the dualism of the role of Lear as man and King, Lamb restored the original play of Shakespeare, with all its immense possibilities, to the general audience.

Besides the interpretation of Lear's character, which is indeed the main problem confronting the actor as well as the reader, the understanding of the central meaning of the play perplexes the thoughtful reader. Why did Shakespear, in the first place, base *Lear* on so many negatives in speech, action, and resolution? The play bristles with negatives, starting with Cordelia's assertion of "Nothing" in the very beginning of the play, to Lear's five times repeated "Never" at the end when he enters with Cordelia's body in his arms. The lingering impression left in the minds of the readers is that of a final realization of the futility or inefficacy of the basic feeling in life called love.

Maynard Mack believes that *King Lear* is not to be taken as realistic, psychological drama, but is to be considered more as a "...Romance, Morality play, and Vision."[2] Accordingly, he believes that the play ends with "... Lear's new acquistion of self-knowledge and devotion to Cordelia, the majesty of his integrity and endurance, the invicinibleness of his hope."[3] Although it is granted that it would not do to convert Lear into a domestic tragedy, it cannot be denied that the deepest meaning of the play can emerge for the modern reader only when he considers the events in the tragedy in relation to his own existence and the reality of the life around him. After a close analysis of one such universally related, basic theme in the play, namely, the love theme - one wonders if *King Lear* really ends on such a high, edifying note as Maynard Mack credits it with.

Just as the three daughters of Lear are to stand or fall by the profession of their love for their father, the play itself is to be judged according to the meaning and efficacy it invests on the love theme. Criticism has been overly kind to the King. Following his own exclamations of self-pity and declarations of bewilderment, readers have a tendency to treat Lear more as a man sinned against than sinning. Yet Lear is the most culpable of Shakespeare's tragic heroes and he himself must undoubtedly bear the responsibility for the tragic occurrences in the Lear-world from the beginning. He commits the worst crime given to a human being to commit - he kills love. In doing so, he commits a crime that is more violent than that of the Ancient Mariner, and the consequences of his act cut deeper than his own selfish heart. His act is knowingly wilful and vicious, unlike that of the Mariner who killed a stray bird idly, and thus Lear perceptibly throws out of gear the very cosmic pattern of the universe and destroys the essential order at the heart of human relationships. Macbeth kills sleep and peace when he kills Duncan, but Lear kills the meaning of life when he banishes love from his kingdom. His is a crime that goes beyond folly and beyond tragedy, taking us to the dead centre of chaos, a void where love is proved to be no more than a delusion, utterly impotent and ineffectual by the time it is given some recognition.

Wilson Knight believes that Lear's tragedy is a failure of the mind. He writes: "His judgement is nothing. He understands neither himself nor his daughters. Lear starts his own tragedy by a foolish misjudgement. Lear's fault is a fault of the mind, a mind unwarrantably, because selfishly, foolish."[4]

But in my opinion, the more significant failure in Lear is the failure in understanding love. The very first scene in the play is a vivid mockery of love and it is Lear who has reduced it to this state. That Lear was ignorant of parental love, as ignorant as a weak old man, can be seen even before our attention is focussed on the actual events of the first scene. At the very beginning, when he is dividing the kingdom, he starts by doing it unequally with a larger portion for Cordelia than for Goneril and Regan. Why should he do this? Is he not forcing Goneril and Regan to play their game of flattery and deception? This was unwarranted in his responsibility as a father. It was not just a failure of judgement in Lear, it was a deeper a failure of character in Lear for Lear appears to be incapable of the instinct of loving his daughters equally. In the violence of his rhetoric, he is quicker in using the word "hate" than "love". In the very first scene, Kent becomes a "hated back" and Cordelia is "... new-adopted to .... hate ...." in no time. He dwells on his hate for Cordelia and advises the Duke of France to ".... avert (his) liking a more worthier way." (*King Lear*, I, ii. 210).

Not only is Lear himself incapable of proper love, but he is also the cause of lovelessness and growing hatred in others around him. This is especially seen in the way the characters of Goneril and Regan develop. Though it must be granted that their professions of love at the beginning are to be taken more as flattery than as the expression of their genuine feelings,we realize that they do not change suddenly into monsters, as we look at their characters unfold. Goneril's complaint that the retainers of Lear are noisy and troublesome might very well be justifiable. The King himself has not shown many signs of order and balance, and it is not difficult to imagine that his followers would be disorderly. We notice that Lear provokes and goads Goneril's displeasure considerably by his incapacity to understand her predicament when she complains initially, just as he had sanctioned her hollow profession of love in the beginning unquestioningly because to do so suited himself in his mood of indulgence. The root cause of lovelessness in the play is Lear himself.

There is no love lost in any relationship in the Lear-world. What little love there is, as between Edgar and his father, or Kent's love for Lear, has to be disguised and concealed in fear. Even when it is revealed it is only at the point of death and thus proves its own impotence. Or it vanishes into thin air, leaving us wondering if ever there was such a thing as love, as in the instance of the Fool who loves Lear in his own fashion, but is made to disappear unaccountably in the middle of the play; or in the instance of the love between Cordelia and the Duke of France, who are removed from the main action into the background quickly. There is no relationship based on romantic love in the play. When all the kinds of basic and instinctual love had failed, there was no place for romantic love, apparently.

Pictures of lust are more pervasive in the play. Lear himself hints at his own feelings of lust when he says: "It was this flesh begot/Those pelican daughters" (III, iv, 74-75). It does not occur to him that love might also be responsible for begetting off spring. The picture of lust is re-inforced in Gloucester's begetting of Edmund. Gloucester is so wrong-headed as to even be proud of the "good sport at his making...." (I, i, 24-25). Gloucester impulsively maintains that he loves his bastard son as much as he loves Egar, but we realize that he obviously did not know what love meant. His treatment of Edgar on hearing the false accusations of Edmund against Edgar shows that Gloucester's love was shallow and without meaning. He had himself committed adultery in his youth and had begotten a son after he had a son in lawful wedlock.

Although Edmund is a character in the sub-plot, his actions are crucial to an understanding of the theme of love in *King Lear*. Edmund is an eloquent symbol of the failure of love in the play. He was begotten in lust and perpetuates the feeling of lust. The villainy that he commits symbolizes the evil that is bred out of lovelessness. His dying scene is a meaningful commentary on the efficacy - or inefficacy - of love. Analysing the scene, John Masefield maintains that Edmund keeps silent about the order that he has given to have Lear and Cordelia killed because he loves Goneril and Goneril stands to gain by the death of Lear. Masefield further believes that Edmund at last confesses about the plot to kill Lear because the message of Goneril's death is brough in.[5] Masefield's interpretation irons out the dramatic transformation in the character of Edmund. Edmund remains a calculating villain to the end, according to that interpretation. Whereas, in truth, the main point in the scene is the conversion of Edmund from evil to good, and the emphasis here is on the theme of the power of love. We should carefully notice the point at which the change in Edmund takes place. The bodies of Goneril and Regan are brought in and it is revealed that their deaths were the consequence of the jealousy involved in their love for Edmund. Edmund says:

> Yet Edmund was belov'd:
> The one the other poison'd for my sake,
> And after slew herself.
>
> (iv, iii, 238-240)

It would be a mistake to take these lines as being in bad taste, that here Edmund is pluming his vanity. Such a view continues to represent him as a villain. But it is only after that observation that Edmund decided to revoke the order of death on Lear and Cordelia. He says:

> I pant for life; some good I mean to do
> Despite of my own nature. Quickly send
> Be brief in it, to th' castle; for my writ
> Is on the life of Lear and on Cordelia.
>
> (iv,iii,243-245)

The crucial point here is that the evil in Edmund was conquered by "love". To an illegitimate son the very idea of love was enough to change his character. We realize the significance of the conversion when we compare Edmund's case with that of Iago in Othello. When confronted with the consequences of his evil machinations, all that Iago has to say is:

> Demand me nothing: what you know, you know:
> From this time forth I never will speak word.
>
> (*Othello*, v, ii, 303-304)

But the ultimate irony in the dying scene is, neither Goneril nor Regan truly loved Edmund. What they felt was nothing more than selfish passion and base lust. Love remains an illusion or delusion for Edmund, and being such, it is impotent, for Lear and Cordelia are already dead. The conquest of love is meaningless in this crucial section of the play.

The saving grace is *King Lear* is supposed to be Cordelia's love. Although Cordelia towards the end symbolises the best aspect of love - namely, love as selfless suffering, forgiveness, and sacrifice - she is not totally blameless at the beginning. She expresses her dislike of her sisters openly, which is not entirely a noble act, well deserved though that dislike is. Goneril and Regan do not show such open hostility towards Cordelia. And even when they plot against each other later, it is in the name of love, misguided love, which was fed by Lear's sanction of it in the beginning.

Lear himself believes in the love of Cordelia at the very end. He dies in joy, imagining that Cordelia loves him, that her lips move in love. But she is already dead in Lear's arms, and love remains a delusion for King Lear. Once again, love is ironically as elusive at the end of the play as at the beginning.

What remains in the world that Lear has left behind? Not the youthful Fortinbras as in *Hamlet* or Macduff as in *Macbeth*, but a prematurely old Edgar "...hearing the weight of this sad time".

At the end of *King Lear* love never really succeeds in transporting us to the other side of despair. The bleakness of the world where love cannot dwell continues to haunt us. To be shown that love fails, is to be given a cut that is as mortal as it is subtle. The tragedy in *Lear* is not that Cordelia dies after all that suffering, or that Lear cannot live after his self-knowledge. *King Lear* takes us into realms more frightening than this idea of tragic waste. It leaves us in the emptiness of a wasteland where love fails to be the alchemy transforming suffering into joy.

Is this the essential hollowness and the delusive nature of that very feeling which human beings call love that we see, or are we to take *King Lear* as an example of the failure of a very real, and natural feeling in life called love which contributes its positiveness to life's meaning substantially even when we do not perceive it? Whatever the answer, *King Lear* emphasizes the negation.

REFERENCES

1. "On the Tragedies of Shakespeare", *The Writings of Charles Lamb*, ed. Percey Fitzgerald, IV, p. 206.

2. Maynard Mack, *'King Lear' in our time* (London: Methuen Co., 1966), p. 83.

3. *Ibid.*, p. 87.

4. G. Wilson Knight, *The Wheel of Fire* (N.Y.: World Publishing Co., 1957).

5. John Masefield, *William Shakespeare* (N.Y.: Henry Holt and Co., 1927), pp. 193-194.

2

John Galsworthy's *Justice*: A Problem Play

John Galsworthy can well be described as one of the first modern dramatists. In his dramas he deals with the problems of a technological, industrialised, urbanised society. Class divisions, the power of money, the inherent regulations and demands of social institutions, and their influence on the individuals of a society form the subject matter of his plays.

Published in 1910 *Justice* is the story of a young man who turns into a criminal because of adverse circumstances and accidental temptations. William Falder, who is 23 years old, is a weak and nervous man who works in the legal firm of John How and his son, Walter How. As he is also a sentimental young man, he gets emotionally involved with an older married woman named Ruth Honeywill. Ruth's plight of being married to a drunken husband and having two small children evokes his sympathy and he suggestes to her that they go away together to South America as man and wife. As they needed a large amount of money for the purpose he commits felony by changing the figure £ 90/- on an official cheque and drawing the money. But his criminal act is discovered and his senior employer, John How, reports him to the police. He is put on trial and despite the able defence of his lawyer, Hector Frome, he is sentenced to imprisonment for a period of three years.

After a bitter, degrading spell in the harsh atmoshpere of prison Falder is released from the prison six months earlier than his full term, on ticket-of-leave. His criminal record sticks to him despite his best efforts to begin a new life and he finds that no one is willing to employ him.

He meets Ruth Honeywill again and approaches John and Walter How for a job in their firm. On his son Walter's persuasion John reluctantly agrees to take back Falder, but on the condition that he cut himself off from Ruth Honeywill, who, John believes was the root cause of Falder's temptation to commit felony. At the same time, a police officer hunts down Falder with the charge that he has forged references to find employment and has also failed to report to the authorities during his ticket-of-leave. He is once again to be taken back into custody, but in extreme desperation Falder throws himself down the stairs and breaks his neck. Ruth Honeywill is left alone to mourn over his dead body.

Galsworthy in *Justice* deals with the problems of the deterioration of a man's character owing to adverse pressures from society. Ironically enough, although the play is titled *Justice*, it is injustice that stands out as the theme of the play.

Galsworthy appears to suggest that Justice, in a society which is rigid and mechanical, can also be rigid and mechanical. If a society acts blindly, justice in such a society will also act blindly. It is like a machine and will move by itself when it is given the smallest push. It is for the human beings to see that the machine runs properly and in the proper direction. Frome, in his long speech in Act II, comparing society and Justice, establishes the point that the quality of "Mercy is not strained", it must flow from human insight and thus save the destruction of the machine that is justice.

On the other hand, the judge in his long speech in the same act upholds the law on which the Court must depend. Society is based on certain laws of morality, criminality, etc. and the judge justifies these Laws as necessicities. He maintains that "Law is what it is—a majestic edifice, sheltering all of us...." and that he as judge has his "duty to society", which he must discharge even if it is unpleasant.

Galsworthy himself seems to believe that Society acts as Fate. It can crush an individual by holding him in its grip. Equally important is a man's character. But many times Society proves stronger and more powerful and the result is the destruction of the man. This is the tragic nature of the situation involving society and a man with some character.

When James says at the beginning of the play, "There is something in character, Cokeson," the theme of the drama is set. *Justice* deals with this theme of a man's character and how society imposes its own demands, sometimes blindly, in defining these terms of a man's character. In a rigid, hierarchical society of class divisions, the demands are rigid and imperative and make no concessions for laxity or compromise. James stands as a symbol of this Society. He has acquired power and prestige by conforming to the rules that govern his class, that is, the ruling class. He is in no mood to relax or make concessions to people who do wrong because if he does so then his own power will be shaken.

When Cokeson is called as witness, the whole cross-examination in the Court trial is about Falder's character. Cokeson has to give the Court his impression of Falder's character as he had observed him in his office for nearly two years.

Frome wants to prove in his defence argument that Falder is a young man of honest character but his one action of stealing the money was due to an unfortunate circumstance, and his circumstance was the one Society had created. Ruth's bad marriage and her inability to leave her drunken husband and marry Falder was because of the social Taboos against breaking even a bad marriage.

Justice can be described to be a social tragedy. In a social tragedy the dramatist depicts a society divided against itself, a society that destroys itself by its ills of injustice, and inequality, and its indifference to human values.

In *Justice* the problem is one of social injustice. There are also other social problems like the one symbolised by Ruth Honeywill's marriage to a drunkard or the social treatment extended to a prisoner after he comes out of prison, as seen in Falder's case. Although Galsworthy never considered himself as a social reformer, his concern for truth and his distress at the sight of senseless social ills drove him into exposing these ills in drama after drama. In this connection he himself has observed that his is an "... art for man's sake," and that "...he is not conscious of any desire to solve problems in his plays, or to effect direct reforms. His only ambition in drama is to present truth as he sees it and, gripping with it his readers or his audience, to produce in them a sort of mental ferment whereby vision may be enlarged, imagination livened, and understanding promoted." (Galsworthy, *Complete Works*: Manaton edition, Vol. XVIII, p. XIV.)

Galsworthy was deeply interested in dealing with the problems of his own contemporary society. The social, economic, and humanitarian problems of his own society were the sources of inspiration for his art. Living in an age of science and technology he realised that the fruits of modern civilization were far from being admirable. Modern life was actually troubled by problems and conflicts, and strife. Being a man of serious temperament Galsworthy was inclined to see the devastation and waste that resulted from these conflicts. Hence his dramas have a sombre, largely pessimistic tone. There is gloom and melancholy in the atmosphere of most of his dramas and the tragic mood generally prevails.

Galsworthy believed that a dramatist should be a realist in theme and a naturalist in technique. As such, the life he chose to depict in his dramas is everyday reality. He avoided the romantic, fanciful themes that had no bearing on ordinary reality and that only please the imagination. His plays reflect the social realism. His artistic technique of naturalism unfolds the realistic life in a natural order, with a natural forcefulness and form.

His artistic purpose as a dramatist was to enlighten the public through his dramatic representations. For Galsworthy the function of art is not just to delight but also to provide a moral. He has said in this connection: "A drama must be shaped so as to have a spire of meaning. Every grouping of life and character has its inherent moral and the business of the dramatist is to pose the group as to bring that moral poignantly to the light of day." (In his essay, "Some Platitudes concerning Drama").

As his dramas are mainly social tragedies concerning life in a society at large, his characters are invariably ordinary men and women. The hero, specifically, is only an ordinary man, an average mortal. He is more often than not a victim of society and so appears to be a pitiable character. He deserves pure compassion because of the social wrong that he has suffered. The character is a victim of social deterioration and disintegration.

William Falder in *Justice* is to be pitied more than condemned. He is not criminal but is driven to a criminal act because of an unfortunate combination of circumstance and weakness of character and an instance of impulse and temptation. The result is the tragic progress towards destruction of Falder.

The evils of circumstance are Falder's poverty, and his being attracted towards this poor, suffering woman, Ruth Honeywill. The evils of his weakness are his belonging to a consumptive family, and his having neurotic feelings and of possessing a sentimental, chivalrous temperament.

In depicting the miseries of Falder Galsworthy shows that not only is society cruel and indifferent to an individual but even his own fellowmen may be inhuman towards him. Falder has paid for his mistake by serving in prison but when he comes out no one is willing to help him. His past pursues him and nobody is willing to forget and forgive even after he has served his sentence in prison.

The two dire agents of society that hold an individual, especially a weak individual, in their grip are the Law and the prison. They are the agents of Society and they are too powerful, nearly tyrannial. In this way, because of their rigid, literal nature, they spell out the self-defeating effects of these social institutions. The literal principles of a Law carried out in letter rather than in spirit can destroy, rather than discipline, a man. This seems to be the sincere, sympathetic view that Galsworthy seems to hold in the play.

Although Galsworthy's play, *Justice,* is a "problem" play, this does not mean that his plays are abstract and theoretical or that they are un-dramatic. Through skilful handling of character and dialogue Galsworthy manages to maintain the tension of dramatic representation. His characters even bear names that underline the qualities of their nature and thus their very names add to the vivid effect of their characters. These names act as clues to the main characteristics of these persons. Falder, for instance, is a man who has faltered, stumbled and fallen from the main path of duty. He is not a criminal, but in some weak moment he has faltered and commits felony.

Similarly Cokesen appears as a man who tries his best to keep things pleasant and jolly in the office. He coaxes James to excuse Falder, he is in turn coaxed by Ruth into giving her permission to see Falder in the office. He is a man who cajoles and coaxes rather than acts rigidly.

In still a similar way, Harold Cleaver, Counsel for the Crown, is like a meat cleaver, a meat cutter, that cuts clean straight to the bone, without leaving anything half-way. He is a man who comes down heavily with his questions to cut through Falder's faltering answers.

Hecter Frome, the Counsel for the defence, on the other hand, is a young man who hectors, that is, who boldly questions, argues, and uses violent rhetoric and strong discussions, and arguments, in order to win his case. He has a powerful, argumentative, persuasive power as a lawyer.

Ruth Honeywill also bears a name that reveals her character. She is a sweet-natured woman and cannot get on with her drunken husband. She loves her children and brings them to the office when she comes to see Falder. It is her sweetness and firm will that have made Falder agree to go with her to start life in another country.

Not only do the characters bear significant names but they also carry the whole meaning of the play. For instance, Walter How in *Justice*, is one such meaningful character. It may be seen that Galsworthy keeps Walter as the norm, as the standard of a balanced, understanding human being, who tries to be just even to a criminal. When Falder comes back to the legal firm after serving his term it is Walter who tries to persuade his father to give Falder his due. The true significance of justice is seen in this behaviour of Walter How.

By creating a character like Walter How Galsworthy justifies his choice of title for his play as *Justice*. Justice is after all in the hands of a human being, not within the cold brick walls of a law-court or imprisoned in legal language, Galsworthy seems to suggest in his play *Justice*.

3

Murder and Mayhem in T.S. Eliot's Plays

One strong reason for the immediate success on the stage of T.S. Eliot's plays is his skillful use of popular modes of entertainment like the music hall comedy and the bar room chit chat in the construction of scenes and dialogue. That the reading of detective fiction was also another popular pastime for the general public Eliot well knew during his editorship of *The Criterion*. Eliot himself obviously depends on this well-known canon for creating a fine sense of suspense and drama, and even an odd kind of tragi-comedy in the atmosphere of his plays.

That Eliot was seriously interested in detective fiction is evidenced by some of his reviews in *The Criterion*. In a lengthy critical review titled, "Homage to Wilkie Collins", he discusses nine detective novels covering a wide variety of crime stories (Elliot, "Homage to Wilkie Collins" 139-43). He traces the tradition of the form from mainstream novels like *The Count of Monte Cristo* to Wilkie Collin's *The Woman in White,* sets down rules for good and bad detective fiction in a well-informed manner, and places the nine writers under consideration according to gradations of skill and craft in story telling. Eliot apparently knew the English, American and European forms of the genre.

In another lengthy essay on Collins written as an Introduction to *The Moonstone,* Eliot once again shows his familiarity with stories that appeal to the sense of mystery and suspense in general readers. He draws a discussion of Dickens's novels into his argument and points out the elements of foreboding and fatality that both Collins and Dickens used in a dramatic way in their novels. (Eliot, "Introduction" v-xii).

Besides these instances Eliot has also made clear his fascination for the Sherlock Holmes stories of Sir Arthur Conan Doyle. In a review of *The Complete Sherlock Holmes Stories* he writes with enthusiasm of the supersleuth who is the father of all later sleuths in modern detective fiction. (Eliot, "Sherlock Holmes and His Times" 552-56). Several critics have testified to Eliot's life-long fascination for the stories of Sherlock Holmes. Sir Herbert Read has recorded that Eliot would play literary games and quizzes with his friends, more especially with Frank Morley, sometimes the Boswell-Johnsonian ones and at others "the same game, on a somewhat more frivolous level was played with the complete works of Conan Doyle and more (arcanely), with the complete works of Wilkie Collins." Read adds that once even he joined in the game "and earned his surprised admiration by answering some ploy of this kind with a question from Poor *Miss Finch,* a novel by Wilkie Collins" (Read, 31-58).

Frank Morley corroborates Read's observations in his own memoir on Eliot. He refers to an article that he wrote for a festschrift celebrating Eliot's 60th birthday and says that he "did so only after strictly limiting the circle of discourse. In that conversation the scheme of reference was the canon of the Sherlock Holmes stories, for that was a canon familiar to Eliot and me, and it provided an appropriate puppet-stage setting within which to convey, with a trifle of badinage, something of the spirit of the first decade of Faber and Faber" (all quotes are from Morley's *Memoirs,* 110-33).

Morley's second memoir written on the death of Eliot is also replete with references to the Sherlock Holmes stories. He records the occasion when Eliot came to visit him at Pikes Farm in Surrey: "We met him next morning at our local station with a dog-cart, which at once reminded him of Sherlock Holmes and appeared to please him very much." Morley also says that about his oldest sister, Ada, for whose intelligence Tom always expressed the greatest respect, "Eliot often said that she was the Mycroft to his Sherlock Holmes." True to the style of Sherlock Holmes, Morley and Eliot also had their publishers' messengers whom they called the "Baker Street Irregulars." When *The Criterion* ceased publication, Morley refers to the events that led to the decision: "The lady who had been paying the bills for *The Criterion* was in Switzerland. At a meeting at the Grove after his return he [Eliot] re-appeared with the announcement, to put it in Sherlock Holmes language, The Red-Headed League Is Dissolved."

Eliot himself appropriated the Holmesean talent more than once. In his "Sherlockian Eliot" Jenkins records the letter that Eliot wrote to Christopher Morley, offering some of his own sleuth-on-the-scent tips regarding Conan Doyle's *The Hound of the Baskervilles*:

> I wish indeed, that I were staying long enough to attend your annual dinner, as I should have been delighted to participate, and, especially, if I had time to prepare a short travelogue with lantern slides on the topography of the Great Grimpen, and certain incidental details which have never been investigated, such as the diet of the hound. That might lead to investigations in Chicago, as I suspect Mr. Stapleton covered his tracks by importing a good deal of canned beef. If he had obtained his supplies of meat for a dog of that size from the local butcher, I am sure that suspicion would have been aroused. (Jenkins, 82)

Robert Giroux, the publisher friend of Eliot, says in his memoir of Eliot that on another occasion, Eliot was to go to Sweden to receive the Nobel Prize: "When he left for Stockholm, the Kauffers and I took him to the airport where a porter asked, 'Mr. Eliot, what book did they give the Nobel Prize for?' 'I believe it's for the entire corpus,' he replied 'When did you publish that?' the man wanted to know.

When he had gone, Eliot said to us, 'It really might make a good title for a mystery-The Entire Corpus.'" (Giroux, 334)

Obviously it is because of such personal experiences as with the porter at the airport that Eliot saw the need for creating a dramatic style that would appeal to a wide cross-section of audience in the modern theatre. Helen Gardner observes in her essay on Eliot's Comedies that in present times the dramatist must give his audiences what they want, otherwise there will be no audiences. No one knew better than Eliot how true that was. It is not for nothing that in one of his review articles in *The Criterion* he discussed at length no less than sixteen detective novels, a kind of fiction that is supposed to appeal to low-brow readers.

Eliot himself has provided the explanation as to why mystery and detective fiction had its perennial appeal to him. His introduction to Collin's *The Moonstone* reveals that he had a liking not only for Collin's novels but also for those of Dickens. He especially liked *The Moonstone* and felt that modern detective writers had added scientific methods but had not improved upon Sergeant Cuff's methods. Eliot clearly indicated the familiarity that he had with different types of detective fiction. For all his later reviews of detective fiction, Eliot keeps *The Moonstone* as the touchstone of excellence in the canon.

Although Eliot himself has not written full fledged fictional work, one of his earliest prose pieces, *Eeldrop and Appleplex*, published in two parts in *The Little Review* in 1917, appears to be a light-hearted take-off on a Sherlockian short story. Eliot is imitating the method of the famous sleuth when he makes the two characters have a dialogue in a scientific analytical style about philosophical questions. They employ the deductive method in order to arrive at an understanding of human nature from their study of human behaviour. Facts matter, no surmise before knowing facts. The relationship between Eeldrop and Appleplex is similar to that between Holmes and Watson. They are in rented rooms and they return to their rooms only at nightfall. When they disperse in the morning there is an element of mystery-they go toward destinations unknown to each other. Evil lurks in the street where they live. The description of the scene is worthy of Conan Doyle or Dickens in his most gothic moments:

> It was a shady street, its windows were heavily curtained and over it hung the cloud of a respectability which has something to conceal.... Eeldrop and Appleplex commanded from their windows the entrance of a police station across the way.

Whenever some malefactor was arrested in the street, Eeldrop and Appleplex would "rush out to mingle with the mob." They were alien visitors, lingering, looking mysterious in their caps. "Each pursued his own line of inquiry. Appleplex questioned the lower classes of both sexes... and usually extracted full and inconsistent histories." Eeldrop "preserved a more passive demeanor, listened to the conversation of the people among themselves, registered in his mind their oaths, their redundance of phrase, their various manners of spitting. When the crowd dispersed Eeldrop and Appleplex returned to their rooms: Appleplex entered the results of his inquiries into large notebooks, filed according to the nature of the case, from A (adultery) to Y (yeggmen). Eeldrop smoked reflectively." They observe the Spaniard eating at their next table and come up with the Case of the Spaniard. Their study is human nature: "In Gopsum Street man murders his mistress... For the man's neighbours the important fact is what the man killed her with? And at precisely what time? And who found the body? For the 'enlightened public' the 'case' is different."

What Eliot enjoyed most about detective fiction, apparently, was to see an intelligent mind at work. In

Eeldrop and Appleplex Eliot hoists such a mind with its own petard. This early piece of pastiche by Eliot hovers on the edge of parody of a typical Sherlock Holmes story. Some of the techniques of a crime story writer are used with a masterly hand in this short sketch, for instance, the creation of an atmosphere of menace and intrigue in an ordinary, everyday street scene, and the pattern of a duo of detectives that is common to most detective stories, as evidenced in famous pairs like Sherlock Holmes and Watson, and Lord Wimsey and Bunter.

Several critics have pointed out Eliot's use of the Sherlock Holmes stories in some of his poems and also in his play, *Murder in the Cathedral.* (See, for example, essays by Smith, Nicholas, Loesch, Preston, Webster and Starr.) Some phrases in "Macavity: the Mystery Cat", the reference to the Baskerville Hound in "Lines to Ralph Hodgson, Esqre ,"the use of the word grimpen in "East Coker" and the cryptic lines of dialogue spoken between Archbishop Thomas and the Second Tempter regarding the wielding of power in the drama, *Murder in the Cathedral,* echo back to the source of the Conan Doyle canon.

The very title of his first full-length play, *Murder in the Cathedral,* is evocative of the sense of a coldly plotted killing of the Archbishop. On one level, it has the horror and bloodshed associated with gang killing, and it is only by dint of historical and by gradual heightening of the intensity of tone that Eliot raises the play to its tragic climax of sacrifice and martyrdom. It is the best example of what can be called an anti-detective play, where the principles of detective fiction are used without their appearing as formulas. Martin Browne records as to how his wife, Henzie Raeburn, came to suggest the title to the play. Eliot "had always wanted the ritual aspect of the play to be balanced by the homicidal; he was a devotee of Sherlock Holmes; and this title, with its sardonic implications, had a contemporary quality which would induce in an audience an attitude favourable to the acceptance of the ironies... the title was a 'selling one'... (Browne, 55-56)."

Eliot's later plays were also "sell-outs" precisely because of his skilful use of coincidences, surprises, mysteries and violent deaths. His dependence on the technique of detective and murder mystery stories was never stronger than in his play, *The Family Reunion*. This most complex of all plays of Eliot has not one, but two murders-one attempted, the other actually happening under mysterious circumstances. Eliot himself was conscious of his use of the elements of a murder mystery in the play, but as he wanted it to be something more than that he makes Agatha declare: "What we have written is not a story of detection/Of crime and punishment, but of sin and expiation." In fact, *The Family Reunion* is both a murder mystery and a spiritual mystery play in a modern setting. At the heart of the play is the mysterious incident of the death of Harry's wife when she falls from the deck of an ocean liner in Harry's presence and is drowned. We are told the body was not recovered. Whether Harry pushes her or not is also left in doubt, for first he makes a confession and then withdraws it. After that point it becomes a mystery play of Harry's course of sin and expiation. In spite of Eliot's denying that it is a murder story, *The Family Reunion* is replete with the stock-in-trade of such a story. Charles hints at it broadly when he says: "Well-known Peeress vanishes from a Liner" and sets the tone for the drama.

In his essay on detective fiction W.H. Auden made the observation that has now become very well-known to all mystery buffs: Chandler took the body out of the vicarage garden and gave murder back to those good at it. But Auden himself believes that as for the proper setting, the "more Eden-like it is the greater the contradiction of murder." According to that formula, Wishwood House in the English countryside is an ideally contrasting background to the horror of a murder story of the Lord Monchensey family. It becomes the "Great Wrong Place" where evil lurks. The drawing room scene where the members of the family are gathered to exchange neighbourhood gossip and family news, with the butler and the maid discreetly slipping in and out with trays of sherry and whiskey and the mother awaiting the arrival of her sons to celebrate her birthday party, is worthy of the setting of an Agatha Christie detective novel. There is also the local policeman, Sergeant Winchell, the faithful servant and chauffeur, Downing and, of course, the hearty, bluff family doctor, Doctor Warburton. The reference to Wishwood House as a haunted dwelling is also there, with "the unspoken voice of sorrow in the ancient bedroom/at three o'clock in the morning." The words murder, murderer, crime, detective, death, body, carcass and blood occur more often than one would expect in a drawing room comedy.

Although *The Family Reunion* is not a detective drama in a hard-boiled way, it has a surprising number of technical devices that are characteristic of detective fiction. The point of view is different in a drama than in fiction, to that extent Eliot's use of the devices is necessarily muted in the shorter, more compact dramatic form. He also does not use guns and pistols as openly as Ibsen does in his dramas. The character of Harry is poised between those of a hero of tragic drama on the one hand and of a cloak-and-dagger detective-murder story on the other. From a repressed, sadistic man, he turns into a self-torturing, masochistic seeker of salvation. In the course of the play we are put into the haunted mind of Harry who thinks he is a killer. Harry is no ordinary murderer but he is a murderer with a conscience, a sinner.

Karen Vander Ven, while analyzing the character of Travis McGee, the criminal-hero of John Macdonald's detective novels, observes that McGee suffers from an effect a person who has committed a murder might suffer. In psychological terms she explains these as "mood swings" that someone who has "wound himself up to accomplishing a deed experiences" after he had accomplished that deed. In psychoanalytical terms, such a killer would be described as a "cyclothymic" person. Harry appears to suffer from the depressive effects of being a weak man who has committed or participated in a violent killing or death. Vander Ven observes that such a man in a depressive trauma tends to go backward into memory by trying to think what his childhood was, how he came to be what he is. Harry also thinks about his past and his childhood extensively. It is significant that Harry is shown as being ill, as someone who needs the care of Dr. Warburton. Harry's condition adds to the effect of the play as a psychological thriller.

In a typical murder-detective story it may be observed that there is always the chain effect of murder. After one murder, the pattern trends to repeat itself and there may be more than one murder in the course of the story. Eliot also has strengthened the criminal instinct of Harry by making his father a failed murderer. The motive for murder in Harry's father's case is well-established as being his illicit love for his wife's sister,Agatha, but in Harry's case it appears to be motiveless malignity. But on the other hand it may be the deep-seated instinct, as of Sweeney in Sweeney Agonistes, of killing a woman because:

> Any man has to, needs to, wants to,
> Once in a lifetime, do a girl in.

Thus murder as a compulsive act and the murderer as being under some compulsion when he commits the horrible act is common to both *The Family Reunion* and a typical serial-killer story.

Harry is apparently cast in the role of a murderer but who is the detective in Eliot's play? Ultimately *The Family Reunion* remains an unsolved mystery, because no actual detective pursues the clues in solving the drowning incident of Harry's wife. This is not to say that Eliot has forgotten the detective totally. Downing and Mary, at the end of the play, in their conversation between them try to establish the motive for murder and the need to cover the tracks of the murderer. They try to find reasons for extenuation of Harry's culpability under the circumstances that his wife was a domineering woman.

To add to the effect of the mysterious murder there is also the chain of accidents of John and Alex and the building up of the atmosphere of violence and horror. There are curious coincidences and connections that lead from one violent incident to another.

In most detective fiction there is the curious pattern of the duo of opposites of the murderer and the detective, the murderer appearing as a dark underside, the subconscious, submerged self of the detective. The famous example of this pattern is the duo of Sherlock Holmes and Prof. Moriarty. In a way, the relationship between Harry and Downing appears to be of this type. Harry is the murderer and Downing, while speaking to the family at Wishwood House, appears to be acting as the detective who has a deep, uncanny understanding of the murderer and his motives.

Harry's murderous conscience has to find its peace in the precincts of Wishwood House, the scene of the attempted murder of his mother. Wishwood House is truly a haunted house, haunted by the ghost of Harry's father and his murderous thoughts and the ghosts springing from Harry's own guilty conscience. Eliot has used the Greek dramatic device of the Eumenides to suggest the spiritual level of the culpability of the sinner Harry, but they serve well also toward creating the effect of a house of horror, a haunted house of thrilling suspense.

Eliot's next play, *The Cocktail Party*, intrigued the critics even more than *The Family Reunion*. Cecil Wilson of the *Daily*

Mail observed that "Reilly turns out to be a kind of Sherlock Holmes of the soul with an unearthly genius for exposing their secret fears..." (*Daily Mail* [London] 4 May 1950). Many other critics echoed the same sentiments, calling the play an "enigma," a "mystery" with the "Mysterious Stranger" as the psychiatrist, and generally agreed that it was "baffling".

Although there is no direct murder in *The Cocktail Party*, there is the violent killing of Celia by the natives. Reilly sends her to her death in an indirect way, when he brainwashes her into embracing the hard way of faith and sacrifice. The mystery in *The Cocktail Party* is not about "whodunit" but "what's up?" And that question can be answered by every reader for himself.

In *The Confidential Clerk* Eliot once again employs the plot of surprises, coincidences, and double identities to create an effect of suspense. It is the single comedy in which Eliot does not introduce a violent death either directly or indirectly.

But his last play. *The Elder Statesman*, once again creaks with an overload of the stock-in-trade devices of a crime murder story. A plot of embezzlement, forgery, killing, and cheating, which are essentially the ingredients of crime fiction, becomes, by Eliot's verbal sleight of hand, a drama of manslaughter, breach of promise, self-betrayal and expiation. From almost being a story of criminals who are fugitives from justice, it becomes a story of people who are fugitives from ordinary reality. Sir Claude himself puts it aptly when he says:

> There are many things not crimes, Monica,
> Beyond anything of which the law takes cognisance,
> Temporary failures, irreflective aberrations,
> Reckless surrenders, unexplainable impulses.

In the play, Mrs. Cargill and Gomez come back like ghosts from the past of Lord Claverton and hold him responsible for what they consider as his crimes toward them. But his daughter, Monica, judging his checkered life in the scales of Portia's justice by her gesture of reassuring love, releases him from the haunting memories and damaging accusations of the avengers. The plot and characterization in *The Elder Statesman* are modeled on those of detective fiction to a large extent. It is this which made one of the critics observe: "Striving for popular taste, he writes the first act as high-class Agatha Christie's, the second as a parody of Terence Rattigan, and the third as an extract from `True Confessions!' This is a play any low-brow can enjoy" (*Daily Herald* 26 Sept. 1958).

Gomez appears on the scene of domestic harmony at the Lord Claverton household in a mysterious way. He is a "foreign person," as Lambert calls him, looking exotic like the Indians in Wilkie Collin's *The Moonstone*. He has assumed this name to conceal his identity. In his opinion Lord Claverton is also a man with an assumed name, concealing his true identity. In their conversation they refer to their disreputable past and reveal themselves in a criminal light, Gomez as a forger and Richard as a possible murderer. The hints and threats of blackmail that Gomez and Mrs. Cargill bring with them appear to add to the thickening of the murder mystery. But time is on the side of the elder Statesman and what should have been "Crime in relation to the law" has now become "sin in relation to the sinner." Lord Claverton gets himself off the hook of guilt by his confession to his daughter Monica, which becomes his act of expiation.

Even in *The Elder Statesman* the "whodunit" formula of chain effect of crime is maintained. Lord Claverton's son, Michael, links up with Gomez to continue in the shady business of some money transactions. Lord Claverton is afraid that his son will continue the chain of hit-and-run accidents, but that does not actually happen in the play. Charles, with his legal mind, serves as the detective or problem-solver. The play ends without there actually being a murder, breach of promise, or black-mail case, and Lord Claverton dies a natural death, it is hoped. This is indeed a tame ending for a writer who was fascinated with Sherlock Holmes and the detective novels of Peter Cheyney!

Critics were quick to observe the distinctive nature of Eliot's last play. It was mostly declared to be an outstanding success, although the drama critic of *The Scottish Mail* had this to say: "The opening scene might be by Charles Morgan out of Agatha Christie. The scenes are as from a horror film. *The Elder Statesman* is a zombie play designed for the living dead" (*The Scottish Mail* 21 Aug. 1958). But the majority of the critics agreed with the opinion of the drama reviewer of *The New York Times* that "Mr. Eliot departed from his expected style to produce a new kind of thriller and with it all he has contrived to give an unusual warmth in his handling of human relations" (19 Aug. 1958).

By the time he wrote *The Elder Statesman,* Eliot had honed the edges of his use of murder and mystery to create dramatic effects. The coincidence and melodrama of *The Family Reunion* are replaced by the genuinely dramatic scenes of interactions between Mrs. Cargill, Gomez and Lord Claverton, and their revealing confessions of possible criminal behaviour on their part. All the usual elements of detective fiction are used only to be transcended. As the drama critic of *The Daily Herald* put it: "This is really something! T.S. Eliot has come out with a thriller. It's no ordinary thriller, of course. It's far more than that but it's full of suspense packed with surprises and loaded with exciting twists! It's a better thriller than 'The Mousetrap'" (19 Aug. 1958).

The economy of plot and dialogue and more especially the lyricism of the theme of love in *The Elder Statesman* make it obvious that Eliot was producing a play that was antithetical to the life of crime and violence and the philosophy of negation on which the hard-boiled detective story depends. Eliot's message appears to be that in a life that is necessarily filled with the basic instincts of hatred, violence, crime and death, the answer is not in incrimination of oneself or of others, but the answer is in love. The final gestures of assertion of love between Lord Claverton and Monica, and then between Monica and Charles, spell out this message . Such a message, needless to say, is missing in a straight-die detective story.

Eliot's employment of the elements of the Sherlock Holmes stories and detective fiction makes it clear that he could use the canon in several ways to suit his purpose. He was not above parodying it, as evidenced in his poem, Macavity: *The Mystery Cat*. He could use it for literary pastiche, as in his prose piece *Eeldrop and Appleplex*. He could also use it with a subversive, antithetical effect, as in his major plays, mainly to create his special kind of dark comedy.

This subversive use of the canon in an extended way in his plays results in his writing anti-detective dramas. Like Faulkner and Nabokov in their fiction, Eliot deliberately employs the principles of detective fiction, but knows better than to use them as a formula. It is in this effect of transcendence that the lasting nature of this use of the canon lies.

It also lies in the mutual fertilizing exchanges that one finds between his works and his attraction for popular forms of entertainment like music hall comedy and the reading of detective fiction. He was not too snobbish an artist to take from these popular forms, nor was he too snobbish to give something back to them. In a note in *English Miscellany*, T.N. Marsh points out the possibility of Dorothy Sayers' having used some of the lines from Eliot's poems "The Triumphal March" and "Burnt Norton" in her detective novel, *The Gaudy Night*. There is also Robert Giroux's comments in his

Memoir that when he heard Eartha Kitts, the queen of music hall comedy, sing the line, "T.S. Eliot writes poems to me" in her song "Monotonous" in the Broadway musical comedy, "New Faces", he told Eliot about it. (Giroux 338). Eliot was delighted and had flowers sent to her. The true measure of Eliot's success as a modern dramatist lies in this living interaction between his art and the popular art forms.

WORKS CITED

Auden, W.H., "The Guilty Vicarage," *The Dyer's Hand*, New York: Random, 1962, 146-58.

Browne, E. Martin, *The Making of T.S. Eliot's Plays*, Cambridge: Cambridge UP, 1969, 55-56.

The Daily Herald [Manchester], 19 Aug. 1958.

—,[Manchester], 26 Sept. 1958.

The Daily Mail [London], 4 May 1950.

Eliot, T.S., "Homage to Wilkie Collins," *The Criterion*, V 1 (Jan. 1927), 139-43.

—, "Introduction," *The Moonstone*, The World's Classics, 316(1928), v-xii.

—, "Sherlock Holmes and His Times," *The Criterion*, VIII 32 (Apr. 1929), 552-56.

Gardner, Helen, "The Comedies of T.S. Eliot," *Sewanee Review*, LXXIV (Winter, 1965/66), 153-76.

Giroux, Robert.,"A Personal Memoir," *Sewanee Review*, LXXIV (Winter, 1965/66), 331-39.

Jenkins, William I, "The Sherlockian Eliot," *Baker Street Journal*, 62 (1962), 81-84.

Joesch, Katherine, "A Dangerous Still at Large," *Notes and Queries*, 6 (Jan. 1959), 88.

Marsh, T.N, "The Turning World, Eliot, and the Detective Story," *English Miscellany*, 8 (1957), 143-45.

Morley, Frank, "A Few Recollections of Eliot," *Sewanee Review*, LXXIV (Winter, 1965/66), 110-33.

The New York Times, 19 Aug. 1958.

Nicholas, C., "The Murders of Doyle and Eliot," *Modern Language Notes,* LXX (1955), 269-71.

Preston, Priscilla, "A Note on T.S. Eliot and Sherlock Holmes," *Modern Language Review,* 54 (July 1959), 397-99.

Read, Herbert, "T.S. Eliot-A Memoir," *Sewanee Review,* LXXIV (Winter, 1965/66), 31-58.

The Scotish Mail, 21 Aug. 1958.

Smith, Grover, Addendum, *Baker Street Journal,* 62 (1962), 84, 128.

—, "T.S. Eliot and Sherlock Holmes," *Notes and Queries,* 193 (2 Oct. 1948), 431-32.

Vander Ven, Karen, "Psychological Genesis of the Prototype Hero in Mystery/Detective Fiction," *Clues: A Journal of Detection,* 2.1 (Spring/Summer, 1990), 31-36.

Webster, H.T., and W.H. Starr, "Macavity: An Attempt to Unravel His Mystery," *Baker Street Journal,* 4 (Oct. 1954), 205-10.

4

T.S. Eliot's *The Cocktail Party* and the *Bhagavad-Gita*

By and large, critics have had the tendency to slight Eliot's interest in Eastern thought. Except for short comments dropped incidentally in the course of discussions of Eliot's deep interest in philosophical questions, the importance of his references to Eastern thought has not been treated in full-length critical works. Even these short comments have been, more often than not, impatient dismissals of its significance. For instance, F.O. Matthiessen, though he recognizes the pertinence of Eliot's notes to *The Waste Land* where the poet points out the significance of the juxtaposition of Buddha's and St. Augustine's cries about the fire of lust and the fire of purgation, believes that a reading of Buddha's Fire Sermon is not necessary for an understanding of the "Fire Sermon" section in *The Waste Land,* and continues that he himself had not yet read the *Upanishads* from which Eliot borrowed the onomatopoeic representation of "What the Thunder Said."[1] This is nonchalantly ignoring Eliot's own notes to "What the Thunder Said" where he draws our attention to the fable in the *Upanishads* and comments on the meaning of the word "Shantih."[2] Cleanth Brooks, like Matthiessen, notices the onomatopoeic effect of the words "datta", "dayadhwam", and "damyata" and drops it at that.[3]

Helen Gardner and H.H. Waggoner are highly displeased at Eliot's introduction of Eastern thought in *Four Quartets*. Gardner believes that "though it is perfectly in consonance with the poem's themes of annunciation to use these great scriptures to bear witness to man's recognition of the divine, it might be objected that to introduce Krishna at this point is an error and destroys the imaginative harmony of the poem, since it is precisely in their view of history and the time process that Christianity and Hinduism are most opposed."[4] Waggoner carries Gardner's argument further and says: "The III Section of `The Dry Salvages' is somewhat weakened by its dependence on Indian Scriptures, since the ideas which are attributed to Krishna may be found within the Christian tradition unmixed with the element of negative detachment or quietism."[5] In his own cryptic way B. Rajan agrees with them and says that the III Section of "The Dry Salvages" "begins badly."[6]

Eliot himself might be largely responsible for warding off closer, more serious studies of his interest in Indian philosophy. Though he Enrolled in Charles Lanman's course in Indic Philology at Harvard in 1911, soon after his return from the Sorbonne, and initially expressed admiration for Indian philosophy, in the same breath he has also expressed reservations about his submission to the Oriental influence. In 1913, at the time he abandoned his study of Indian philosophy and bought himself a copy of F.H. Bradley's *Appearance and Reality*, he observed:

> Two years spent in the study of Sanskrit under Charles Lanman, and a year in the mazes of Patanjali's metaphysics under the guidance of James Woods, left me in a state of enlightened mystification. A good deal of the effort of understanding what Indian philosophers were after - and their subtleties make most of the great European philosophers look like schoolboys - lay in trying to erase from my mind all the categories and kinds of distinctions common to European philosophy

> from the time of Greeks . . . And I came to the conclusion . . . that my only hope of really penetrating the heart of that mystery would lie in forgetting how to think and feel as an American or European; which, for practical as well as sentimental reasons I did not wish to do.[7]

Eliot also expressed his skeptical thoughts about the successful blending of the Western and Eastern philosophies. Although he admired his teacher Irving Babbitt a great deal, he says of him in this context: ". . . I cannot but feel that in some respects Irving Babbitt, with the noblest intentions, has merely made matters worse instead of better."[8]

Eliot's self-appraisal and comment about Babbitt, though extremely helpful, must be accepted with caution. It is well known that most of his personal references, which are very few, are characteristically modest, diffident, and skeptical. Furthermore, we have also to remember that Eliot the critic is different from Eliot the poet. The critic might have critical theories and principles that the poet could not, or would not, practice. Although personally he might have felt the impossibility of coming under the influence of Indian philosophy, as a poet he could not wipe out the intellectual and philosophical background in Indology that had contributed so much to his mental development. The obvious Oriental references in significant parts of his major poems need to be explained more fully. Some very fine recent critical endeavours, such as that of Herbert Howarth in his *Notes on Some Figures behind T.S. Eliot*,[9] and of Harold McCarthy, Russel Fowler, and K.S.N. Rao in some shorter articles, point to the possibility of deeper meanings emerging from a closer reading of the Oriental references in the poems.[10] The recent critical controversy in *The Times Literary Supplement* following the article by Craig Raine, emphasizes the need for such closer studies.[11]

When perceptive major critics have summarily dismissed Eliot's overt references to Eastern thought in crucial parts of his poems, a reading of his very "British" play, *The Cocktail Party*, in the light of the *Bhagavad-Gita* may appear irrelevant, if not impertinent. But considering the significance that the Gita has had to all Orientalists and to Eliot himself, such a study of *The Cocktail Party* is not only justified, but becomes necessary in order to clarify the resolution of some of Eliot's ideas in the play.

The Bhagavad-Gita is the Holy Grail of Indian Philosophy. Any quest for the understanding of Hindu religion and thought must begin there and end there. In the significant words of Ananda Coomaraswamy, the book may be considered as a "compendium of the whole Vedic doctrine to be found in the earlier Vedas, Brahmanas, and Upanishads, and being therefore the basis of all later developments, it can be regarded as the focus of all Indian religion."[12]

It is well known that the Gita was a book of gold to earlier American writers like Emerson, Thoreau, and Whitman. Eliot himself with his American background soon came under the spell of the Song. In his essay on Dante he had made this comment: "... *the Bhagavad-Gita*... is the next greatest philosophical poem to the *Divine Comedy* within my experience."[13] He has taken care to point out that he has read the work in Sanskrit.[14] He went to it specifically for inspiration in "The Dry Salvages" section of the *Four Quartets*. In his little known poem " To the Indians who Died in South Africa," he once again brought the Gita alive. He identified a contemporary World War situation in Africa with the situation of the mythological Battle of Kurukshetra in the Gita, and became Krishna to the Indian soldiers in Africa, advising them to fight a battle which was not their own really, with a true sense of duty towards the principles.

In light of such significant handling of the Gita, it can be maintained that thematically and technically Eliot once again packed a great deal of the poem into *The Cocktail Party*, this time more covertly, or even unconsciously. That certain Indian philosophical concepts were uppermost in his mind can be seen by one of the key sentences in the play repeated in three places: "Work out your salvation with diligence."[15] The line is a reference to the death-bed injunction of the Buddha to his disciples. Paul Elmer More, who had also studied Indic Philosophy at Harvard, points out that Babbitt, who was very much attracted by Buddhism because of its rigorous, ascetic qualities, was constantly reiterating this injunction. But despite the obvious Buddhist reference it would be a mistake to confine our reading of the play to the Buddhist angle. The play gains in meaning if placed in the Brahmanic or Hindu context, especially that of the *Bhagavad-Gita*. In his otherwise perceptive analysis of the Indian influence on Eliot, Howarth makes the mistake of reading *The Cocktail Party* only from the Buddhist angle. He points out that up to *The Cocktail Party* Eliot was advocating ascetic detachment but "in *The Cocktail Party* a tremendous change occured: an acceptance of humanity. He made a distinction between the opportunity of the saint and the opportunity of the common man, and admitted a decent value on the latter. Buddha had called renunciation the abandonment of the `household life' and the election of the 'houseless one.' The household life covers what the common man values most. But it is worthless, said the Buddha, a source of inevitable sin and thus of the prolongation of the agony of the incarnate soul. By a moving concession in *The Cocktail Party* Eliot made himself the champion of the household life as well as of the sacrificing martyr."[16] If *The Cocktail Party* is read in the tradition of the *Bhagavad-Gita* instead of the Buddhist doctrine, it can be seen that Eliot did not introduce any new or original concept countering the one that he started out with, but that he was merely mixing the Buddhist and Brahmanic backgrounds in the play, himself leaning more towards the Brahmanic in *The Cocktail Party*.

A perceptive student can realize that the Buddhist doctrine is radically different from the Brahmanic one. The relation between Buddhism and Brahmanism is like that between Christianity and Judaism. Gautama expounded his philosophy as a reaction against the romantic, idealistic aspects of the Hindu Vedic outlook. As a consequence, Buddhism depended on a stark, spartan attitude of life. Extreme asceticism is not uncommon in certain kinds of Buddhism. Life, said the Buddha, is the cradle of desire and consequent sorrow; withdrawal is the first step in eschewing this sorrow. The aim of the soul is to attain nirvana or total Nothingness. This is the kind of negative detachment or quietism that Waggoner mistakenly reads into the philosophy of detachment that is advocated by Krishna in the *Bhagavad-Gita*. The Buddhist and Brahmanic ideas of non-attachment to life are not one and the same. One leads to nirvana through withdrawal; the other leads to moksha through detached action. Nirvana is the avoidance of worldly life; moksha is the transcendence of it.

According to the Gita and the Brahmanic tradition in general, life in this world is unreal; it is an illusion or maya and the soul must not be attached to it. Enlightened knowledge and the realization of the nature of this world lead one into participating in this life without involvement or attachment. A total withdrawal, which can only lead to the Buddhist nirvana, is not necessary. Thus the important duty of a human being is to participate in life with the proper attitude. So, in the tradition of *The Bhagavad-Gita*, Reilly points out to Edward and Lavinia that the householder's life is as important as that of the ascetic. According to the four stages of life, termed as the ashramas in the *Upanishads*, an individual has to recognize the value of all four stages - that of the novitiate, the householder, the anchorite, and the ascetic. Instead of discounting the value of family life in this world, as Buddhism does, the Vedic sources consider the order of the householder "as the most important because it is at this stage that the individual enters into the first unit of society, i.e. the family, and the responsibility of supporting his wife and his children falls on him."[17]

From this point of view *The Cocktail Party* can be read as an epitome of the situation described in the *Bhagavad-Gita*, that life is a matter of choice, of involvement in action with proper attitudes. The pattern of dialogue between Reilly and his patients resembles that between Krishna and Arjuna in the Gita. Arjuna is at the crossroads of experience and is bewildered, and so seeks answers to his questions. At one point Krishna places intellect above action but still bids Arjuna to act. When Arjuna points out that Krishna's statements seem to contradict each other, Krishna replies:

> I have already told you, that in this world, aspirants may find enlightenment by two different paths. For the contemplative is the path of knowledge: for the active is the path of selfless action.
>
> Freedom from activity is never achieved by abstaining from action.[18]

Krishna's words are similar to Reilly's where he tells Celia about the two paths by which individuals may achieve salvation. The ways are different and are suitable to individuals according to their temperaments. Edward and Lavinia's way will not suit Celia and so Reilly tells her of the way of knowledge or faith, a way appropriate for her. The dialogue between Celia and Reilly further echoes a passage from the Gita:

> Celia: That sounds like what I want. But what is my duty?
> Reilly: Whichever way you choose will prescribe its own duty.
> Celia: Which way is better?
> Reilly: Neither way is better. Both ways are necessary. It is also necessary to make a choice between them.[19]

The parallel passage in the Gita is as follows:

Krishna

The wise see knowledge and action as one;
They see truly.
Take either path
And tread it to the end:
The end is the same.
There the followers of action
Meet the seekers after knowledge
In equal freedom.[20]

When Krishna speaks of the two-fold path the reference is to the Hindu idea of salvation by faith and salvation by works, metaphorically described as the "way of the cat" and the "way of the monkey," respectively.[21] Reilly too makes a similar distinction and prescribes the way of faith for Celia, and the way of works or action for Edward and Lavinia.

Reilly's job, like that of Krishna in the *Gita* is to bring the questioner to a proper state of mind. This is done through detailed dialogue in both works. *The Cocktail Party* bears not a little resemblance to the *Gita* in this very didactical structure. They are both philosophical works reflecting the dramatic qualities of the cosmic comedy.

More than anything, the central theme of both Eliot's play and the *Gita* is that one does not separate religion from secular life, and one cannot separate action or knowledge from love. According to the *Gita*, the proper state for an individual is achieved when he practices in this life the two all-inclusive virtues - love and non-attachment. As the *Gita* puts it:

Krishna

United with Brahman
Cut free from the fruit of the act,
A man finds peace
In the work of the spirit.
Without Brahman,
Man is a prisoner,
Enslaved by action
Dragged onward by desire.[22]

Though the resemblance is not explicit, the message that Reilly gives to Celia, and to Edward and Lavinia is similar to this. They have to understand themselves only after understanding the true nature of love. All three of them were caught in different distortions of love - self love, selfish love, and lovelessness. Celia's infatuation for Edward had to be transmuted into a more universal love for the sake of her individual redemption. Edward's self love had to change into his selfless love for Lavinia, just as Lavinia's lovelessness had to change into responsible love for Edward in the interest of their mutual redemption.

Even the rhythms in the lines in *The Cocktail Party* remind one of patterns of rhythms in the *Gita* and some Vedic hymns. Eliot knew both Pali and Sanskrit. One can safely presume that he had read some Indian poetry in their original Sanskrit verses. In a radio talk in 1946 Eliot himself had remarked:

> Long ago I studied the ancient Indian languages, and while I was chiefly interested at that time in Philosophy. I read a little poetry too; and I know that my own poetry shows the influence of Indian thought and sensibility.[23]

Significantly, the libation scene at the end of Act Two obviously shows the influence of Indian poetics on Eliot's work. Though the scene also bears resemblance to Greek dramatic techniques, the cryptic invocations and blessings pronounced by Alex, Reilly, and Julia are close to the invocations of Vedic hymbs. According to the *Rigveda*, one offers libation to *Agni* or the God of Fire, for he is the "God of the Hearth." Similarly, when a new house is built, a ceremony called "the purification of the house" is performed. The invocation then is: "Lord of the House, be our increase, furthering our wealth with kine and horses. May we be free from old age in thy friendship."[24] Julia and Alex call upon the "Protector of Travellers" in words similar to those addressed to the God of Rain: "May he who is the increaser of plants and waters, who as God rules over everything living, give threefold shelter and protection... May this hymn be to the heart of the monarch. May he accept it. May the rains that give pleasure be ours. . . ."[25]

In conclusion, one can say that tracing the influence of an external force on a writer's work is a difficult job. But notwithstanding that, one can easily determine the obvious similarities between two works involved in an inexplicable way. In the light of that possibility one cannot dispute that technically and thematically Eliot's play gains a new dimension of meaning if read along with a background of the *Gita*. Such a reading would be quite in keeping with a cocktail conversation peppered with reference to "saffron monkeys," "curry powder," and "tigers."

NOTES

1. F.O. Matthiessen, *The Achievement of T.S. Eliot* (N.Y.: Oxford Univ. Press, 1947), p. 51.

2. T.S. Eliot, *The Waste Land,* ed. Valeric Eliot (London: Faber and Faber, 1971), pp. 148-149.

3. Cleanth Brooks, "*The Waste Land:* An Analysis" in *T.S. Eliot - A Study of his Writings by Several Hands,* ed. R. Rajan (N.Y.: Funk & Wagnalls, 1948), p. 29.

4. Helen Gardner, *The Art of T.S. Eliot* (London: Cresset Press, 1949), p. 173.

5. Hyatt Howe Waggoner, *The Heel of Elohin* (Norman: Univ. of Oklahoma Press, 1950), p. 43.

6. B. Rajan, "The Unity of Four Quartets," in T.S. Eliot: *A Study of his Writings by Several Hands, op. cit.,* p. 87.

7. T.S. Eliot, *After Strange Gods* (N.Y.: Harcourt Brace & Co., 1934), pp. 43-44.

8. *Ibid.,* p. 44.

9. Herbert Howarth, *Notes on Some Figures behind T.S. Eliot* (Boston: Houghton Mifflin & Co., 1964), pp. 200-206.

10. Harold McCarthy, "T.S. Eliot and Buddhism," *Philosophy East and West*, 2, no. 1 (Aprl 1952), 31-53.

    Russel K. Fowler, "Krishna and the 'Still Point': A Study of the *Bhagavad-Gita's* influence on *Four Quartets*," *Sewanee Review*, 79 (Summer 1971), 407-23.

    K.S.N. Rao, "T.S. Eliot and *Bhagavad-Gita*," *American Quarterly*, 15, no. 4 (Winter 1963), 572-78.

11. Craig Raine, "Methim Pikehoses: *The Waste Land* as a Buddhist Poem," *The Times Literary Supplement*, May 4, 1973, pp. 503-505. Followed by correspondence on May 11, 1973, p. 556; May 25, 1973, p. 587; June 15, 1973, p. 749.

12. *Bhagavad Gita*, tr. Christopher Isherwood and Swami Prabhavananda (California: Vedanta Press, 1944), p. 6. Quotations from the *Gita* in this paper are also from this edition.

13. T.S. Eliot, *Selected Essays* (N.Y.: Harcourt Brace & Co., 1932), p. 209.

14. Information in a letter to K.S.N. Rao, *Indian Literature* (Sahitya Akademi: New Delhi, 1970), XIV, no. 1, p. 97.

15. Henry Clarke Warren, *Buddhism in Translation* (N.Y.: Atheneum, 1972), p. 109.

16. Howarth, *Notes*, p. 205.

17. I.C. Sharma, *Ethical Philosophies of India* (N.Y.: Harper and Row, 1965), p. 79.

18. *Bhagavad-Gita*, p. 50.

19. T.S. Eliot, *The Cocktail Party* (Harcourt Brace & Co., 1950), p. 141.

20. *Bhagavad-Gita*, p. 70.

21. The kitten puts its faith in the mother's mouth to be carried around to reach its destination: the baby monkey clings to the mother by its own effort.

22. *Ibid.*, p. 72.

23. Quoted by Howrah, *Notes*, p. 201.

24. *Vedic Hymns*, tr. Edward J. Thomas (London: John Murray, 1923), p. 72.

25. *Ibid.*

5

"Across a Whole Thibet of Broken Stones . . ." Eliot's *The Family Reunion* and His Indic Studies

T.S. Eliot's second play, *The Family Reunion,* was considered a failure when it was staged for the first time in the Westminster Theatre in 1939. It closed after only five weeks of the show and the reason for the closure was attributed to the intervention of the World War. But critical consensus of the time makes it clear that it failed largely because of inherent literary flaws. Even when it was revived for a second showing between 1946-1947, it did not win critical acclaim. For instance, the drama reviewer of *The Daily Worker* (9 Nov., 1946) comments: "Everything happens offstage, and its coincidence and melodrama strain incredulity." The opinion of the *Sunday Graphic* critic was stronger (3 Nov., 1939) before that, when he had said: "I can hardly trust myself to speak—its dullness and pretentiousness seemed to me awful."

But reading the play as Eliot's first drama dealing with contemporary society recent critics like Lyndall Gordon and Tony Pinkney have seen the theme of *The Family Reunion* as a complex one. Gordon, for instance, in *Eliot's Early Years* and *Eliot's New Life* draws attention to Eliot's tortured relationship with his first wife, Vivienne, between 1915 and 1933, and his lifelong friendship with his young American friend, Emily

Hale, and studies the play as a dramataized version of his personal struggles immediately preceding the composition of the play. Pinkney, also depending on recently discovered information regarding Eliot's personal life, reads the play, along with the earlier unfinished *Samson Agonistes,* in terms of Freudian psychoanalysis.

In his *Women in the Poetry of T.S. Eliot,* he draws attention to Eliot's preoccupation with the theme of betrayal of a woman and resulting feeling of guilt, and once again associates them with the sexual and psychological problems Eliot faced in his personal life.

Gordon reads *The Family Reunion* as a thinly visualized representation of Eliot's own feeling of sin, guilt, and expiation in the context of his Puritan religious belief. Thus Harry's self-torture about his own and his family's sin and guilt is seen by her to be projections of Eliot's "pure New England" inheritance.[1] But considering Eliot's deep involvement with Eastern religion and philosophy, one can question such a reading of *The Family Reunion* within the narrow confines of Puritan belief. Cleo McNelly Kearns's recent critical work, *T.S. Eliot and Indic Traditions,* (1988), brings to light clearly Eliot's involvement with Eastern language (Sanskrit and Pali), literature, and religion, starting from his early years as a student at Harvard and later as a reviewer and critic for various philosophical journals when he worked in an editorial position at Faber and Faber. Basing her study on hitherto unpublished material of his Note books on courses that he took at Harvard, and his yet uncollected articles and reviews that he wrote for philosophical journals, Kearns draws our attention to the large number of Indic texts that he knew. Edwin Arnold's *Light of Asia,* Henry Clarke Warren's *Buddhism in Translations,* the *Upanishads,* and the *Gita,* were the chief among these. This present extended knowledge that we have of Eliot's readings of Indic works makes possible a re-reading of *The Family Reunion* in the light of Buddhist philosophy. There are also several overt references in the play that invite an interpretation of the predicament of Harry in other terms than just the New England religious belief.

For instance, Violet at the very beginning of the play speaks of the "strong cold stewed bad Indian tea," almost providing a metaphor for the rehashings of Harry's ideas of sin and guilt and expiation and his expression of his feelings in terms of a "contamination," of something that leaves a bad taste in the mouth.

There are also frequent references to tropical landscape. At one point when Violet and Charles are dwelling on the excessive cold of Wishwood House, Gerald says he'd:

> . . . just as soon be a subaltren again
> To be back in the East. An incomparable climate
> For a man who can exercise a little common prudence;
> And your servants look after you very much better.

And much later Gerald once again refers to the exotic atmosphere:

> There's nothing wrong with a tropical climate!
> But you have to go in for some sort of training;
> The medical knowledge is the first thing.
> And don't forget
> That you'll need various inoculations —

We learn that Harry himself has been travelling in the East, in the tropics, when he says

> In the Java Straits, in the Sunda Sea
> In the sweet sickly tropical night
> I knew they were coming.

Agatha's description of the day when she and Harry's father came together are in similar terms:

> I remember
> A summer day of unusual heat

For this cold country
Only a present moment of pointed light
When you want to burn. When you stretch out your hand
To the flames. They only come once,
Thank God, that kind. Perhaps there is another kind,
I believe, across a whole Thibet of broken stones
That lie, fang up,a lifetime's march.

Besides the tropical landscape there are repeated references in the play to the image of the Wheel.The wheel is an important symbol in Buddhist and Hindu scriptures. In Warren's *Buddhism in Translations*, it is mentioned: "The Wheel of Existence is without known beginning ... Respecting theWheel of Existence it is to be understood that the two factors ignorance and desire are at the root."[2]

Harry speaks of the moment when he pushed his wife overboard on the ocean liner with a curious reference to the image of the wheel:

It was only reversing the senseless direction
For a momentary rest on the burning wheel
That cloudless night in the mid-Atlantic
When I pushed her over.

At another crucial point later in his talk with Agatha when a full awareness of his father's guilt compounded with his own is laid bare in front of him he again speaks with reference to being bound to a wheel;

To and fro, dragging my feet
Among inner shadows in the smoky wilderness'
Trying to avoid the clasping branches
And the gazing lizard. To and fro.
Until the chain breaks.
The chain breaks
The wheel stops, and the noise of machinery,
And the desert is cleared, under the judicial sun
Of the final eye

The Wheel is also the wheel of time, for past and present have neither beginning nor end. Harry refers to his experience of life as being:

In and out, in an endless drift
Of shrinking forms in a circular desert
Weaving with contagion of putrescent embraces
On dissolving bone.

The Wheel as the wheel of Existence spels out the cycle of birth and death. This wheel also symbolises the wheel of karma, of endless rebirth as a consequence of one's sin. Warren's *Buddhism* explains: "Karma expresses not that which a man inherits from his ancestors, but that which he inherits from himself in some previous state of existence. Karma covers two distinct ideas namely, karma is the deed itself and the effects of that deed in modifying the subsequent character and fortunes of the doer. The Buddhists say that this subjective effect continues after death into the next life. The countless influences that affected the ancestors . . . and the numberless actions performed under those influences are in some mysterious way stored up . . . and must bear their own fruit and none other."[3]

This concept of karma in Buddhist terms is better explained by Eliot himself in *The Confidential Clerk*. At one point in the play Lady Elizabeth says:

I took up the Wisdom of the East
And believed for a while in reincarnation. That seemed to explain it all. I don't
Believe it now. That was only a phase.
But it made it all so simple!
To be able to think that one's earthly parents
Are only that we have to employ
To become incarnate. And that one's real ancestry
Is one's previous existences. Of course, there's something in us,
In all of us, which isn't just heredity,

But something unique. Something we have been
From eternity.

Thus in terms of the Buddhist doctrine of sin the causal connection between the acts of Harry and his father are not to be disputed. The evil thought of the father has blighted the spirit of the son he has fathered. The seed of his intended murderous act must naturally find its logical fruition in the son's completed act of actually participating in his wife's death on the deck of the ocean liner. Harry has to reap the consequences of his karma or fate which has been prepared for him by his present act as well as by the actions of the past by his father. The evil in him, the sin that he commits, is predetermined.

Throughout the play there is the discourse of sin and evil being like a disease. Harry's predicament is like that of a sick man and he, and others around him, must find a cure for that sickness. Several passages in the play bring out this discourse of sin and sickness vividly. Violet remembers Harry's childhood illnesses:

It was always the same with your minor ailments
And children's epidemics; you would never stay in bed
Because you were convinced that you would rever get well.

And Harry replies cryptically:

Not, I think, without some justification:
For what you call restoration to health
Is only incubation of another malady.

Dr. Warburton adds his professional comment to this view and says:

We're all of us ill in one way or another:
We call it health when we find no symptom
of illness.
My first patient, now —

You wouldn't believe it, ladies — was a murderer,
Who suffered from an incurable cancer.

It is significant to note that not only in *The Family Reunion* but also in *The Cocktail Party* and *The Elder Statesman* Eliot speaks of sin and suffering in terms of sickness and medication.

According to the Buddhist doctrine, sin, or evil in life, which is inseparable from misery and suffering, is like a disease, an illness. At Harvard in 1913 - 1914, Eliot had attended the lectures of the visiting Buddhist scholar, Masaharu Anesaki on Buddhism and had taken down copious notes and carefully preserved the additional typed and printed notes and translations of certain texts that Anesaki presumably handed out during the lectures. The very first lines that Eliot has noted in his Notebook refer to the Buddhist doctrine thatLife is pain; *aniccha, asubha*, as Eliot has transcribed it in the Notebook (*Aniccha* in Pali means affliction, which the implication that worldly life is like a disease.) Buddha propounded his doctrine and his teachings as parables describing diagnosis in medical treatment. In his Notebooks Eliot has also recorded the story of Ajata Catru who is believed to have killed his father and imprisoned his mother. With the help of Devadàtta he wanted to kill Buddha himself. As a result he was attacked by leprosy. But when he repented his sins he was pardoned and his disease was cured.[5]

In his *Buddhism in Translations* Warren has the following account about the birth of the Buddha:

> Just as he was issuing from his mother's womb, Sakka, the king of gods, came and placed in his hand some choice sandal wood and deparated. And he closed his first upon it and issued forth.
>
> "My child," said his mother, "what is it you bring with you in your hand?"
>
> "Medicine, mother," he said.
>
> Accordingly he was born with medicine in his hand, they gave him the name of Osadha-Daraka (Medicine-child).

Harry's speech at the end draws our attention to his belief that he has been sick and that he is also surrounded in this world by sickness:

Harry: Where does one go from a world of insanity?
To the worship in the desert, the thirst of deprivation,
A stony sanctuary and a primitive altar,
The heat of the sun and the icy vigil
A care over lives of humble people,
The lesson of ignorance, of incurable diseases.

In Harry's mind, associated with the idea of disease was the feeling of "contamination," that has "reached the marrow." Buddhist doctrine holds the same belief, hence the medicine of Buddha's teachings was to have its effect as purification. Thus Buddha taught his Visuddhi-Magga,the doctrine of the path of purification. Eliot's Notebooks record also the date on which Anesaki explained this doctrine in his lectures.

Many of Harry's speeches in which he dwells on his feeling of sin appear to fit into the context of the Buddhist concept of sin rather than the "pure New England" one, as Gordon calls it. In Buddhist ethics no distinction is made between sin and human passion and the resulting ills. The origin of sin is not according to Christian terms of Adam's fall, his transgression of God by his free will. Various doctrines of the Buddha insist on the dreadfulness of human passions; the origin of sin or pain is not sought in the objective world but in our own mind and act. It may be noted that in *The Family Reunion* Eliot has significantly marginalized the actual act of sin, both Harry's and his father's. Although Harry might not even have pushed his wife, it has happened that she has died, and it is clear in the play that he has wished it, just as his father had wished his wife's death earlier. Considering that the only fault that Harry's wife might have had was her over-possessive, demanding nature, Harry's "wish for her death" or his action of having pushed her appears to be more strongly prompted by Harry's own degenerative spirit, his lack of emotional or spiritual faith or power. This degenerative spirit, if we have wondered what might have caused it, is later tied to the suppressed act of his own father, who also had not loved his wife. Many times Harry refers to this idea of sin as a general depravity in the human condition, a depravity that is bound up with desire and ignorance mainly:

Harry: In a thick smoke, many creatures moving
Without direction, for no direction
Leads anywhere but round and round in that vapour—
Without purpose, and without principle of conduct
In flickering intervals of light and darkness

And at another point he says: "It is not my conscience. / Not my mind, that is diseased, but the world I have to live in."

Harry also insists:

What matters is the filthiness. I can clean my skin,
Purify my life, void my mind.
But always the filthiness, that lies a little deeper.

Harry sees his own sin and guilt not just as aberrations of his individual abnormal nature but as something that is a part of the depravity and degeneration that is inherent in the human condition. He maintains:

Harry: What you call the normal
Is merely the unreal and the unimportant.
I was like that in a way, so long as I could think
Even of my own life as an isolated ruin,
A casual bit of waste in an orderly universe.
But it begins to seem just part of some huge disaster,
Some monstrous mistake and aberration
Of all men, of the world, which I cannot put in order.

Speeches such as these make it clear that Eliot has foregrounded the theme of sin and human suffering in *The*

Family Reunion and placed it in the bilateral context of the Greek (pagan) and English (Christian) thought in order to consider it from the points of view of different ethical philosophies. After all, he was writing a drama, not a religious treatise.

In this context the opinions of some critics regarding both *The Family Reunion* and *The Cocktail Party*, the two plays in which Eliot treats the theme of sin and suffering and salvation with considerable spritual intensity, are interesting. Walter Stein says of *The Cocktail Party*:

> Its vision is not that of a human - 'Incarnational' and 'sacramental' - Christianity, but approximates to a radical division of existence into spheres of Nature and Transcendence sharpy separated from each other: where the transcendent is not merely approached by way of the disclosure of Nature's essential imperfections, but finally embraced as a - literally - desperate alternative to the latter's graceless essence.

What Stein says of *The Cocktail Party* he might very well have said about *The Family Reunion* also.

Middleton Murry's comments about *The Family Reunion* are even more acute when he observes that there is "a confusion of values" in the play, ". . . as though there were an element irreducibly pagan at the heart of a Christian mystery." He is also of the opinion that "the curse does not become sin" in the drama.[8]

Associated with this idea of sin as contained in the depravity and degeneration of the human condition is the metaphor of the body as a house, a house where disease and befoulment dwell. This is a much used metaphor in Buddhist ethics as well as in the *Upanishads*. For instance, in the Maitri Upanishad it is observed: "Now, as there is no one to touch harlots who have entered into a vacant house, so he who does not touch objects of sense that enter into him is an ascetic and a devotee."[9]

Harry's fate is very closely associated with Wishwood House. In the play the house becomes the objective correlative of Harry's and his father's festering feelings of sin. The sense of disease and contamination that he feels in himself he feels in the atmosphere of the house also:

You do not know
The noxious smell untraceable in the drains,
Inaccessible to the plumbers, that has its hour of the night;

Although the Eumenides have haunted him in other places he perceives them clearly only in Wishwood House. Harry himself is struck by this when he says:

They were always there but I did not see them.
Why should they wait until I came to Wishwood?
There were a thousand places where I might have met them!
Why here? Why here?

Necessarily, Wishwood House has be the meeting place where Harry is to have his illumination about the true magnitude of his sin. The prolonged theme of the play is the dispelling of Harry's ignorance of his burden. He has been like a man in the dark, like someone asleep and dreaming. Eliot uses the dramatic device of light and darkness tellingly in the play to emphasize the theme of Harry's awakening. The play opens with Amy telling Denham not to draw the curtains but to turn on the lights. When Harry enters the house the first thing that he notices and comments on is the glaring light:

Harry: How can you sit in this blaze of light for all the world to look at? If you knew how you looked, when I saw you through the window!

And at the end of the play when the "curse" has come "To complete fruition" (Agatha) Mary and Agatha "walk slowly in single file round and round the table" clockwise, "and at each revolution they blow out a few candles, so that their last words are spoken in the dark." After his knowledge of the sin Harry has to go on his own course of expiation.

> (Agatha:) . . . in the night time
> And in the nether world
> Where the meshes we have woven
> Bind us to each other.

In between these states of ignorance and knowledge are the states of sleep and dream that Harry repeatedly refers to. He feels that he is only dreaming that he pushed his wife and later calls it "The accident of a dreaming moment / of a dreaming age, when I was someone else." He believes: "What I see is one dream or another." For Harry this state of being half-awake and half-asleep has been the worst state for it is then that he has felt the doubts, the misgivings, and the horror. But this was the necessary vale through which he had to traverse for his soul-making. Eliot's description of Harry's state closely follows the description of such a state in one of the *Upanishads* that he knew well as evidenced in *The Waste Land*, namely, the Brihadaranyaka Upanishad:

> Verily this person, by being born and obtaining a body, is joined with evils. When he departs,on dying, he leaves evil behind. Verily, there are just two conditions of this person: the condition of being in this world and the condition of being in the other world. There is an intermediate third condition, namely, that of being in sleep. By standing in this intermediate condition one sees both those conditions. . . . Now whatever the approach is to the condition of being in the other world, by making that approach one sees the evils(of this world and the joys of (the one yonder.)[10]

After the shock of recognition administered by Agatha Harry is fully awakened to the magnitude of the sinful situation in which he is placed. He passes through a period of self-torture and severe thoughts of self-judgement, because he must be rid of many kinds of ignorance before he can set himself on the path of expiation. The passage from the Abhidhamma Pitaka which Warren has translated in *Buddhism in Translations* spells out the kinds of ignorance:

> Ignorance is want of knowledge concerning misery, want of knowledge concerning the origin of misery, want of knowledge concerning the cessation of misery, want of knowledge concerning the path leading to the cessation of misery, want of knowledge concerning anteriority, want of knowledge concerning posteriority, want of knowledge concerning anteriority and posteriority, want of knowledge concerning definite dependence and of the elements of being sprung from dependence.[11]

Harry himself best describes his state towards the end of the play when he has been able to face the horror and fight it:

> Harry: It is quite irrational, but now
> I feel quite happy, as if happiness
> Did not consist in getting what one wanted
> Or in getting rid of what can't be got rid of
> But in a different vision.

It is after acquiring this "different vision" that Harry decides to leave Wishwood House as the first step towards his path of salvation. Where he will go, he himself is not sure of yet, he has" . . . not yet had the precise directions," "he shall have to learn". Amy and Violet believe that he is going to a tropical country to be a missionary. Gerald, who has himself served in the North West Frontier, believes that there is nothing wrong with going as a missionary to a tropical climate, only hewill need various inoculations.

But in the end Harry leaves amidst this speculation of the family and takes his faithful chauffeur, Downing, with him. The finality of Harry's leaving Wishwood House after all that suffering and self-torture, with only Downing as his faithful attendant, is, within the context of Eliot's Indic studies, reminiscent on a mundane level, of the young Gautama Buddha's final departure from the palace with his horse-keeper, Channa. Edwin Arnold had recounted the story of the Buddha movingly in his narrative poem, *The Light of Asia*. Eliot was familiar with Arnold's poem even in his youth. In his essay, "What is Minor Poetry?" Eliot refers to Arnold's book and says: "I must have had a latent sympathy for the subject matter, for I read it through with gusto, and more than once."[12]

One particular stanza in Arnold's poem suggests a link with Eliot's *The Family Reunion*:

> If ye lay bound upon the wheel of change,
> And no way of breaking from the chain
> The heart of boundless being is a curse,
> The soul of things, fell pain.
> ... Ye suffer from yourselves. None else compels
> ...You that live and die
> and whirl upon the wheel.[13]

In the play Eliot consciously used the double dramatic structure of the anacient Greek and the modern English not only for the sake of new technical device but also to suggest the universality of a predicament such as Harry's. In one way or another, in everyone's life such a situation of facing the truth and taking a decision might arise, bitter as it might be. Eliot indicates this by marginalizing the actual dimension of the particular act of sin and by concentrating on the sinner. No amount of quotations can prove that what we have in *The Family Reunion* is the pure New England experience of Eliot or the deep Indic philosophical knowledge of his Harvard years. Eliot's life was composed of the complex inheritance of a man born from Puritan stock in a Southern town in the United States, who was trained in the systems of Indic, Greek, and Western philosophies, and who finally converted to Anglo-Catholicism in England and settled down there as a typical British gentleman, complete with bowler hat and furled umbrella. In such a context, *The Family Reunion* is the story of any Tom, Dick, or Harry who comes to know that he is a sinner who needs to expiate his sin. And that is all we need to know.

NOTES

Quotations from *The Family Reunion* are from T.S. Eliot's, *The Complete Poems and Plays 1909 - 1950;*

N.Y.: Harcourt, Brace & Company, 1950

1. Lyndall Gordon, *Eliot's New Life;* N.Y.: Farrar, Straus, Giroux, 1988, p. 84.
2. Henry Clarke Warren, *Buddhism in Translations,* Cambridge, Mass.: Harvard University Press, 1922, p. 175.
3. *Ibid.,* pp. 210-211.
4. Eliot's Notebooks on the lectures of Anesaki, along with some typed and printed notes are in the Houghton Library, Harvard University.
5. *Ibid.*
6. Warren, *Buddhism in Translations,* p. 47.
7. Walter Stein, "After the Cocktails," *Essays in Criticism,* 3, January, 1953, pp. 85-104.
8. John Middleton Murry, "A Note on *The Family Reunion*", *Essays in Criticism,* 1, January, 1951, pp. 53-67.
9. Robert Hume, *The Thirteen Principal Upanishads,* Tr. by 1921, 2nd ed. rev. London: Oxford Univ. Press, 1931, 6. 10.
10. *Ibid.,* 4. 3. 8-9.
11. Warren, *Buddhism in Translations,* p. 170.
12. T.S. Eliot, "What is Minor Poetry?" in *On Poetry and Poets,* N.Y.: Noonday Press, 1961, p. 38.
13. Edwin Arnold, *The Light of Asia,* London: Routledge and Kegan Paul, 1954, p. 139.

6

Another Source for Ralph Waldo Emerson's "BRAHMA"?

First published in the *Atlantic Monthly* in 1857, Emerson's poem "Brahma" has intrigued scholars and critics endlessly. The first most famous reaction to the poem was expressed by the scientifically trained doctor, Oliver Wendell Holmes, He dismissed it as the "... nearest approach to a Torricellian vacuum of intelligibility that language can pump out of itself" (Holmes, 1885:397). Yet Emerson himself would not agree to its being omitted from the 1876 edition of his *Selected Poems*, and told his publishers that whatever went overboard. "Brahma" was to stay [Bartol, 1888:104].

The poem was written late in Emerson's life and came as a culmination of his abiding interest in Oriental thought. He had been fascinated by the central idea in the poem, i.e. the idea of the One in All, for a long time. In the course of his *Journals* one comes across a number of references to Oriental texts in which he had found the idea of the Oneness of Deity. For instance, as early as 1845 he had copied the following passage soon after reading the Hindu work. *Vishnu Purana*. What living creature preserves or is preserved? Each is his own destroyer, as he follows evil or good [Emerson, 1993:127].

The following sketch of a poem came a little later:

What creature slayeth or is slain?
What creature saves or saved is?
His life will either lose or gain,
As he shall follow harm or bliss

[Emerson , 1903: 465].

Although in the above sketch the emphasis is more on another predominant. Hindu concept, i.e. the theory of *karma*, rather than on the idea of Oneness of Deity, it is obvious that at least in the first two lines Emerson's "Brahma" was germinating. Further in 1844, apparently after reading some Oriental work that he does not clearly specify, he had written:

> Then I discovered the Secret of the World, that all things subsist, and do not die, but only retire a little from sight and afterwards return again [Emerson, 1883:494].

In his essay on Plato written in 1850, he developed the idea more lengthily in prose.

It is true that most of the lines that he transcribed in his *Journals* when his mind was fermenting under the idea that was later to become the central theme of his verse "Brahma," came from Hindu sources. Indeed, the lines from certain Hindu works seem to reappear in the poem without too much re-working on Emerson's part. This has no doubt led scholars interested in the origin of Emerson's famous poem to confine their study only to a comparison of "Brahma" with the relevant portions of Hindu texts. In this connection K.R. Chandresekharan [1960:507-510] and Andrew MacShane [1969:115-122] have thrown invaluable light on the topic. Between them, the two critics traced every step of the transformation of certain lines in the *Katha Upanishad* and the *Bhagavad-Gita* into the finished product of "Brahma." Chandrasekharan points out the important difference between the Hindu concpts of *Brahman* and *Brahma* and does well to clarify that Emerson was thinking of the concept of Brahman although he called the poem "Brahma." According to the

Hindu Triad of gods, Brahma stands for Creation, Vishnu for Preservation, and Maheswara for Destruction. *Brahman* is the spirit transcending these three manifestations of the universe. It is this spirit that is celebrated in Emerson's poem "Brahma." Obviously the title Emerson gave to his poem is misleading. Brahma as such is not present in the poem. Ther are more overt references to Maheswara than to Brahma, as for instance, in the phrase "red slayer." The "red slayer" appears to be almost a literal translation of *Rudra*, another name for Maheswara, the god of Destruction. In this connection, Chandrasekharan attempts to give an interesting explanation to the "red slayer" in Emerson's poem. Endeavoring to relate it closely to Hindu texts, phonetics and semantics, he believes that the world *rudhira* is at the root of the word *Rudra*. He points out that rudhira in Sanskrit means "blood" jor "red", and the word is also connected with the English word "ruddy." Although this appears to be a convincing etymology for vividly explaining the phrase "red slayer," the correctness of the explanation can be questioned in the light of Joseph Campbell's [1962:208-209] explanation of the word *Rudra*. Campbell believes that *Rudhra* is derived from the Sanskrit root word *rud,* which means to "cry" or "howl." Thus Rudra is more convincingly the Howler, howling in anger and destructive power. Campbell's etymology is more precise according to the accent and spelling used in the Sanskrit pronunciation. Siva is symbolized as the powerful god who cries in anger or triumph in the process of striking apocalytic destruction, rather than as a primitivistic god showing his hands dripping with blood.

The difference of opinion possible even in the matter of etymology of just one phrase is cited to show that one cannot, after all, be certain about the background sources for the poem "Brahma." It is true that the similarity in phraseology places it closer to Hindu sources. But the nature of so subtle an operation as influence being what it is, one must consider other possible sources of inspiration behind the poem.

Arthur Christy [1932:355] refers to the claim of an anonymous correspondent in *The Galaxy* [July 1968] who maintained that "Brahma" may have been influenced by John Fletcher's "Hymn to Venus," which poem, according to the correspondent, Emerson knew very well. Fletcher's [1932:358] "Hymn" runs thus:

> O divinest star of heaven
> Thou, in power above the seven;
> Thou, kindler of sweet desires
> Till they grow to mutual fires;
> Thou, the gentle queen, that art
> Curer of each wounded heart;
> Thou, the fuel and the flame,
> Thou, in heaven, here, the same;
> Thou, the wooer and the wooed;
> Thou, the hunger and the food;
> Thou, the prayer and the prayed
> Thou, what is or shall be said;
> Thou, still young and golden-tressed
> Make me by thine answer blessed.

It cannot be denied that lines 7-11 in the "Hymn" are close echoes of the first stanza of "Brahma." If nothing else, Emerson's awareness of the poem may have added to his already existing fascination for the Hindu texts, and thus contributed to the inspiration behind the poem.

Similarly, it can now be argued that even more than the "Hymn." "Brahma" may have been influenced by the following poem by Jelaluddin Rumi, a Persian mystic poet of the thirtreenth century. Rumi's poem runs thus:

> I am the mote from the sun. I am the sun's circuit;
> To the mote I say, Hither! And to the sun I say, Hence!
> I am the glimmer of the dawn, I am the air of the eventide;
> I am the rustling of the branch, the roar of the sea
> I am the mast, rudder; steersman, ship; and I am the reef
> On which the ship founders.

I am the bird-catcher, bird net; I am the face and mirror.
Voice and its echo;
I am the tree of life and the parrot in its branches;
I am silence and thought, tongue and talking;
I am the breath and the flute, I am the spirit of man;
I am the spark from the stone, the sheen of metals.
I am drunkenness, I am vine, I am vinepress, I am "must".
tapper and tavern, the crystal of the cup;
The candle and the moth that circles around it; the
rose and the rose-drunk nightingale
I am physician and sickness, poison and antidote; sweet
and bitter, honey and gall.
I am plaster and trowel; the builder and the plan,
corner and root tree, the building and its ruin.
I am hart and lion, lamb and wolf, I am the shepherd
who gathers all into one fold;
I am the chain of being, I am the ring of the worlds
the ladder of creation mounting and fall
I am what is and is not, I am - O you who know
Jelaluddin, say it - I am the soul in All

[O'Brien, 1962:108-110].

It is quite possible that Emerson may have had a close knowledge of the poems of Rumi. He mentions him in his essay on "Persian Poetry" that he published in 1858. Emerson's interest in Persian poetry had started simultaneously with his interest in Hindu literature. In many entries of the *Journals*, Emerson lists Persian works simultaneously with Hindu ones. Even as early as 1832, one of the entries is an extract from an article on Zoroastrianism.In 1850, he wrote his excellent essay "Persian Poetry," admiring some Persian poets. His next significant gesture was writing the preface to the American edition of Francis Gladwin's translations of the Persian poet, Saadi, published in 1865. William Rounceville Alger had sent him a copy of Eastern poems called *Poetry of the East*. The "Ethical Scriptures" that Emerson and Thoreau edited for the *Dial* between 1842-43 contained extracts from Persian works.

"Days" is one of his poems that has been directly influenced by his reading of Persian literature. His long poem "Saadi" is an eloquent appreciation of a major Persian poet that he admired. The short poem at the end of his essay on "Heroism," which significantly has one of Mahomet's sayings as an epigraph, is written in the concrete, imagistic style that is characteristic of Persian poetry. His poem"Bacchus" can be said to be influenced by the poetry of Hafiz, whom Emerson called "the Prince of Persian poets." He shows an excellent understanding of Hafiz in his essay on Persian poetry. In this essay Emerson mentions the names of many Persian poets, namely, Nisami, Enwari, Ibn Jemin, Feisi and Feradiddin Attar, and provides samples from their poetry. Although he mentions Rumi in the beginning of the essay, he does not provide any quotations from his poetry. According to present evidence found in Carpenter's study of Emerson's Orientalism, Emerson had knowledge of at least six different volumes of Persian poetry. Whether this particular poem of Rumi was in any of the volumes that Emerson knew is a matter for further investigation.

One of the volumes that he knew was Von Hammer Purgstall's German Anthology of Persian poetry, which he had read as early as 1846.He admired some of the poems so much that he was inspired to translate some of them into English [Emerson, 1903]. Around 1847, he had also come across Chodzco's *Specimens of Ancient Persian Poetry*. At the end of the Chapter on Emerson's interest in Persian literature, Carpenter [1930:194] in his book *Emerson and Asia*, lists a number of Persian works that Emerson knew, the list being drawn up from refrences that Emerson himself had made in his *Journals*. The catalogue is formidable for a New England reader of that time. Considering the provenly unmethodical way of Emerson's own recordings of his readings, one may suspect that he knew more Persian works than he himself has mentioned in his *Journals*.

Alger's volume contains numerous poetic fragments from Hindu and Persian sources. But it is disappointing to note that it does not contain this particular poem by Rumi. It only contains four short fragments from Rumi's poetry, only one of them slightly close to the poem under discussion. But these fragments along with the poem quoted above, strongly suggest the influence of Rumi on Emerson's thought. Besides the idea of the unity or oneness of the Deity, the above poem by Rumi echoes certain central concepts to be found in Emerson's philosophy. For instance, the last phrase in the poem, "soul in the All," comes close to the phrase, Over-Soul. Although it is obvious that Rumi's poem did not provide him with the exact phrase, Over-Soul, no doubt it emphasized and intensified Emerson's belief in the spirit of the Over-Soul. One of the fragments from Rumi in the Alger [1856:149-150] *Anthology* is a poem called "All in Each, Each is All," and it is very close to Emerson's poem called "Each is All." It has already been seen in the beginning of this essay how Emerson changed the line of argument as he kept developing the poem "Brahma." He changed the emphasis from the idea of *karma* to an emphasis onthe all-inclusiveness and oneness of deity. Rumi's poem may have decided the change in the emphasis, even if it did not provide the phraseology as strongly as the Hindu sources.

Even if it has to be conceded that Rumi's poem might not have been directly behind the inspiration for "Brahma," the discussion serves to illustrate the complex nature of poetic composition of so eclectic a reader as Emerson. Unlike his younger contemporary Thoreau, who was a bold practitioner of an original, individualistic personal philosophy, Emerson was apparently a man who lived by his mental energy which fed upon ideas and books. This is not to deny originality to Emerson. It is only a reminder of the unique qualities of a thinker who could so well amalgamate the disparate ideas derived from his reading of his Neo-platonic, Hindu, Persian,

Arabic and Chinese literatures. Under these circumstances, "Brahma" appears to be more of an enigma than Holmes thought it to be.

But today, the enigma can be solved a little more by looking more closely into Emerson's*Journals* dealing with Orientalia. Although he was a New England Brahmin, it is clear that he was fascinated by the florid nature of Persian literature. It is interesting to note that besides writing the imitative poem "Brahma," he has also written his poem "Bacchus" in imitation of Hafiz. Compare, for instance, Emerson's [1903:215] translation of Hafiz:

> On turnpikes of wonder
> Wine leads the mind forth,
> Straight, sidewise and upward,
> West, southward, and north:
>
> Stands the vault adamantine
> Until the doomsday.
> The wine-cup shall ferry
> Thee o'er it away

With some of his own lines in "Bacchus".

> Give me of the true -
> Whose ample leaves and tendrils curled
> Among the silver hills of heaven
> Drew everlasting dew.
> Wine of wine.
> Blood of the world,
> Form of forms, and mould of statures,
> That I intoxicated,
> And by the draught assimilated.
> May float at pleasure through all natures
>
> [Alger, 1856:149-150]

His poem "Days," based on his understanding of Persian philosophy, is a more fully realized poetic composition than his staccato verse composition, "Brahma." He showed his enthusiasm for Persian poetry by writing separate essays on Saadi and Hafiz. All this makes one believe that his imagination was more in rapport with the rich, romantic nature of Persian thought than with the subtle, complex ideology of Hindu thought although his intellect found the latter attractive. Obviously he fed eagerly on both Hindu and Persian literature to sustain his poetic imagination and intellectual thinking.

But as in T.S. Eliot, another eclectic poet who borrowed from the Orient, there were some strains in the Oriental philosophy that particularly fascinated Emerson. It is well known that Eliot fully used both Buddhist and Hindu concepts in his writings, but the Buddhist attitude to the world stayed with him more than the Hindu one, as is evident in his play *The Cocktail Poetry* and even in his poem *The Waste Land* despite the significant Hindu philosophical ending of the last section. In the same way, the romantic, optimistic affirmative content in Emerson's idea of Transcendentalism shows that Persian philosophy influenced him no less than Hindu philosophy, perhaps it influenced him more.

But the nature of "influence" being what it is in the nebulous realm of ideas, one cannot be categorical about placing a finger on where and how this influence operates. In this essay, I have only attempted to point out that knowing Emerson's interest in Persian literature, Rumi's poem may have played a part in crystallizing his ideas in "Brahma". The more important thing for us is to see how our assessment of the poem "Brahma," and our understanding of Emerson's theory of Transcendentalism will be affected by this further knowledge about Rumi's poem.

The caustic Doctor Holmes [1885:396] had also observed thus in connection with the poem "Brahma".

> Of course no one can hold Emerson responsible for the "Yoga" doctrine of Brahmanism, which he amused himself

> with putting into verse. The oriental side of Emerson's nature delighted itself in these naracotic dreams, born in the land of poppy and hashish. They lend a peculiar charm to his poems, but it is not worthwhile to try to construct a philosophy out of them.

That is just the point. If one dismisses the idea of possible influence because of lack of proof, one's understanding of a writer's work would be woefully limited. The knowledge of Emerson's acquaintance with Rumi's poetry, although not of this above poem by Rumi, should suffice for us to provide the connection between Emerson's poem and the poem we know by Rumi, and help further in our judgement of the poetic work. Merely drawing parallels of the factors of the influence would no doubt lead to reductive criticism. But a comprehensive knowledge of a background of a writer's readings should enhance our understanding of all works involved in the process of evolution of a creative work.

Why did Emerson fail in incorporating the Hindu concepts that he knew so well in his poetic compositions but succeed enormously in absorbing them into his essays that breathe the spirit of Transcendentalism? Was it simply because he was a bad poet but a good prose writer? For despite the interest aroused in a reader by his poems "Brahma," "Hamatraya" and "Maia," one must conclude that they remain as intellectualized, unimaginative versifications rather than succeed as poems.

One can in this connection again compare Emerson with T.S. Eliot. In so short a poem as "To the Indians who Died in Africa." Eliot could subtly and symbolically assimilate his understanding of the whole of the *Bhagvad-Gita*. He takes the central theme of the *Gita*, applies it to a contemporary military situation where the Indian soldiers are urged to face the battle in the name of duty without questioning other political or personal motives, and concretizes the concept in that particular situation into a vivid poem. Emerson could not achieve the same "conceptual enactment" in his three Indian poems. If "Brahma," "Hamatreya" and "Maia" succeed at all as poems, they do so because the poetry is in the philosophy underlying them.

Then did the Hindu concept of Oneness of Deity that Emerson emphasized and explained so brilliantly in his essay "The Over-Soul" gain something of its strength from his understanding of Persian literature? Perhaps the Neo-Platonic, Hindu and Persian backgrounds of Emerson's reading interact more successfully in his essays than in his poems, in which he had to confine himself to narrower limits. Thus Rumi's poem might not be behind "Brahma" at all but it may be in his essay on the Over-Soul. Once again remembering the shortcomings of such a study as I have undertaken in this essay. I would like to answer the worthy Doctor Holmes belatedly by saying that it is indeed worthwhile to construct a philosophy out of Emerson's interest in Orientalia.

REFERENCES

Alger, William Rounceville, 1856, *Poetry of the East*, Boston: Whittemore, Niles and Hall.

Bartol, C.A., 1888, "Letter to the Editors," *Critic* [New Series], IX, 3 March, 1: 104.

Carpenter, Frederic Ives, 1930, *Emerson and Asia*, Cambridge: Harvard University Press.

Campbell, Joseph, 1962, *The Masks of God: Oriental Mythology*, New York: Viking Press.

Cambridge: Harvard University Press.

Chandrasekharan, K.R., 1960, "Emerson's Brahma': An Indian Interpretation," *New England Quarterly*, XXX, 4:507-510.

Christy, Arthur, 1932, *The Orient in American Transcendentalism: A Study of Emerson, Thoreau and Alcott*, New York: Octagon Books.

Emerson, Ralph Waldo, 1883, *Journals*, Volume VI, Boston: Houghton Mifflin and Company.

—1903, *Completed Works*, Volume IX, Edited by Edward Emerson, Boston: Houghton Mifflin and Company.

Fletcher, John, 1832, "Hymn to Venus", In Christy.

Holmes, Oliver Wendell, 1885, *Ralph Waldo Emerson*, London: Kegan Paul.

MacShane, Andrew, 1969, "Emerson's Brahma' as an Expression of Brahman," *New England Quarterly*, XXXXX, 1:115-122.

O'Brien, Elmer, 1962, *The Varieties of Mystic Experience*, New York: Holt, Rinehart and Winston.

7

William Faulkner's *"A Rose for Emily"*: A Feminist Interpretation

Faulkner's short story, "A Rose For Emily," which was published for the first time in *The Forum* for April, 1930, was one of his early writings. It is generally taken to be a macabre Gothic tale, full of horror and unnaturalness about a "crazy" woman's treatment of her lover. Any reader can notice the several types of polarities and opposing tensions working in the story that contribute towards the ambiguity and the final tragic effect of the story. The chief of them are the contrast between the individual and the community or society, (Miss Emily and the townspeople), the aristocracy and the ordinary citizens, the past and the present, tradition and modernity, the serious and the comic, and love and hate—to mention only a few of them. But one must see that the most crucial opposition determining the meaning of the story is that established between the socially stereotyped identities of the male and female as understood in the American South of the post-Civil war period.

Dorothy Tuck, one of the earliest critics of the story, believes that "Miss Emily desperately sought love with an unworthy partner, murdered him rather than lose him." (Crowell's *Handbook of Faulkner*, N.Y., 1964, p. 175). But a closer look at the story brings out the inadequacy of Tuck's romantic interpretation of the story.

"A Rose for Emily" is set in Faulkner's imaginary locale of Yoknapatawpha County as most of Faulkner's important works are. Yoknapatawpha County is closely modeled on the actual Lafayatte County, Mississippi. Jefferson, the seat of the imaginary county corresponds to Oxford, Mississippi, where Faulkner lived most of his life. The action takes place in the countryside of the post-bellum South of the United States. In the background we feel the conflict between the ante-bellum South of the Civil war days where white women were sheltered and protected from contact with ordinary folk and kept ignorant of the new, post Civil War atmosphere of railroads and progress. The old artistocracy was fighting a losing battle for survival at the turn of the century. There was their inability to come to terms with the post-bellum world. Mainly they hated the substitution of mechanical and commercial values for the human ones of old times. But as we see, their stubborn belief in artificial distinctions and a stiff regard for mere" appearance, itself carried the seeds of their own decay for the fading aristocracy.

These tensions of the aristocracy are best exemplified in Faulkner's description of the old house of Miss Emily, sitting like an eyesore amidst the growing bustle of garages and road construction workers. The central characters in the story are Emily on the one hand and the townspeople on the other. There is also Miss Emily as against her father, and Miss Emily as against Homer Barron. All in all, Miss Emily carries the burden of the story, thus lending the story the inevitability of a heavy feminist interpretation.

The townspeople themselves are unsure about Emily. Their reactions to her are from a distance - sometimes they are indulgent in a typically Southern old-world graciousness and at others veer towards resentment and jeering.

The biggest mistake that a reader can make in interpreting the story is to view Miss Emily from the same perspective as the towns-people, who in a collective way represent the narrative voice within the action of the story. From this perspective Miss Emily's story is full of horror and unnaturalness and she herself seems to be no more than a "crazy" woman who was killed her lover in order to possess him - a sort of inverted similarity to the situation in Browning's poem, "Porphyria's Lover", can be seen here.

But looking at the story from Miss Emily's point of view, which is a view from a world of suppression and silence, or Faulkner's point of view we find that this judgement about her is far from true. Although there was insanity in her family - her aunt the old Lady Wyatt had turned mad during her old age - it is the circumstances in her life rather than heredity that have pushed her to the brink of madness.

Taking her youth we see how her father had domineered, literally with whip in hand, to drive away any sultors that might come to the door. This itself was the beginning of an enforced perverse life for her, almost one of incestuousness. When he died she did not want to part with his body, we are told. But once he was buried the past also was buried with him and there was a new lease of life for Emily.

But then comes another man Homer Barron, the Northener the Yankee, the young man from the modern world and he becomes the "Other" for Miss Emily. Soon, within the year, the town itself hears from Homer that he is not a marrying man, he likes men, he sits with the boys to drink, young boys follow him to hear him curse the niggers, the workmen. He appears as domineeringly offensively male as Emily's father was. It is then that Miss Emily goes to the druggist for arsenic. She asks for the best poison. It is the druggist who writes on the box: "for rats." In Miss Emily's mind Homer Barron was the "rat".

Added to his homosexual leanings. Homer Barron also seems to be born of miscegenation—he was a"dark" man, with eyes lighter than his face, we are told. Miss Emily, the flower of Southern aristocracy is caught in the grip of a man who may have negro blood in his veins. She has only changed hands from one man with a whip to another man with another whip—Homer Barron sat in the buggy with the "reins and whip in his hand," it is observed.

Thus "poor Miss Emily" appears to be betrayed for the second time by a man. The change in her because of these betrayals is drastic. We are told that she had cut her hair short and it turned into pepper and - salt grey - "like an active man's". When at the end of the story it is hinted that she had lain on the pillow next to the corpse of Homer Barron, it appears to be as unnatural as the homosexual leanings of Barron himself.

This "craziness" of Emily is comparable to that of Miss Havisham in the Charles Dickens's novel *Great Expectations*. It is a "craziness" rooted in sexuality and it is the woman who becomes the victim of the perverted sexual leanings of the father or the lover and is driven out of her mind. It is Compeyson's criminality and betrayal on her wedding day that has driven Miss Havisham, the bride-to-be, to arrest time, to freeze her dream within the wedding chamber, the room in which she confines herself until death releases her. Yet Dickens, like Faulkner, has highlighted the "crizeness" of the victim, the woman, to caricature her, to place her in a situation of eccentricity and grim irony. Her bridegroom-to-be, Compeyson, is sketchily treated and his villainy is reported in an oblique style by Dickens.

Also similar is the case of Blanche Dubois, another Southern belle like Miss Emily, in Tennesses William's, *A Streetcar Named Desire*. Blanche is taken away almost in a straight-jacket to a nursing home because she is "crazy", as the he-man who has raped her, her brother-in-law, Stanley Kowalski, stands by and jeers at her. Kowalski, her younger sister Stella's husband is incensed by her "superior" attitude and believes that raping is the just treatment for her. But at the beginning of the play in a scarcely perceptive way, Williams has indicated that Blanche had found her young husband with a boy just a few nights after their wedding day. Williams' reference to this detail is so brushingly done that many a reader of the play misses the connection between the reality of the situation and Blanche's behaviour .

Miss Emily's character then can hardly be considered as that of a "crazy", unnatural, "superior" woman, as the townspeople seem to believe. Instead, we see the ironical twist at the end that refers us back to the title, that Homer Barron was the Rose, the dried rose from a wedding bouquet that Miss Emily has kept pressed between her sheets. Like Miss Havisham who tries to avenge her betrayal by a man through the young beauty, Estella, Miss Emily too has avenged her betrayal by first drying and then preserving her Rose, i.e., Homer Barron. Hers is a gesture of hate like Miss Havisham's rather than of love. "A Rose for Emily" is obviously set in a strongly patriarchal framework. Emily is mostly seen to be a marginal figure, hovering about in a silent way behind drawnshades or hiding in complete silence or standing at the end of the drawing room to repeat a few words to the townspeople who have called on her, or appearing to be lost behind a strong bad smell coming out of a shuttered house. She is treated as a symbol from the very beginning by her father initially, then by her lover and later by the community. She has no way of asserting her individuality in this context of totally male discourse except by her violent act. In the beginning of the story we have the vivid picture of the daughter standing behind the domineering father, later of the woman sitting beside the cigar smoking lover and then the citizen standing at the edge of the group of officials representing the community. She is a "tradition, a duty and a care", never a woman in the story.

Her self assertion perforce gets a twist of perversion in

this situation. The father's possessiveness of the daughter after driving away the suitors was the incestuous beginning of this. Later she falls into the trap of a man who likes other young men. In confused response as a woman towards a man of homosexual leanings she tries to cut her hair short and adjust to the male-dominated world around her. Her last act of killing the lover and withdrawing into the house were she lies/lives with the body is an act of self-annihilation in answer to this frustrating, destructive treatment of her womanhood. It is not love for Homer Barron that makes her kill him and lie with his body, but hate. She buys the poison for "rats" we must remember in the grim situation at the drug-store.

Thus Homer Barron is hardly the rose from a bridal bouquet that is pressed and dried between paper by a young bride in fond memory of love, but he is the rat-poisoned body, the symbol of death and decay, which Emily has embraced for herself in her thwarted life, even as she ironically lives on in a rose-coloured chamber.

8

White Masks, Black Faces: Poetic Subversion in Claude McKay and Langston Hughes

The Harlem Renaissance, although it is believed to have failed, is an important index for determining the nature and development of American cultural history and literary achievement, especially in the early decades of the 20th century. One prominent landmark from the direction of which we can attempt to make a study of this renaissance is by looking into Alain Locke's volume, *The New Negro* (1922) and the resulting critical responses to the volume. Alain Locke's image of the new negro was represented through photographs, portraits, paintings, prose, poetry, drama, songs, and poems, by black artists and writers. The volume also contained poems by poets like Countee Cullen and Claude McKay. This publication by Locke was a seminal work enormously influencing not only the Harlem Renaissance in America but also spreading even beyond to influence the Caribbean and African writers.

The explicit message of Locke's work came through as a declaration of black intellectual and cultural independence, an assertion of a community of black artists and writers concerning their freedom from white dominance in thought and cultural attitudes. The need of the day was to emphasize negro experience and further express this experience in their own terms.

Much of the writing of these black writers was protest writing and necessarily so. For the first time these educated negroes of the 20s and 30s were trying to forge an identity for themselves and their race even when they were living in a predominantly white society. Their repressed anger and protest showed themselves not only through street riots and agitational movements but also in the practice of literary conventions. Indeed, the works of writers like McKay and Hughes expressed their protest in different ways. Protest was not just the theme and content of their poems but it was also the very substance of form. Each of them had his own way of subverting the existing poetic conventions of their white counterparts.

A study of the poetry of writers like McKay and Cullen shows that their employment of conventional poetic forms like the sonnet, ballad, and lyric was a subtle way of establishing their difference as black writers. These conventional forms acted as masks to a poet like McKay. The derivative, imitative use of the familiar form in a certain way concealed the desperate difference that he felt as a double exile - of being an immigrant from Jamaica, and being a black. He blackened the white form of the sonnet by introducing experiences and feelings, dark and angry experiences and feelings, felt by a different race in different rhythms. His way of subverting the conventions of the form was to indirectly expose the inadequacy and the limitations of the rigid unit to express the deep feelings of the new negro. The poetic mask conceals as much as it reveals of the protest and frustration McKay doubtless felt as an in ambitious writer in a society where he was an outsider twice removed.

His sonnet "The Harlem Dancer" supports this observation. The repressed nature of the dancer, the resulting listlessness and weariness, the victimised feeling, are brought out in McKay's description of the atmosphere in the bar and the mechanical movements of the dancer. The precision of the sonnet form is totally unsuited for the undulating, meditative dance-theme McKay has chosen for the poem. One can contrast this poem with Hughes's "The Weary Blues," where the poet's use of the negro blues form is itself a way of showing his defiance of white poetic conventions. The atmosphere of the cabaret scene, the negro singer's despair and frustration and at the same time his inborn panache as he touches the piano off into melody are brought out through a poetic form which is essentially expressive of negro experience. Negro blues particularly conveyed the mood of pathos and irony, that subtle blend of humour and despair, that is so much a part of the negro's attitude to the world. Hughes was clever enough to tap this source of negro expressiveness in his lyrical poems. McKay, on the other hand, attempts to fit personal, lyrical expression into the rigid form of the sonnet and this only results in his sounding artificial and pretentious. A sonnet like "I know My Soul" is a good example of this.

McKay uses the soonet form in a naive and uncritical way. In many sonnets, for example, "Moscow", "This negro's Tragedy", he appears to be straining after effect, showing an ambition to appear genteel in order to appeal to a genteel audience. When McKay started writing in America his fellow blacks were not quite the well-equipped audience, there was no proper black audience for writers like him. Besides this, it appears that McKay deliberately chose to write to a white audience—they were the "Other" whom to measure himself by, they were the ones who were writing and reading poetry.

The challenge for McKay was to imitate the forms of the white poets, the masterrace. Mastering the form was mastering the race. This was a colonial compulsion, perhaps that he could not resist. Writing of the black poets' use of conventional forms like the ballad and the sonnet, Houston Baker observes: "Theirs were standard artistic postures, 'ballads' of Cullen or sonnets of McKay. These are mastered masks. Their trick was denigration of form - a necessary ('forced' as it were) adoption of the standard that results in an effective blackening." (Houston A. Baker, Jr., : *Modernism and the Harlem Renaissance*: Univ. of Chicago Press, 1987: p.85.)

The use of the sonnet form by poets like McKay is a desire for mastery of form, as well as deformation of form. By adopting the sonnet, a form of poem perfected by generations of white Anglo-Saxon poets, the Afro-American poet was deliberately imitating his masters and trying to do one better in the process. It was his way of triumphing over his own masters.

At the same time it was a subtly manipulated mask, a mask concealing the irony and rejection, a parody against the rigid code of the white man. Instead of celebrating the use of their own folk art and folk expression the group of Harlem Rensissance poets like Countee Cullen and Claude McKay stiffly went about imitating the sonnet form and the romantic tone of their white counterpart, crippling the form and crippling themselves in the process.

McKay's "Africa" is a good example of these crippling effects, as also his "Enslaved" and "I know My Soul." It is well known that the classical sonnet and the Shakespearen or English Sonnet each has its own internal laws of end-rhyme arrangement in the octave and sestet parts. The content and the form fall into neat patterns - in the classical sonnet the octave develops the theme in a rising argument, there is then a turn of thought and the sestet works out the resolution (abba, abba, cd, cd, cd, for example, in "I Know my Soul."). Whereas in an English sonnet there is no such neat division of octave and sestet, for the thought moves through three quatrains and than ends in a clinching couplet (ab, ab, cd, cd, ef, ef, gg, for example, in "Africa.").

Now, when McKay writes an English sonnet like "Africa," he is so taken up with the correct form of the sonnet that he goes off focus in fitting the theme to the form. We observe that in the sestet part in "Africa" the idea runs on into one unit of six lines, but the rhyme pattern is divided into quatrain and couplet, indicating a kind of development in idea which is not really there:

> The Hebrews humbled them at Pharoah's name.
> Cradle of Power! yet all things were in vain!
> Honor and Glory, Arrogance and Fame!
> They went. The darkness swallowed thee again.
> Thou art the harlot, now thy time is done.
> Of all the mighty nations of the sun.

Not only is the division of line units mixed up in "Africa" but even the imagery is vague and confusing. What may the poet mean in the line —

"When all the world was young in pregnant night."? Further, the sonnet is a series of exclamations and ejaculations without any logical development. Starting from an idea of being a cosmic force in the first line, Africa strangely becomes a harlot in the penultimate line.

Similarly, in the sonnet "Enslaved" the sestet is very loosely managed and the six lines are repetitious without any development of idea to justify the quatrain and couplet rhymes that have been used:

> Then from the dark depth of my soul I cry
> To the avenging angel to consume
> The white man's world of wonders utterly.
> Let it be swallowed up in earth's vast womb.
> Or upward roll as sacrifical smoke
> To liberate my people from its yoke!

"Enslaved", which is so much like Milton's sonnet on "His Blindness" in vocabulary, tone, as well as idea, is strangely cast in an English sonnet form, and not in a classical form. It is very clearly seen in this sonnet that McKay's control of sonnet conventions was rather poor. His idea of the sonnet just seems to be that it must be a poem of 14 lines with certain rhyme sounds at the end of the lines.

So to say that McKay chose the sonnet form because it helped him to represent his sense of duality, doubleness, split, twoness, is quite wrong. It is not true to say that in the sonnet this duality was neatly presented in the octave and resolved in the sestet, in the form of a classical argument. So to say that McKay chose the sonnet form because it helped him to represent his own inherent sense of duality, doubleness, split, twoness, is quite wrong.

In the above brief analysis of "Enslaved" it can be seen that McKay has not been able to fit the theme to the art form. We cannot say that in his sonnet the duality has been neatly presented in the octave and resolved in the sestet, as in a classical form, as in Milton's "Sonneton On His Blindness", for instance. His predominant use of the English sonnet and not the classical sonnet, and the vagueness and diffusiveness of his theme like "Negro's Tragedy," "Truth", "Like a Strong Tree," etc., defeat such critical opinion offered in explanation of his obsessive use of the sonnet form.

There was another fault McKay was blind to in his eagerness to use the sonnet form. No doubt he adopted it believing that his poetry would be in the mainstream of poetic development when he used this popular and often-tested sonnet form. But McKay overlooked the fact that the sonnets by earlier writers had deliberately limited themes, like love or certain strictly subjective moods. McKay was reckless in using the familiar sonnet for all kinds of themes, ranging from abstract, philosophical idea ("Truth"), to religion ("Baptism", "St. Isaac's Church,Petrograd), race ("Lynching", "The White House"), and social criticism ("The White City").

His best known sonnet, "If we must Die" is a good example of how theme militates against form, and how McKay's desire to be a great poet and to be a spokesman for the negro race pull him in different directions. He wanted to be considered a poet of universal significance and also be a special poet of the black psyche. He has himself admitted that he was happy that a copy of the poem was found in the bag of a dead white Russian soldier, and has implied that he did not mean it to be a call for courage for the negro who was facing lynching or who was embattled by the white race in other ways. His idea of art and idea of race are kept separate and this was the fatal split for McKay, unfortunately.

McKay's use of the sonnet had become so habitual to him and so hackneyed that even his lyrics just narrowly escape turning into sonnets - poems like "Adolescence," "Tropics in New York," "After the Winter," are examples of this, with 12 lines or 16 lines in each.

With the too frequent use of this mask - the sonnet - McKay developed the style of over-dramatizing his feelings, striking poses of theatrical attitudes, blowing up his imagery and vocabulary. The mask succeeded in totally concealing the real McKay even from himself, as is evident in the resulting confusion and unresolved tensions expressed in the body of his poetry covering themes touching on colonialism, communism, racism, Nature, religion, and divided self.

Although Langston Hughes's poetry also covered similarly wide themes and concerns, yet his dedication to the cause of the common man and the ordinary negroes came to his aid in maintaining a poetic integrity. In all his poems the concern of the poet is to express negro experience in authentic terms. And this meant asserting the identity of the black American in the face of the overwhelming power of the white master race. Hughes realized that there could never be competition or imitation, it had to be total defiance and change of direction as far as poetic practice want. As a black American he had the confidence of an insider, unlike the unsureness of an immigrant like McKay.

To be a good poet one needs not only one's own talent but also a proper receptive audience. And, of courses, one also needs good critics who will show proper directions. Appearing first among the founder members of the Harlem Renaissance McKay missed the audience and the critics. Speaking of the theme of audiences and critics for black poets, Charles Scrugge in his book, *The Sage in Harlem* (Baltomore: Johns Hopkins Press, 1984, p. 94), monitored the development of the Harlem Renaissance through the dynamic relations of the journalist - writer, H.L. Mencken. Scrugge points out that it was Mencken's severe criticism of black writing that made the black writers sit up and think about the realism in their writings, to see for themselves the stereotyping of forms and theme they were trapping themselves in, in their works, to acquire the confidence to write critically about white culture. Writers like McKay and Cullen would have benefited a great deal by such helpful criticism as Mencken's but unfortunately their paths did not cross.

It was left to a gifted black poet like Langston Hughes to break out of this imitativeness that he saw in his friends like McKay and Cullen. Hughes plunged into the world of negro spirituals and blues and came up forging haunting poems in a stirring combination of the deeply moody blues, sad and tearful in their evocation of the group sorrow of the negroes, so different from the "egotistical sublime" of the Anglo-Sexon white poets. His "Minstrel Man", and "The Negro speaks of River," are good examples of this.

Hughee's way of subverting the poetry of the master race, the conventions of the Western poets of the white race, was open, defiant and individualistic. From the beginning he realized that he would be nowhere if he attempted to take the poetry of his masters as his models. His genuine talent sought the roots of his poetry in his own racial, traditional expressions of music—the cabaret, jazz, and minstrel shows, gospel songs, and music. Thus his ironical stance is obvious in every word and image in his poem. It is clear that he is striving for effects that are very diffrent from those of his white fellow poets because he himself is a very different man from them. The finest examples of such subversion of conventional poetic form leading to original, inspired black poetry can be found in his poems like "The Weary Blues", "America," "Pride," etc. In poems such as these one is struck not by just the note of irony or gentle mockery, but also of pathos, of beauty, of suffering that the negro poet feels in being a negro.

Even when he employed a conventional poetic form like the ballad, Hughes was capable of deforming the form by his ironical attitude. His "Ballad of Roosevelt," criticising the New Deal of Roosevelt, is ironical in the extreme and it shows the impact of Roosevelt's policy on the black citizens of the U.S. "The Ballad of Lenin" works in a similar way.

Hughes never missed the deep grain of irony that was found in the borderline between the black and white Anglo-Sexon cultures. He too was aware that many of his readers might be white, but he does not appear to have written to a white audience deliberately or exclusively, as McKay appears to have done. Even in Harlem Hughes had observed that most of the night-clubs and theatres were owned by whites - they did not employ even negro clerks, he had learnt from his own experience. He was quite disillusioned. Harlem appeared to be only a ghetto where, once again the poet saw the blacks being exploited. And seeing this he wrote about them and also for them. McKay and Hughes were two of the early, prominent black poets who experimented with poetic form. McKay, who suffered from the double bind of colonialism as well as blackness, curiously adopted the sonnet form and the lyric form, two of the popular poetic forms of the master-race. Hughes, on the other hand tapped the negro music sources like blues and soul, for forging his poetic thoughts.

Whatever the difference between McKay and Hughes, whether they were imitative or original, subversive or conforming, they were successful in stimulating and making possible a dynamic body of poetry like black poetry.

9

Reading a Frost...y Poem: "The Road Not Taken"

Robert Frost is a writer who can be described as an early modern poet. Although he is a modern poet ther is no characteristic obscurity in this poetry, there is rather a kind of obscurantism. His style appears to be puzzing in its simplicity. But even this simplicity is only a seeming simplicity.

"The Road not Taken" is one of Frost's typical poems. It illustrates his own statement about a poem being a metaphor, saying one thing and meaning another. It is a poem in which sound and sense are to be considerd as being equally important in order to arrive at some meaningful interpretation. In fact, the sound effects, the prosody, in the poem is so important that by reading it aloud in certain ways one can make or mar the meaning of the poem.

The metrical pattern is unusual and very ingeniously managed. The line is generally a four-stress line at arranged in stanzas of five lines, as is usual in ballads. The pattern of the rhyme in the first stanza is a-b-a-a-b, and this pattern is repeated in the next three stanzas. Although the rhyme scheme is simple enough, determining the stresses is a hard task, for the poem has a reflective, speaking voice without much variety of emphasis, except perhaps, for line 13. The diction is also extraordinarily simple, if not simplistic, and also flat. There are not many words with more than two syllables and no word that is not used in the most ordinary conversation. There is not much pressure or tension in either the vocabulary or the line, and one is hard put to scan a line like the 1st, or 14th for instance. The unmelodious consonants *w* and *v* appear to figure more frequently than any other, starting with the very central word, wood.

Not only does this poem say one thing and mean another but it must also be noted that the poet says one thing and does another. He looks at one road but takes the other. Even in the second and third stanzas there are unreconciled thoughts and actions. He argues that one road looked better than the other but says that both were really the same. He hopefully kept the other for another day and immediately cancels all hope by wondering it one ever comes back. And finally, although the poet has taken a road, the poem is not about that,but as the title of the poem emphasises it is supposed to be about the one not taken. Between the title and the poem it is difficult for the reader to decide which road it is about. Not only is the metaphor of the diverging roads an adequate objective co-relative to the poet's journey of life, but the poem itself appears to be an objective correlative to the poet's feeling of confusion on that day when he stood at the road's meeting point. The uncertainty of the poet's mood goes beyond what could be termed as ambiguity or paradox, which effects, after all do contribute to making a poem a complex piece of poetic expression. It is only in the third stanza that one finds the poet in a definite coherent mood. He allows himself some feeling when he exclaims. "Oh, I kept the first for another day!" and soberly adds that knowing how one way leads onto way in life, he doubted if he should ever come back. The thought here is more mature and clear than that expressed in the final stanza, although the final stanza is supposed to be the resolution.

The tired lack of emphasis in the last line and the hesitant repetition of the "I" in the penultimate line indicate that the poet regrets having taken the road that was less traveled by. There is also a sigh but still one cannot be sure if this is of regret, for it may be a sigh of relief and not of sadness of regret. The repetition of the "I" may be in an assertive, triumphant tone and the poet may be proud that he has taken the one less travelled by and which has made a real difference to his life. It is here that one is once again reminded of the title and that the lure of the unknown and untried possibility is what the poet is returning to and so the sigh could be taken to indicate regret, definitely.

In spite of the oppositions in the poem one can say that there is no ambiguity in the poem, but it is full of a feeling of ambivalence. This ambivalence only adds to the tightness of the structure of the poem. The poet then is to be taken as a drifter, someone who has no particular philosophical stance when faced with a situation of choice.

Poets writing about youth or age tend to take extreme views about the times of promise or of fulfilment. As the last stanza indicates "The Road Not" taken is a poem of middle age wherein the poet remembers the choice he made "...that morning..." and thinks of the ages hence when he will be telling of that choice. That it is a poem of autumn and not of spring or winter is made clear by the "yellow wood." The poem is made out of an ordinary, routine moment in the poet's experience, and this experience is made use of in the poem without much stylisation or sophistication of poetic structure. Although the incident relatd could have actually taken place in the poet's life, that is, the necessity of having to choose between two roads at some time, the action is not worked out to its logical conclusion in the poem. Somewhere in the middle of the poem we realize that the poet started out with the deliberate intention of symbolising the way life goes by using the metaphor of the road, for he never speaks conclusively about his journey in the wood itself. The road as a symbol, signifying the journey of life, is obviously a hackneyed stock metaphor. The banality and vagueness of the metaphor here can be seen in contrast with his justifiably better known poem, "Stopping by Woods on a Snowy Evening."

The actual experience in "Stopping by Woods" is clearly, concretely specified and further used in order to heighten it into metaphorical meaning. The poet's meaning is coherently based on this vividly worked out metaphor. In "The Road not taken," however,a reader has the uneasy feeling that the actual, real experience and the metaphorical expression are not genuinely fused.

The Road Not Taken

Two roads diverged in a yellow wood.
And sorry I could not travel both
And be one traveler long I stood
And looked down one as far as I could
To where it bent in the undergrowth.
Then took the other, as just as fair.
And having perhaps the better claim.
Because it was grassy and wanted wear;
Though as for that the passing there
Had worn them really about the same.
And both that morning equally lay.
In leaves no step had trodden black.
Oh, I kept the first for another day!
Yet knowing how way leads on to way.
I doubted if I should ever come back.
I shall be telling this with a sigh.
Somewhere ages and ages hence:
Two roads diverged in a wood, and I—
I took the one less traveled by.
And that has made all the difference.

[Robert Frost]

While discussing the nature of the actual and metaphorical experience in the poem it is interesting to note the observation of Frost himself in this connection. E.S. Sergeant, in his *Robert Frost: The Trial by Existence* (N.Y. 1960 pp.87-88) quotes a letter from Frost written Feb 10th, 1912, in which he describes how, going down a lonely cross-road on an evening he saw someone "who looked for all the world like myself coming down the other, his approach to the point where our paths must interest being so limited that unless one of us pulled up we must inevitably collide. I felt as if I was going to meet my own image in a slanting mirror...I stood still in wonderment and let him pass by."

It will be observed that unlike as in the poem where the word "roads" is used, Frost uses the term "paths" in his letter, a substantial difference that affects the poem, as already pointed out above.

With such mixed up imagery and metaphor in the poem, what then can one say about the philosophical consistency in the lines? It is true that a poet need not have all the answers but the formulation of some personal attitude to life is something that is expected of a poet especially in a contemplative lyric.

The poet in the poem neither decides for individual volition/free will and responsibility, not for natural determinism. His individual action of choosing one road has no self-conviction, admittedly. Even though he has taken one of the roads the action has no positive, decisive quality about it. It is a weak choice and he makes it because a choice has to be made. In the course of things one cannot decide whether the "grassy" one attracted him because of its softness or because of its unbeaten, challenging quality. He cancels any decisiveness there might have been by adding that both were worn nearly the same.

If on the other hand he believes in natural determinism as he seems to hint when he says he knows how way leads on to way, preventing him from fulfilling his own wish, then why the sighing that it could have been some other life if he had chosen the other road? Would not that road have had similar predetermined trials and tribulations? The poet's stance is so indecisive and chameleon-like that the poem fails to have any character. One has the uneasy feeling that the poet has had the experience but has missed the meaning.

At this point it must be emphasised that the metrical reading of the poem is highly important and the voice emphasis might provide some clue to the poet's belief. Especially in the last three lines there can be important variations. Reading the lines thus:

I made the one less travelled by

And that has made all the difference.

By putting the emphasis on "I" in different ways one can indicate a self-assertive, joyous choice or it could in another way, argue for a sad, disappointed traveler. Since the poem is in a conversational tone of voice rather than in regular metrical beats one can take the liberty of varying the stresses without violating the rules of metre to force one's meaning.

Frost appears to be hinging all the possibility of ambiguity on this ingenious device of using a conversational tone of voice in poetry.

And when the nature of the experience itself lacks depth and complexity, such a device becomes the only admirable point in the poem. The expression of his regret at what is, is as unwarranted and unconvincing as his wistful dream of what the other road could have been. The poem, instead of embodying an unresolved ambiguity as it set out to do in the beginning appears finally to be a masterpiece of evasiveness and incompleteness. The poet is still in confusion and, perhaps, has to wait to "drink deep" elsewhere "to be whole again".

10

The Regionalism of Richard Wright's *Native Son*

Regionalism, in essence, is the social reality that has survived in a geographical background. The fabric of social reality is woven with the threads of the psycho-social behaviour of the individual and community of a region over a number of generations. A living tradition flourishes in such a society and lends meaning to the particular life of that region. The eternal verieties of human existence, such as love, fidelity, loyalty, faith, and trust between human beings find a particular shape, and organize themselves into a distinct set of values that are special to the region. The region is thus more than a physical boundary, for it has life hovering around it. The topographical entity has nourished the roots of this life; the topography itself in its turn has come to life in the bole, the leaf, the flower, and the fragrance of this life that has grown out of its nourishment. How do you separate the region from its regionalism? How do you separate the dancer from the dance?

Centering a literary work in a region gives the work a core of communal culture. American writers who have appeared relatively late on the world literary scene have depended on this communal culture to give body and substance to their literary imaginations. Many of them like Mark Twain, Bret Harte, James Fenimore Cooper, and William

Faulkner have drawn inspiration for their work from the strength of regionalism. The dynamism of migratory regionalism is reflected in the work of Mark Twain. *Huckleberry Finn*, for instance, represents the migatory, frontier-type cultural and social norms of people who lived casually and close to the earth, with few belongings and fewer pretensions. Twain's close understanding of life in the region of the Mississippi led to his immortalization of the aspects of the region that are as inseparable from the environment as the Mississippi river itself. The hilarious half-truths and half-fictions of the extravagant Frontier yarns and the innocent superstitions of the Indian and Negro folk fill his writings with color and nostalgia. Huck Finn's life near the Mississippi river transcends the limits of regional realism and becomes the archetypal symbol of the young American's search for himself, for the world.

William Faulkner, on the other hand, describes in his works the deep-rootedness of the sedentary regionalism of the South. The more permanent and haunting images of family feuds and racial oppositions in his stories reflect the cultural patterns of Southern Society in the early part of this century. Pictures of the spirited Southernbelle, as Drusilla in "An Odor of Verbena," in*The Unvanquished*, the aristocratic white lady of the mansion as Miss Habersham in *Intruder in the Dust*, the morbid spinster of the white upper-class such as Emily in "A Rose for Emily,"and the stolid, loyal Negro servant as Dilsey in *The Sound and the Fury*, have helped to fix the typical characteristics of life in the Southern Region into sharp focus.

If earlier American writers dealt with rural regionalism, more recent American writers are increasingly depicting an urban regionalism. The shift is a natural one, as the younger generation turns from the country to the city according to the demands of the time. Rapid industrialization has helped in developing New York, Chicago and Los Angeles as the pivotal points for American as well as foreign migrants. Each one of these cities, with its multi-leveled living patterns ranging from skyscraping rooftops to invisible holes in basements, has developed a complex cultural milieu around it. Of these cities, Chicago, being the heart-throb of America in more than one sense, has accumulated a vast reservoir of regional culture upon which artists can draw.

As a distinct background with its own special characteristics, Chicago has left its imprint on many a major American writer. Carl Sandburg, Sherwood Anderson, Theodore Dreiser, James T. Farrell, Jack Conroy, Frank Norris, and more recently, Saul Bellow, have all drawn powerful inspiration from their close association with this city. Its claim to literary regionalism, by which one may mean the importance of an environment in providing more than a more geographical coherence to a group of people, came to be realized in the emergence of the Chicago School of neo-Aristotelian critics. Even a recent American pop-music group has chosen the name of the city for itself. The raw, frightening beauty of this city on the edge of Lake Michigan, with its streets of icy winds, iron-and-glass skyscrapers and sweeping freedom, lurks behind scenes as the most important character in significant works like Drieser's *Sister Carrie* or Wright's *Native Son*. It shapes the lives of Carrie and BiggerThomas as their creators have shaped its image in their novels. It hypnotizes them all equally. It lends its hopelessness and negativism to the spirit in Bellow's*The Dangling Man* just as it instigates the tone of radicalism in the thinking of the Chicago critics. Its South Side has come to stand as the symbol of defeat for black migrants seeking the American Dream, just as its Loop spirals as the symbol of achievement for the capitalists. The squalid, hand-to-mouth existence of the Irish Catholics in Farrell's *No Star is Lost*, the stunted, violence-lined lives of the American Negroes in Wright's *Native Son*, the sad, money-grubbing ambitions of the small-town youth in Dreiser's *Sister Carrie,* speak of the cultural endowment of this metropolis. Chicago, in these writer's works, has many realities, many identities, all contributing to a distinct type of regionalism. Indeed, this single city not only attains the stature of a region, but it multiplies itself into many regions with its plurality of ethnic and cultural zones.

The saga of Richard Wright's own life shows that ethnicity is no longer regional in America. The shift in regional background from the South to the North that Wright so vividly describes in his autobiographical *Black Boy* symbolizes the shift in values, ambitions and aspirations of America in general. It was an emergence of the old world into the new. The change is not only in place but also in time. Like Wright, many American Negroes have left the deep South, which was once their country outside a country, and have sought new fortunes in Northern cities.

Richard Wright left his boyhood in Memphis, Tennessee, and came to Chicago believing that it could be his first home. His bid for individual identity came when he started expressing himself as a writer. Two of his significant novels, *Native Son* and *The Outsider*, were inspired by his experiences in Chicago. If, in his *Black Boy* Wright describes the characteristics of life for the Negroes in the South as an "insider," in *Native Son* and *The Outsider* he describes the life of Negroes in the North. In Natchez and Jackson, and in Memphis, the atmosphere of the old world persisted for they were essentially still rural in atmosphere. The feudalistic attitudes of the Southern whites towards the Negroes served as the seed-bed for the nurturing of the rebellious spirit in the young Wright. He sought to realize the fractured dreams of his boyhood in another background, in a different cultural setting. The road led upwards towards Chicago.

Unfortunately, the white, snow-covered Chicago, as one invariably sees it in Wright's vision, becomes a cold, impersonal, logical extension of what the South had been to the Negro despite its sunniness and warmth. The conflicts are merely urbanized, not solved. There still remains the South side and the North side even in Chicago.

Wright's autobiographical *Black Boy* and fictional *Native Son* are complementary to each other. As evidenced by Wright's own analysis of Bigger Thomas' character in his introduction to *Native Son,* Bigger is not so fictitious a character.[1] Wright even identifies himself with Bigger in a certain context in his introduction.[2] Bigger must be seen as a complex figure, a unique combination of the racially burdened Southern Negro and socially free Chicago black youth.

The story of Bigger Thomas unfolds in the heart of Chicago's black belt. The black belt had its own subculture to set it apart from the white culture surrounding it. For Bigger and his friends there was Ernie's Kitchen Shack on 47th and Indiana, where one could eat Southern fried chicken and guzzle beer, or there was Doc's poolroom around the corner, where one could shoot off one's frustrations. If they were inclined toward quieter pleasures there were the movie houses where they could see white films. Bigger and the other boys could re-live, then, their real-life situations of being idle "outsiders" and spectators viewing the action and happenings in a white world. The cultural milieu of Bronzeville compelled one to escapist solutions - either to take to these cheap and trival pleasures, or go under the opiate of religion as Bigger's mother had done.

Bigger's life is shaped by the background in which he lives. He starts to live only in the nexus of the city's images, its attractions, its aspirations. The white world of Chicago tempts him but the burden of life in the South Side crushes him. Between the two worlds he cannot find his identity. Commenting on the inter-action between the individual and his external world in forging an identity, psychologist Erik H. Erikson remarks: "The individual belonging to an oppressed and exploited minority, which is aware of the dominant cultural ideals but prevented from emulating them, is apt to fuse the negative images held up to him by the dominant majority with the negative identity cultivated in his own group."[3] Just so, Bigger becomes a victim of identity-confusion because of his essential rootlessness. The impersonal, "faceless" city of Chicago contributes to this confusion. It precipitates the inchoate urges of an adolescent like Bigger. As an urbanized black youth, he has no racial inheritance that can act as a psychic ballast to his growing confusion. Bigger carries no images of a region where his roots are set, for he has no such region. He does not belong to Chicago; Chicago merely externalizes the negativism and "facelessness" of Bigger.

Throughout the novel Wright mercilessly exposes the part the world around him had played in contributing to the negated impulses of Bigger's existence. At the heart of *Native Son* is the flight-and-pursuit scene when Bigger is cornered on a rooftop and is captured near-dead, in a fashion that reminds us of his cornering the rat and killing it in their one-room tenement at the beginning of the novel. The hunt for Bigger closes in on the black belt area. During his last hours of freedom, when he is deseperately moving secretly from one Negro home into another in order to conceal himself, Bigger comes closest to an understanding of the background from which he had sprung. In unshaded rooms he overlooks upon black men and women in sexual intercourse in one-room homes full of wide-eyed children, large families eating skimpy meals, or arguing loudly about white dominance. In a nearby church a group of his people lose themselves in prayer. Bigger revolts with his whole being against this limited, characterless trap which has been his background. He cannot identify himself with the kind of life that was given to him. It is obvious that there were no shared experiences between Bigger and the community to which he belonged. Although his behaviour cannot be fully explained, one can understand why he acts as a rapist-murderer. Life in the black belt region was only a negative inheritance, and Bigger's violence and destructiveness only testify to the rootlessness that was a part of his life as a product ofthe black belt. The deadness of the region does not only surround him, it is in him. It had provided him with no ideological pattern for his life for it itself possessed no ideological structure. An adolescent, as Bigger is, especially depends upon the stability that his environment or regional culture can give him. But the black belt area, surrounded by the white region, as it is in the map that the Chicago police have as they hunt Bigger, is simply a blotted-out spot. It has no regional strength to bestow on Bigger.

As the heart of the novel testifies, Chicago becomes myth, symbol, and fact in *Native Son*. Wright himself had felt the importance of this city as region at the time he was contemplating writing the novel. In the introduction he emphasizes the part played by it in the story and says:

> Then there was the fabulous city in which Bigger lived, an indescribable city, huge, roaring, dirty, noisy, raw, stark, brutal; a city of extremes: torrid summers and sub-zero winters, white people and black people, the English language and strange tongues, foreign-born and native-born, scabby poverty and gaudy luxury, high idealism and hard cynicism! Acity so young that, in thinking of its short history, one's mind as it travels backward in time, is stopped abruptly by the barren stretches of wind-swept prairie! But acity old enough to have caught within the homes of its long, straight streels the symbols and images of man's age-old destiny, of truths as old as the mountains and seas, of dreams as abiding as the soul of man itself! A city which has become the pivot of the Eastern, Western, Northern and Southern poles of the nation. But acity whose black smoke clouds shut out the sunshine for seven months of the year; a city in which, on a fine blamy, May morning, one can sniff the stench of the stockyards; a city where people have grown so used to gangs and murders and graft that they have honestly forgotten that government can have a pretense of decency![4]

Chicago, on the whole, exhibts the full development of a mass culture in Wright's *Native Son*. There are the capitalists and the working class living their separate lives in their own pockets. Mr. and Mrs. Dalton are rich people, occupying a fine house on Drexel Boulevard. The very street on which they live excudes a confidence and certainty that are totally lacking in Bigger and his background. His own family of four occupies a one-room tenement on the South Side. Charity flows now and then from the Drexel Boulevard area to the South Side, but the division between the whites and the blacks is strictly maintained. Sometimes, some representatives of Marxist groups who inevitably would be active in such an urban, industrialized background, attempt to bridge the gap. Jan, Mary Dalton's boyfriend, and Max, the Jewish lawyer, attempt to fight Mr. Dalton and his class. They expose the corruption, meanness, and self-interest underlying Mr. Dalton's achievement. He holds large stocks in the South Side Real Estate Company and is involved in the racket of determining rents for the Negro housing. He and people like him do their best to maintain the unbalanced culture of the city in their own interests. They are aided and abetted by city administrators like the Deputy Coroner, and the State's Attorney, Buckley.

The trial of Bigger exposes frighteningly the power politics underlying all levels and classes of people who live in Chicago. Buckley wants to fight the case because he is interested in his own re-election. Max wants to get involved with Bigger because he wishes to work out his own frustrations as a Jewish intellectual. Jan, too, is guilty to a certain extent of being the victim of his own communist leanings when he takes up Bigger's cause, although he appears to be the kindest of all towards the ill-fated boy. Wright succeeds in bringing out in the trial scene all the problems and complexities of life for different groups of people in an impersonal city like Chicago. It is a city which everybody fights to own, but which really remains a no-man's land.

Least of all does Chicago belong to the Negroes, although many of them gravitate towards the city after leaving the South. In both *Native Son* and *The Outsider*, Chicago only symbolizes the disinheritedness of the Negro. Bigger Thomas and Damon Cross actually belong to no region. They suggest that ethnicity is non-regional. Black Americans are no longer associated only with the South. Bronzeville in Chicago and Harlem in New York, to which Damon Cross migrates from Chicago, are equally associated with the American Negro.

The American Negroes have also proved that their ethnic group is regionless, as they are uprooted beings. And uprooted beings are everywhere - in the South, in Chicago,in New York, and even inthe non-white countries. In the preface to the novel. *In the Castle of My Skin*, by the Barbados-born writer George Lamming. Wright observes that the colonial situation of the Negro in the West Indies is a"symbolic repetition of the story of millions of simple folk who, sprawled over half of the human race, are today being catapulted out of their peaceful, indigenously earthy lives and into the turbulence and anxiety of the twentieth century."[5] In addition to being regionless, alienated individuals as the urbanized, mechanized modern men are in an existential world today. Bigger and his race are victims of a racial ostracism. Their cross is to eternally be outsiders in this world. Inthe character of Bigger, Wright depicts the totally negative inheritance of the boy. He is lost between the black and the white world, the adolescent andthe adult stages, the unaware and the aware human consciousness.

After considering the full success Wright has achieved in transforming a single city into a complex, densely eventful regional presence in *Native Son*, one must examine the implications of depicting special, regional characteristics in a literary work. Does the depiction of regionalism limit the appeal of a literary work? The writer's self-confinement to a small, special canvas may suggest a narrowness of approach. The reader may require information external to the text itself in order to understand the full meaning of the regional element in the work. The strength of the regionalism present inthe novel or poem may push the literary work into more vague and confusing realms of history, economies, or anthropology, areas into which a student of literature may not wish to venture too far. In short, does the regional element in the literary work explode the formalist, autotelic shape of the literary text?

Truly enough, a fully-flavored regional poem would prove to be a challenge to the New Critic. The theme of the regional poem would re-inforce the argument that word and language spring from the anthropological, psychic, mythic soil of man's mind, and a study of only the form or the text in isolation is no clue to the full meaning of the poem. To understand why Richard Cory shot himself, one has to place him against his background, if not against E.A. Robinson's background.

As for a novel, regionalism enlarges the scope of a work, for it then becomes the record of the life in a certain region as seen by a sensitive artist who combines in himself the tasks of the historian and the painter. Any individual, including the artist himself, is the product of a socio-genetic evolution. To learn about him, to understand his visions and his failures, one has to take him along with a little bit of the sod in which he has sent his roots. When he has no roots, as is the case with Bigger, there is still the non-sod region, as the pavements of Bronzeville. For nothing is truly rootless, neither men nor dreams.

NOTES

1. Richard Wright, *Native Son* (1940, New York: Harper and Row, 1971), vii-xxxiv.
2. *Ibid.*, xxi.
3. Erik H. Erikson, *Identity* : *Youthand Crisis* (New York: 1968), 303.
4. Wright, *Native Son*, xxvi.
5. George Lamming, *In the Castle of My Skin* (London and Trinidad: Longman Caribbean Limited, 1970), jacket blurb.

11

Text, Textile, and Context, in Sylvia Plath's Works

Sylvia Plath was at no time a conscious feminist activist, nevertheless her life and work have become paradigmatic of the ideals that the feminists later came to struggle for. A strong feeling of her own independence, rebellion against male domination, resentment and protest against women who were passively perpetuating the values of abject, mindless domesticity, are freely expressed in her numerous Letters and in almost all her works. She was in the vanguard of young, American women writers of the 20th century who have tried to assert themselves as writers of professional dedication. In a male-dominated society she sought to establish her identity as a woman and an outstanding writer. This quest for identity becomes the main theme in her short novel, *The Bell Jar*, and in almost all her poems.

The search is primarily undertaken at a personal level to find her true self as a woman called Sylvia Plath, and further extends into an existential level with her anxiety to find her meaningful identity as an individual human being in what she saw in her own life as chaos. There was plenty of cause for her confused feeling of identity because of the sudden deathof her father when she was only nine years old. She never forgave her mother for concealing the news of his death from her for a few days. Later in her life temporary fits of insanity aggravated this sense of loss and confusion. Her leavingher own country and crossing the waters to settle down in a new place after her marriage to an English poet, Ted Hughes, further complicated an already sensitive awareness of rootlessness and confusion. Although in the beginning her love for her husband and the choice of England for a new home appeared to be good augeries for a wholesome personal and artistic existence for Plath, the promise of such hope was soon shattered by the final breaking up of the marriage and a re-surfacing in her mind of a fatally ingrained sense of alienation and loneliness in her adopted country. Indeed, under such circumstances she had to strive hard to find and keep her identity as a woman and a writer. Sylvia Plath had an extremely ambitious and competitive spirit as evidenced in her writings. Under any circumstances, the struggle to find oneself is a difficult business. A human identity defies finding and keeping. One's identity is a mixture of external and internal factors, an inchoate element always in the process of becoming to define a being as fixedly as possible in a world of flux. But in spite of the essentially inchoate nature of it as a developing element, it must be granted that a central, cohering thread runs through the whole process of development. Figuratively speaking, the search for identity may be described as an attempt to find this connecting thread, and by holding on to it, arrive at the endof the quest.

Being fully aware of the importance of this thread, this life-line, Plath curiously expresses her quest to be a woman / Writer through the imagery of clothes. This is no acident, if one remembers that the first job Sylvia worked at was to be an apprentice journalist for the well known fashion magazine, *Mademoiswlle.*

As Roland Barthes maintains in his book, *The Fashion System,* there is a language in clothes, and still another language in a language that deals with clothes. Plath skilfully exploits the use of both these languages in her stories and poems. A semantic and symbolic interpretation of the costume imagery in her work would no doubt lead us to a better understanding of Plath as woman/writer. It would help us to understand whether Plath caught hold of that all important thread, and whether, by its guidance she arrived at the end of her quest.

The persona of the writer, which is always extraordinarily striking especially in her autobiographical novel, *The Bell Jar*, is constantly placed before us in a number of stylized postures and attitudes. The differences in such self-dramatizations are emphatically presented through the visual effects of clothes. The series of images involve this persona in a kind of stage show where the ego is displayed in a revolving change of moods, personalities, and roles. References to dresses, hair styles, accessories, jewellery, mirrors, etc., are cumulatively usedto present this dynamic quest of the female persona to discover her identity.

The subject of dress is often seriously regarded by sociologists as a visible source of knowledge for determining the social and artistic temper of a particular society. Man's, or woman's dress is an expression of the creative impulses, sometimes of the wearer himeself, herself, sometimes of the designer's. Quite often it can be as self-expressive as painting or architecture.

Not merely sociologists, even psychologists may find the subject of dress and undress an indispensable, supportive source of information to gauge the inner urges of their patients. Conceptions of beauty, sex, personality, are represented in a visible dimension in the matter of dress, and one's inner nature and identity are thus made manifest to the outside world through one's dress. Next to one's body one's dress is of importance in the business of living, and being so close to one's self, next to one's own skin, it engages one's innermost feelings without fail.

Lacking a more insightful way of judging a person's inner nature the next best measurement to understand this deeper self in its external expression is through clothes. The outer self reflects, or manifests, the inner self.

Contrary to this, one can also argue that the outer self-hides the inner self and clothes it from being revealed. In this connection we are reminded of the argument between Madame Merle and Isabel Archer in Henry James's *The Portrait of a Lady*. To a worldly-minded society woman like Madame Merle the dress is an important way of displaying and declaring to the world what one's inner nature is. But to an introvert character like Isabel the dress of an individual hides, and what is even worse, distorts the inner being. They express their views characteristically thus:

> (Madame Merle) : ". . .I know that a large part of myself is in the dresses I choose to wear. I have a great respect for 'things'! One'sself — for the people — is one's expression of one's self; and one's house, one's clothes, the books one reads, the company one keeps, . . . these things are all expressive."
>
> (Isabel) : "I don't agree with you. . . I think just the other way . . . . Nothing that belongs to me is an expression of me. Certainly, the clothes, which as you say, I choose to wear, don't express me; and heaven forbid they should . . . . My clothes may express my dress-maker, but they don't express me. To begin with, it's not my own choice that I wear them; they are imposed upon me by society."[1]

Whatever Isabel might say, it cannot be denied that clothing, and costuming of women especially, has been a matter of social significance throughout the ages in all cultures. Susan Gubar points out the crucial symbolic role costuming played in the lives of someof the female modernists in the 19th century.[2] Mary Walker, a doctor, was oneof the first women to discuss the social political, and medical questions of women's clothing,inher two books, *Hit*, and *Unmasked*. She herself, like Amelia Bloomers, discarded the claustrophobic clothing imposed by Victorian society and wore the divided skirt, "bloomers," as a liberated woman. One can safely say that the rhetoric of clothes has turned out to be of even greater importance to the modern woman after her liberation, than to the Victorian woman, in order to define herself.

A good part of our study of Sylvia Plath must be based on a study of her first novel, *The Bell Jar*, some slender volumes of her poems and a collection of her letters published by her mother in 1976 under the title, *Sylvia Plath: Letters Home.* Although Amelia Schober Plath has cautiously — sometimes over-cautiously and hence heavily — edited many of the letters, apparently tailoring the image of her daughter to suit the multipurposes of her own need, the family prestige, and above all the particular identity of Sylvia that she wants to emerge in relation to her poems, still, the forceful spirit behind many of the Letters — that is, of the essential Sylvia Plath — has not been crushed. The Letters serve as a magic mirror drawing out the innermost, inexpressible moods andfeelings of the writer herself. But placed beside her own novel and poems the volume of Letters once again conceal as much as they reveal of what must be her full identity. It is to her creative works that one must return in order to understand the struggle and the triumph or failure of this writer to find and define herself.

In her novel, *The Bell Jar*, the very first suggestions of the heroine's feelingof undermined identity is indirectly referred to in terms of clothing—Esther says : "I knew something was wrong with me that summer because all I could think about was the Rosenbergs and how stupid I'd been to buy all those expensive clothes hanging limp as fish in my closet."[3] Esther further develops the picture of the feeling of confusion by references to her outward appearance, which, by its artificial glitter, of self-possession, sadly belies the disintegration within her. She was to be the envy of all college girls because she was " . . . tripping about in these same size-seven patent leather shoes . . . black patent leather belt and black patent leather pocket books to match." (p. 2). The height of this heady phase of glamour is reached when ". . . in a skimpy, imitation silver-lame bodice struck on to a big fat cloud of white tulle," she drinks martinis on starlit roofs in the company of "all-American youths." (p. 2).

The crash comes as dramatically as that of the Rosenbergs and soon she was losing control of herself. But still, even after the crack-up she hangs on to the remnants of the make-up kit that the office of the fashion magazine where she was working had presented to the girls that summer, ". . . fitted out for a person with brown eyes and brown hair . . . complete with mascara, eye-shadow, lipstick and . . . a gilt box with a mirror on one side." (p. 3). That indicates Esther's instinctive attempt to cling to her normal identity, her worldly self, through her possession of these objects of dress and make-up from a former gay life.

The bourgeois nature of Esther Greenwood is also suggested by her rather resentful comparisons of herself with her well-dressed companions. She admires Doreen and envies her for her peach pink silk and lace dressing gown. She herself has to make do with starched" . . . cotton summer nighties and terry cloth robe that doubled as beach robe . . ." (p. 4).

As in the case of Doreen, even in regard to her boss, Jay Cee, Esther's feelings are expressed through her reactions to her clothes, her appearance. She finds her to be in " . . . strict office suit and luncheon-duty hat . . . " (p. 5). Esther likes her a great deal from the beginning. Jay Cee becomes the model for a successful career woman that Esther secretly wants herself to be.

Esther's admiration for Doreen's personality grows with her increasing admiration for Doreen's daring style of dress and deportment. Indeed, Doreen gradually appears to become a bolder side of Esther herself. To a party that they both attend Doreen wears white and she herself wears black shantung sheath, under which she could wear no bra. Woman speaks biological language through her dress, and throughout her descriptions of the Doreen - Esther episode Plath skillfully exploits the different levels of language.

In spite of her bourgeios upbringing Esther herself is a bold girl independent and ambitious. Throughout the novel we see her trying to keep in top form and learn about whatever might help her to be herself, to be successful as an intelligent woman. She sets the goal high for herself and in many situations she is frustrated about her own feelings, especially in situations which involve her with young men like Buddy and Irwin. These swings between ambition and depression are vividly expressed in terms of clothing and unclothing. In one instance she returns to the hotel from a party where she feels totally frustrated and standing alone on the balcony of her room in the middle of the night, lets fly all her clothes, one by one, over the spires of Manhattan. That was her last day in New York and her short term on the editorial staff of Mademoiselle had ended. The next morning she is to return to her suburban existence. In her gesture of throwing away a particular set of clothes, Esther seems to be symbolizing the destruction of one typical identity, that of the glamour girl she had attempted to be. This gesture is also reflective of an urge for self-destructiveness. At the same time, it is this self-destructiveness that releases her and reveals her naked self. It makes way for a remodelling of her self. Lacking any dress the next day she has to trade her cornflowered gown with Betsy and go home as an imitation Betsy, a "Polyanna cowgirl," as she had called her in contrast to the flashy Doreen. In the midst of all these rapidly changing identities, it is obvious that Esther is heading towards a breakdown.

In *The Bell Jar* although Plath narrates the story in the first person, much of which story is obviously thinly veiled fact presented as fiction, she assumes the name of Esther Greenwood. Even this persona-mask is not firmly assumed. Esther is diffident and unsure about herself. At a party with Doreen and her friend Lenny, she suddenly assumes the name of Elly Higginbottom. (p. 9). Again, at another point, when she is involved in the sexual escapade with Irwin she goes to a gynaecologist, gives herself a false name, and quickly forgets this name. It is curious to note Esther's compulsion to change her names just as quickly and frequently as she changes her clothes. These attitudes of the narrator-persona signify the ambiguous urge for withdrawal as well as the wish to assume a new personality.

While noting these changes of the names of the narrator-persona of *The Bell Jar*, we must also remember that Sylvia Plath herself wrote the novel under the pseudonym of Victoria Lucas. In this, her first, autobiographical novel, Plath maintains an uncanny telescoping effect of the writer, the narrator-persona and her different identities in the novel. She thus introduces the theme of the double and the multiple personality. The character's dramatic change of clothes indicates not only a change in appearance, but it is an attempt to meet the various contingencies of life even inwardly. Rapid changes in life's situations require that there be equally rapid changes in one's adaptability, one's flexibility, if one wants to survive without breaking. But on the other hand, a giddy rapidity of change may itself be the cause of disintegration. Over-playing the game of multiple roles may dangerously lead to neuroses, rather than be a cure for it. Plath effectively brings out these psychological aspects of human personality by using the imagery of clothes.

Esther's mode of dressing becomes a clear indicator of her psychicmoods. From a well-dressed, presentable co-ed, she gradually transforms into, by turns, a defiant, glamorously apparrelled fashion-plate as a sub-editor of a modish women's magazine and then a provocatively under-dressed female as she progresses in her New York adventures, until the crack-up comes and then she discards her clothes altogether as pretentious items, as cover-ups, hindering her in knowing herself. She falls into a state of existential confusion, rejecting her hitherto bourgeios life, rejecting the very act of dressing up decently inorder to be presentable in society. Her dishevelled appearance, wherein she has abandoned the effort to comb her hair every day, bespeaks of this confusion. (p. 105). And similarly, at the end of the novel, her return to normalcy is also indicated in terms of dress, as she sits waiting for her last interview with the doctors : "My stocking seams were straight, my black shoes cracked, but polished, and my red wool suit flamboyant as my plans. Something old, something new . . . ." (p. 199). And the shoes are cracked, we may note.

Related to the donning and doffing of clothes are Esther's hot baths. The hot baths, suggesting a cleansing effect, make her feel like a new baby, a pure, yet unclothed creature, still in its pristinely clean state in this world. Clothes are only the need of an adult. Thus clothes are suggestive of concealment, and in a deeper sense, of hypocrisy and pretention. The new baby does not needto cover up yet. Besides the clothes, the covering of dirt which has been acquired in the process of rubbing against the world also has to be removed. Esther endows these baths with almost ritualistic undertones. Her desire to be naked and pure as nature's original creation suggestsher disenchantment with an adult world and its shattering responsibilities.

Associated with the occasions for dressing and make-up, there are innumerable references to Mirrors in Plath's novel and several poems. The face in the mirror always looks like somebody else's to Esther. Once she thinks that she looks like a sick Indian and another time like an old chinese woman. On the verge of cutting her wrists to commit suicide Esther says: "I moved in front of the medicine cabinet. If I looked in the mirror while I did it, it would be like watching somebody else, in a book or a play. But the person in the mirror was paralysed and too stupid to do a thing." (p. 121).

The mirror is known to be a much used, richly complex symbol in the writings of all cultures. It is, first of all, a fascinating object that not only reflects reality but also transforms it quite often. As a symbol the mirror has magical properties of revealing not merely the surrounding world, but it might also transport into its surface reality the unseen and the unknown backgrounds. In folk and fairy tale it is not uncommon for a witch or a step-mother to use a mirror as a medium for seeking such unseen events of the past or the future.

Most obviously as its main function the mirror reflects oneself. The reflector might also be something other than a mercury-coated glass. In Romantic poetry especially, the image of the poet grazing at his own reflection in a pool or a lake is a constantly used symbol evocative of complex meanings. The image symbolizes the narcissistic impulses of the poet. He contemplates his own importance in the universe through this gazing at his own reflection. From mere surface gazing the poet takes himself to the depths of contemplation about his own psyche and inner impulses. In this way the lake and pool are more natural symbols and deeper reflectors than the surface -coated mirror. The self is thus seen to be a complex evolvement of a number of deeply refracted images.

The reflection itself might act as an externalised presentation of one's own psyche, it might equally strongly signify the idea of the other. What onefaces is the other, the necessary object in the outside world that one learns to confront from one's earlier stage of growth.

Psychologists like D.W. Winnicott have pointd out the meaning of such confrontation in a reflection. "One's self starts defining itself only when it sees the other."[4] Thus the mother becomes the very first mirror for the child and in her face the reality of the world and self shape themselves for the child. The child sees not only himself in the smile or frown on the face of the mother, but it also sees the outside world, the other.

Curiously enough, two of the significant women writers of our time, namely, Virginia Woolf and Sylvia Plath, have seen the fulfilment or the destruction of their lives reflected inthe mother-mirrors. They are known to have had closer involvments with the mother as rival. As many letters in *Letters Home* testify, the relations between Sylvia and her mother were none too cordial, particularly when she started growing up. This strained relationship in real life is reflected even in the fictional Esther's relationship with her mother in the novel, *The Bell Jar*. Sylvia resented the perfectionist, demanding mother. Her final break with her mother came when she realized that the death of her father had been hidden from her as she was then a nine-yearold girl and her mother mistakenly took a protective attitude in order to spare the child the shock of a parent's death. But to Sylvia this was the ultimate cheating for which the daughter never forgave the mother, as her mother herself admits in her Introduction to *Letters Home.*

Thus in much of Plath's works, and especially in *The Bell Jar*, the mother serves as a reflector of the daughter's feelings and reactions. As Winnicott observes: "In individual development the precursor of the other as the mother's face."[5] The very origin of expression, of language for the child, and the first shaping of the self are associated with a child's gazing at the mother's face. The mother was the mirror to be looked at, if not looked into. In *The Bell Jar* Esther's biggest confrontations are with her mother as the Other. The mother-daughter engage in a basic, instinctive struggle in the context of a dominating male figure, the father.

The most significant purpose of the mirror imagery in

literature is to emphasize the existence of the other self in oneself. One's recognition of the Stranger, the other, the outsider, is established in confrontation with the mirror. It is with this kind of confrontation that one starts grappling with the question of one's identity. Slowly there is the recognition of the other self and this perception may very well turn into an obsession, a hallucinatory belief in the power of the other self. And such a hallucinatory image of the other self becomes symbolic of the Dostoevskian ultimate reality of the divided self.

From beginning to end the story in *The Bell Jar* is about this divided self, with the glass of the bell jar reflecting this divisive force. What constitutes identity or personality is the constant juggling and keeping in balance of these two selves, or sometimes more than two selves, as in Sylvia's case. Plath represents the maintaining of this delicate balance, in artistic terms through her poems and novel, as being glued together like a broken thing or stitched up like a torn garment.

The most significant implication of the mirror imagery in *The Bell Jar* is the theme of the double. *The Bell Jar* deals with a number of inter-face relationships between Esther and other characters. There are those of Esher and Doreen, Esther and Betsy, Esther and Joan, Esther and Jay Cee, not to speak of the intra-face relationships of Esther and Esther, Esther and Elly, or Esther and Elaine. These relationships indicate that the divided self need not necessarily be double-faced or neurotic, or negative, or destructive. In feminist terms Esther's relationships with the other women represents both female bonding and female antagonism in a male dominated world. In philosophical terms it may represent the two sides of a coin, the nature of duality or the double principle in nature. All these characters seem to be overlapping.

There is also the cracked mirror, the daemonic mirror, suggesting disintegration and unhappiness in *The Bell Jar*. At one point Esther asks the nurse for a mirror. After some hesitation the nurse hands it to her. As Esther's face had all been distorted as a result of her suicide attempt, Esther cannot recognize her own reflection in the mirror and thinks that it is someone's picture that she is looking at. She drops the mirror and breaks it to a number of pieces, to as many pieces as she herself seems to be broken up into the novel. (p. 143). Again, in another instance, Esther overturns a trayful of thermometers and as they break small balls of shining mercury get scattered about. Esther picks up one slipping ball and says: "I opened my fingers a crack, like a child with a secret, and smiled at the silver globe cupped in my palm. If I dropped it, it would break into a million little replicas of itself, and if I pushed them near each other, they would fuse, without a crack, into a whole again. I smiled and smiled at the small silver ball." (p. 150). This small piece of mercury is Esther's mirror of romantic escape, it reflects her dream of being or becoming whole.

Besides all these is the reflective image of the bell jar itself, a glass surface that distorts or blindly reflects the world outside to the persons inside. This mirror affords no magical flight or dreamscape for Esther.

Associated also with clothing and make-up is the fashioning of hair-styles, a feature contributing distinctively to one's personality or identity. Hair, the crowning glory of a woman's appearance, has always been regarded as a symbol of sexuality and fertility and strength. The colour of the hair or length of the hair or the cut and set of it is taken as an indication of the person's inner nature and character. Long, bound up hair spells bondage just as short, cut up hair announces freedom and liberation for the woman. Examples like the ensnaringly long hair of Rapunzel in the fairy tale, the snaky locks of Medusa in Greek mythology, and the golden net of Browning's Porphyria, or Tennyson's Lady of Shalott, are familiar instances where the woman's hair plays a significant part in the action. Hair is also indicative of mystery, a sinister potency, a primeval force. One remembers the Biblical Samson here.

With true woman's flair Plath makes use of significant references to hair in her imagey in *The Bell Jar* and several poems. In a particular episode in the novel, the first man that Esther encounters in New York is Constantin. He fails to seduce her as she had expected and sitting on the bed under cover of a fall of hair on her face she contemplates him secretly and wonders at this attractive man lying on the bed beside her. Constantin, although he does not touch her that night, while gazing at her the next morning suddenly wonders at her hair and runs his fingers through it from the roots to the tips. "A little electric shocks flared through me and I sat quite still," Esther says. But Constantin brings her down to earth brutally by commenting: "Ah, I know what it is, you've just washed it." (p. 70). Esther's constant fear that she is too homely compared to her glamorous friend Doreen, who had white hair like "cotton candy" is, alas, confirmed by Constantin's attitude. All her roused expectations for herself are crushed.

At another point, when Buddy Willard and she are lying on the bed side by side and talking about sex for the first time during their acquaintance, a similar situation as with Constantin occurs. Esther sits cross-legged on the bed and asks for a comb. When she gets it she says: "I began to comb my hair down over my face so Buddy couldn't see it." And then she asks him if he has ever had an affair with anyone, and continues: "I kept rhythmically combing the hair down over the side of my face nearest to Buddy, and I could feel the little electric filaments clinging to my cheeks and I wanted to shout . . ." (p. 70). Even on this occasion Esther is disappointed in her expectations and she "froze up." She merely continues to comb her hair mechanically. Both sexual encounters turn out to be failures for Esther.

On many occasions in *The Bell Jar*, Esther's, and many

times other characters' being well or ill is indicated by the condition of the hair, as being "fat and greasy," or as "hair that was shaved off and sprouted in bristly chicken-feather tufts all over the head," or as "rusty hair knotted up in a schoolmarmish bun." Esther uses the descriptions of the hair to suggest psychic moods.

With differing personae and changing voices Plath uses the imagery of the fashion system with varied effects in her poems. A poem like "The Applicant" depends entirely on the terminology of clothes to suggest the mood of self-alienation. The metaphors, depending on the different turns of phrase, obliquely refer to society as a hospital, a toyshop, or a graveyard. The individual himself is found to be a misfit in such a background:

> The body itself is all broken and patched up
> A glass eye, false teeth or a crutch
> A brace or a hook
> Rubber breasts or a rubber crotch,
> Stitches to show something's missing?
> I notice you are stark naked
> How about this suit —
> Black and stiff but not a bad fit
> Believe me, they'll bury you in it.

The same kind of imagey to suggest loss of self and identity is kept up in "The Tulips" also. The female persona's identity changes as soon as she hands over her day-clothes to the nurse, and dons the hospital dress, Even in her poem "Getting There" the difference between being well and being ill is suggested through her act of dressing:

> The body of this woman
> Charred skirt and deathmask
> And I stepping from this skin
> Of old bandages, old faces.

Similar imagery is worked out in her long poem, "Three Women," in which there is a complex, intricate detailing of the poet's feelings as woman and mother. There are three different masks and voices in the poem, all of which obviously echo the feelings of the poet. Besides numerous references to the body and the clothes, the poem contains references to the mirror and to a supermarket plate-glass window as objects deflecting or reflecting one's identity:

> How slowly she superimposes her neat self
> On the inferno of African Oranges, the heel-hung pigs.
> She is deferring to reality
> It is I. It is I.
> The mirror gives me back a woman without deformity.
> The nurse gives me back my clothes, and an identity.

Little adhesive tapes with the owner's names written on them marked the clothes of Esther in *The Bell Jar*, and of these personae in the poems when they wore confined in hospitals, thus fixing or unfixing their identities as they went in and out of hospitals and got in and out of the clothes. The fits of illness and nervous breakdown that Plath herself had suffered naturally led her to an acute awareness of her body and its workings. With remarkable ironic distance, she views the workings of her own mind and body through these acts of clothing and unclothing herself.

Contrasting with this is the strip-tease in "Lady Lazarus" shocking the spectators, defying death itself to reduce her body to ashes as she stands divested of all coverings. In telling metaphors of a woman's clothes, the poem "Fever 103", shows the female persona as being alienated and lost in the thraldom of sex:

> Love, Love the low smokes roll
> From me like Isadora's scraves, I'm in a fright
> One scarf will catch and anchor in the Wheel,
> (My selves dissolving, old whore petticoats —)

By such violent and flamboyant rhetoric regarding her clothes, the poet appears to evoke in the reader a shock of recognition of her innermost, inexprissible self. The clothes themselves serve as metaphors to emphasize this shock of recognition as well to actualize it.

Poems like "Totem" and "Edge" go beyond the subject of self-alienation of the poet personally, and extend into comments of the existential alienation of man from the universe, from life itself. Once again Plath draws inspiration from the images of clothes in these poems She declares: in the poem, "Totem":

> There is no terminus, only suitcases
> Out of which the same self unfolds itself suit
> Bald and shiny, with pockets of wishes,
> Notions and tickets, short circuits and folding mirrors.

She observes about the dead woman in "Edge":

> Flows in the scrolls of her toga,
> Her bare
> Feet seem to be saying
> We have come so far, it is over.

For Plath even important relationship like those with her father and mother suggest themselves in the images of familiar personal dress items like raincoat and shoe. In "Daddy" her father is the "black shoe/In which I have lived like a foot", and in "The Moon and the Yew tree," The moon is my mother. She is not sweet like Mary/Her blue garments unloose small bats and owls. In a poem called "Medusa," the snaky hair of Medusa suggests to the poet the "eely tentacles", that with which her mother appears to hold her.

In the poem, "For a Fatherless Son," the mirror image is used in a reverse fashion, wherein the child becomes the mirror in the mother-child relationship:

... right now you are dumb.
And I love your stupidity,
The blind mirror of it, I look in
And find no face but my own.

Sylvia's aloneness after her separation from her husband is sharply pointed out in the image. Again, in the poem, "The Other," the split personality is confronted and the loneliness is emphasized by the mirror: "Cold glass,/How you insert yourself/Between myself and myself." By all these examples it can be seen how Plath again and again indicates the connection between the mystery of the self and the paraphernalia of dress, especially as it relates to the female personae that we find in all her works.

By juxtaposing her novel, *The Bell Jar*, and her poems, with her own letters, and the biographical accounts given by her close friends one can better understand the life-long struggle Sylvia went through to find her own self. The personae in the poems appear to be close images of her real, everyday self that her friends saw. For instance, in her memoir of Sylvia, Nancy Steiner discusses at length the first impact Sylvia made on her. There was generally a distinctive way in which girls at Lawrence House, the scholarship house, in Smith College, would be dressed. They reflected a nonchlance verging on eccentricity — ". . . dirty jeans, bare feet, and deliberate gaucheries to demonstrate their contempt for values they considered superficial . . ." and sometimes . . . "they adopted a sartorial asceticism as a means of advertising their individuality."[6] When Steiner first saw Sylvia, she had placed her " . . . in the nonconforming minority in the House and on the Smith campus — the group that eschewed the cosmetic trappings in favour of a no-nonsense dedication to their work . . ." and looked " . . . plain or dull or deliberately dowdy. . . ."[7] But surprisingly enough, she finds on her first close meeting with Sylvia that her earlier surmises belied the fact. "Her clothes and manner seemed deliberately cultivated to disguise any distinction."[8] Sylvia was extraordinarily neat and careful about her own way of dressing. On the one hand, she dressed herself ordinarily in bourgeois style and avoided any distinction. On the other, she fiercely guarded her individuality and her unique personality under this exterior. She kept her writer's personality inside herself in extreme secretiveness. On one occasion Steiner quotes her as saying that she felt as though she ". . . had been raped intellectually, if anyone disarranged her meticulous arrangement of her laundered clothes in her drawer."[9]

For Plath her outward clothes served as a mask. They effectively concealed her inner being, but at the same time gave her the secret boldness to express what was in her heart fearlessly in her poetry. This was a subversive method of leaving bare her deepest self — her conscious as well as her subconscious urges — frankly in her poetry. It is well known that a mask can be used as a carapace for defence just as it can be used as a device for exposure of the self. Plath fully makes use of this ambivalent nature in the art of dressing and masks to play out the drama of the self in her works.

The picture of Sylvia that Steiner gives is corroborated in Sylvia Plath's own *Letters Home*. We find her discussing hair-dos and clothes carefully with her mother in many of the letters.

But A. Alvarez's account of Plath in his *The Savage God* covers the later period in Plath's life and reveals greater depths in her. Alvarez was a witness to the transformation in Sylvia during the last two years that preceded her suicide. In his poet's way he indicated this change through references to her dress and appearance. When he first met her:

> Sylvia seemed effaced, the poet taking a back seat to the young housewife. She had a long, rather flat body, a longish face, not pretty but alert and full of feeling, with a lively mouth and finebrown eyes.Her brownish hair was scraped sevely into a bun. She wore jeans and a neat shirt,

> briskly American: clean, bright competent, youngwoman in a cookery advertisement, friendly and yet rather distant.[10]

Two years later he met her again for the last time, just two months before her suicide. He records his impression vividly:

> She seemed different. Her hair, which she usually wore in a tight, schoolmistressy bun, was loose. It hung straight to her waist like a tent, giving her pale face and gaunt figure a curiously desolate, rapt air, like a priestess emptied out by the rites of her cult. When she walked in front of me down the hall passage and up the stairs to her apartment . . . her hair gave off a strong smell, sharp as an animal's.[11]

How truly evecative of her psychic moods Alvarez's account of her dress and appearance is!

A woman gives attention to her clothes with the prerogative of an artist. Her sense of beauty, form, and aesthetic values are indicated in this attention. Plath the artist was quite aware of this. Just as her characters and personae play out their roles in different garments, Plath plays out her moods through the medium of words, stitching them into poems or stories. She tries to make and remake and fix her identity as completely as she can by clothing her thoughts, or unclothing them, in the succession of poems and in her novel, *The Bell Jar*.

An over-dependence on the matter of clothes, the attention given to it, indicates a vulnerability, a suggestion of the wish to please the other sex. This vulnerability shows itself at its worst in the spirit of competitiveness that is set up for such a woman in a man's world. Esther's several confrontations with men in *The Bell Jar* come to mind in this context. Her relationships with Marco, Constantin, Irwin, and above all, Buddy Willard are all abrasive and they end in a disastrous way. Even in poem like "Daddy" and "For a Fatherless Son", the persona of the woman is left behind, alone. In her personal life, for Plath, there was the failure of her relationship with her father, and later with her husband, Ted Hughes. There was a combative spirit of competition in Sylvia and this time she was competing with her husband as a poet.

Then, should we say that in spite of all the razzmatazz of her changing clothes and playing different roles in this game of identity hunt and survival, Sylvia Plath was a sad loser? Both as artist and woman?

Once again, the answer can be found in her own writings rather than in her letters or biographical accounts about her. Looking at *The Bell Jar* closely, one notices the neat correlation between theme and structure. During one of her confused gropings to find herself Esther thinks:

> I saw the years of my life spaced along a road in the form of telephone poles, threaded together by wires. I counted one, two, three . . . nineteen telephone poles, and then the wires dangled into space, and try as I would, I couldn't see a single pole beyond the nineteenth.[12]

Significantly enough, the novel had twenty chapters. When we see Esther at the end of the novel, in the twentieth chapter, she is in her twentieth year and is waiting in the anteroom of the hospital to face the interview which will determine the question of her being discharged from that institution. When her name is called she walks up to the threshold of the room where the Doctors are sitting, and she observes:

> The eyes and the faces all turned themselves toward me, and guiding myself by them, as by a magical thread, I stepped into the room.[13]

It is discouraging to see that at the end of the book Esther steps into a room, rather than out of the hospital, as though implying that she was frozen in the twentieth year, and the succeeding, crucial twenty-first year signifying her arrival at full adult identity, had eluded her after all.

But then, turning to one of her very last poems, "Lady Lazarus," one finds a more subtle answer, when the poet says:

> Out of the ash
> I rise with my red hair
> And I eat men like air.

With that, we must conclude that in physical terms of identity Sylvia Plath could only follow the magical thread so far, but when it came to her spiritual identity, her poetic imagination, she could forge wings for herself. In her quest the woman died and lost, but the artist survived to triumph.

NOTES

1. Henry James, *The Portrait of a Lady*, Signet Paperback, p.101.
2. Susan Gubar, "Blessings in Disguise: Cross-dressing as Re-dressing for Female Modernists," *The Massachusetts Review*, Autumn, 1981, 478.
3. Sylvia Plath, *The Bell Jar*, Bantam Paperback; p. 9. All further references to the novel will be in this edition and page numbers only will be mentioned in brackets in the text of the paper.
4. D.W. Winnicott, "Mirror-role of Mother and Family," in *Playing and Reality*, Harmondsworth, England: Penguin Paperback, 1974, pp. 130-137.
5. *Ibid.*, p. 138.
6. Nancy Steiner, *A Close Look at Ariel: A Memory of Sylvia Plath*, London: Faber and Faber, 1973, p. 12.
7. *Ibid.*, pp. 15-16.
8. *Ibid.*, p .31.
9. *Ibid.*, p. 6.
10. A. Alvarez, *The Savage God*, Bantam Paperback, p. 29.
11. *Ibid.*, p. 6.
12. Plath, *The Bell Jar*, Bantam Paperback, p. 101.
13. *Ibid.*, p. 200.

12

Asian American Women's Fiction and their Ethnic Discourse

Some of the most stimulating works of fiction coming out in the U.S. today have been written by individuals who belong to a variety of ethnic groups. American society is now increasingly being recognized to be a multicultural one. Native Americans, African Americans, Jewish, Chicano, Japanese, Chinese, Indian andCanadian Americans are represented by their own writers who voice the hopes, aspirations, and frustrations of their people with empathy and authenticity. Among such groups women writers are raising their voices with increasing assurance. Fiction writers like Leslie Mormon Silko, Amy Tan, Maxine Hong Kingston, Diana Chang, Kyoki Mori, and Bharati Mukherjee among others, have contributed towards enlarging the dominant group's understanding of other cultures and other lives through their writings.

Literary form, style, and language in American writing are also undergoing changes because of these new writers. Humor, pathos, attitude to the family, and human relationships are treated in new contexts, adding to the complexity and richness of life experience in America. As Maxine Hong Kingston says: "When you are a person who comes from a multicultural background it just means that you have more information coming in from the universe. And it's your task to figure out how it all integrates, figure out its order and its beauty. It's a harder, longer struggle." (MELUS, 16.4:63).

Interest in ethnic groups and the writing done by members of such groups has been of long standing importance in American cultural studies, starting with the publication of Israel Zangwill's play, *The Melting Pot,* in 1908. But it has acquired increased attention by the Reverend Jesse Jackson politicising the issue when he stood for the Presidency of the United States in the 1986 elections. In his article, "Beyond Melting Pots," Jules Chametzky maintains that the ". . . lid was off" the melting pot idea in the '60s and '70s, as a consequence of certain events in the U.S. like ". . . the Black consciousness movement in the late `60s and the fragmentation during the Vietnam war period of the previous consensus view of American society," (MELUS, XVI, iv, 3).

It might be pertinent to add here that the biggest reason for the lid to be off was the world-wide phenomenon of decolonization that had started taking place in a dramatic way in countries like India and Africa since the '30s onwards. In fact, the upheavals of the decolonizing process and the more recent breaking up of the U.S.S.R. have resulted in the changing scenario of a possible multipolar world. There are increasing national and ethnic conflicts in every part of the world, not to speak of within the U.S. itself. Writers in the U.S. and elsewhere are naturally engaged in reflecting these conflicts and emerging identities of various ethnic groups. Asian American women writers represent one such important group. Belieing the common idea that "all Asians are alike," their writings reveal marked intercultural differences.

This article will deal with some Asian American women writers in order to contextualize their work amidst the changing trends in the American literary scene of the '80s and '90s. Four writers discussed here, namely, Kyoko Mori, Valerie

Matsumoto, Siu Wai Anderson, and Susan K.C. Lee, are represented in *The Forbidden Stitch: An Asian American Women's Anthology* edited by S. Geok-lin Lim, et al. Published in 1989, it is the first such Anthology in the U.S., according to the editors. The fifth writer, Bharati Mukherjee, is represented in her *The Middleman and Other Stories*, published in 1988.

The Forbidden Stitch contains, among other art works, stories by Japanese, Chinese, Indian, Pakistani, and Hawaiian Americans, besides Filipino and Malayasian American women, each group comprising three or four generations of intermixture. As yet there are not many major works by Asian American women, except for those by Maxine Hong Kingston with her *The Woman Warrior* (1976) and *Tripmaster Monkey: His Fake Book* (1989), and Amy Tan with her *The Joy-Luck Club* and *The Kitchen God's Wife*. The writers have to be studied as a group. Of the five, only Bharati Mukherjee has achieved a major minor status and deserves greater critical attention. Werner Sollors, in his seminal, wide-ranging book, *Beyond Ethnicity*, has not considered the contribution of Asian American writers although he discusses nearly every type of immigrant writing in America.

Trying to trace the very root of the term "ethnicity," and the first significant use of the term, Glazer and Moynihan in *Beyond the Melting Pot* have pointed out: "Ethnicity seems to be a new term. In the sense in which we use it — the character or quality of an ethnic group — it does not appear in the 1933 edition of the Oxford English Dictionary, but it makes its appearance in the 1972 supplement, where the first usage recorded is that of David Reisman in 1953." (1). Subsequent writings by Sollors, Mary Dearborn, and Kristin Herzog, among others have validated the study of certain American writers as ethnic writers, and their writings as representing cultural characteristics. The increasing emergence of such a variety of ethnic cultural writing has given way to speculations regarding "beyond the melting pot" and "beyond ethnicity" in the American scene today.

Kyoko Mori's story, "Yellow Mittens and Early Violets," is set in the rural parts of Kobe, Japan. The story deals with the dawning of friendship between a grandmother and grand-daughter, in the absence of the mother who has committed suicide. Mori is a first generation Asian American woman. Understandably, she is still looking backward, to the memories of life in Japan, rather than turning to the new environment in America where she has come to live, for material for her stories. The narration is clear cut, almost like strokes of Japanese brush painting, with clean strokes of her memory drawing out the beauty and tenderness of relationships in the small Japanese family of grandmother, grandfather, and grand-daughter. Mori's assimilation into American life is confined to her style and language, in her easy use of the expressions like "faucet" and "kind of strange." She does not deal with confrontations and conflicts with culture as theme, or with contrasts between her past and her present, although she is a first generation immigrant. Further, there are a number of ethnic gestures and rituals described in the story which may require a specialized response. But in spite of this, or perhaps because of this, her story is very appealing, enriching our understanding of family relationships and their beauty and depth.

Valerie Matsumoto is a third generation Japanese American. In her story, "Two Deserts," confrontation and conflict between two cultures is the very texture of the story. Emiko, the main character, is a Japanese American who has never been to Japan. She is a second generation, *nissei,* woman living with her husband, Kiyo, and daughter, Jenny, a third generation *sansei,* Japanese American girl. The stubborn resistance to assimilation in the melting pot is shown conceretely in the story in Emiko's protest at being called "Emily" in her American school. When Roy, her neighbour, also tries to call her Emily, she repeats emphatically that she is Emiko, Emi for short and not Emily, and that she was named after her grand mother whom she had never seen. Yet, Emiko has adapted herself to the desert farmland in California much better than Roy and Mattie, her American neighbours. The fine balance between yielding and resisting that second and third generation ethnics manage in order to cling to their distinct identity is unmistakably the very theme of the story that Matsomoto tells. Jenny, the third generation child, has imperceptibility grown away from the more definate Japanese American identity of her mother. She is a child of the future, day dreaming and thinking of the gold to be found in the desert beyond their house, and she is growing up free, without the strong consciousness of her background that her mother has. The name Jenny itself signifies her American acculturation.

In the story the most vivid contrast is shown between the ethnic difference that Emiko, the Japanese American symbolizes and the master race, dominant culture that Roy stands for. In their relationship is shown the conflict that arises when the dominant culture interacts with the minority, ethnic culture and tries to erase it or take it over. There is not only the cultural difference between the two characters, but also the gender and class difference, that contributes to the tension between them. Emiko is a farming woman who deals with the soil whereas Roy is a retired businessman who is after city pleasures. Emiko gets on better with Mattie, Roy's wife, as they are two women working on the same level, in their gardens or kitchens making paper flowers for church bazars. The two deserts of the title are apparently the part of California where they live, and more significantly, the sterile world in which Roy lives, without understanding either his own wife, Mattie, or the neighbour, Emiko.

Roy, in his over-bearing self assurance thinks of Japanese women as Stereotypes, believing that Emiko is just like the geisha girl whom he had known in Tokyo. Hence he underestimates the power of Emiko's anger and her spirit as an independent woman. To Emiko, on the contrary, Roy is clearly the other, and she fights against him to retain her individual identity. At the end of the story we see that she is empowered by the strength of her own convictions to withstand the seductive advances of Roy. This is vividly signified in her action of crushing the scorpion in her own garden with all her might as Roy turns and retreats hastily into his house.

Roy, who does not bother to see Emiko as the other in his assurance as a domineering man, can only think of her in his own terms as Emily rather than Emiko. The tension in the story emphasizes a subtle truth in the melting pot metaphor, that the dominant culture sees its own safety in absorbing rather than maintaining the difference in cultures of ethnic minorities, whereas the ethnic immigrants, of even the later generations, see their safeguard in clinging to their parent culture despite the inevitable adjustments that they make in the dominant culture milieu.

Sui Wai Anderson, a Japanese born in Hong Kong and raised in the U.S. by British parents, depends on the technique of memory to link the lives of two Japanese American women who are survivors of the Hiroshima bombing. Although Mariko and Mitsuye have painful memories of their day in Horishima, they have returned to the U.S. where their parents have continued to live. Mariko settlesdown in New England, but her mind is imprisoned in the past, in her memories of her short trip to Japan, the day of the bombing, and later her relocation experience in camps for Japanese in U.S. under President Roosevelt. Unlike Emiko in "Two Deserts" Mariko makes no attempt to adjust to the life in U.S., and lives unto herself asan island, cultivating alone her small garden which is full of fall leaves and where nothing yet seems to have grown. Her isolated chilly, weed-grown patch of land, is quite in contrast to the farm garden of Emiko laden with zuccini, melons, tomatoes, besides marigolds, petunias, and bougainvillea. Significantly enough, both Matsumoto and Anderson in "Two Deserts"and "Autumn Gardening" respectively, use the metaphors of their women working in gardens, with land and soil, to express the themeof assimilation/alienation in adopted countries. At the end of Anderson's story, it is only when Mariko comes to terms with herself and makes an effort to release herself from the prison of her Japanese past on the urging of another Japanese American friend, that she succeeds in accepting her American present and adjusting to her life as a Japanese American. This is vividly shown in her completing the task of clearing the dead leaves from the frosty garden, painful as the effort is to her old and aching back, and preparing it for planting flower-beds in spring.

Unlike the three stories considered above, Susan K.C. Lee's story, "A Letter for Dar," shows no trace of the writers ethnic background. Lee is a Chinese Hawaiian, third generation. Details in the story show neither the Chinese nor the Hawaiian ethnic flavour specifically. Only in the opening sentence of the story there is an indication that it is a family reunion during Christmas of three grown up sisters and their mother, belonging to a Chinese Hawaiian background. But the story is primarily interesting as a study of women's relationships, especially of the mother-daughter and sister-sister ones. Lee exposes relentlessly the cruelties and jealousies with which women cut themselves, and each other. An elderly man, Mr. Winston, supposed to be a friendly neighbour — one cannot be sure whether he is white — has sexually abused the narrator persona when she was nine years old and left alone in the house, and the mother does not even appear to be aware of it. Lee is perhaps an example of the kind of ethnic writer whose third generation assimilation and acculturation into the dominant culture has removed all traces of the ethnic traits. Consequently her story deals with women's discourse in a general way, in a panethnic style. All these four stories deal with the inter-action of the ethnic culture with the other, the dominant culture of white hegemony.

Unlike the stories of the American women with the Far Eastern background, whose stories are based on a two-culture, or mono-culture theme, Mukherjee's stories present the multicultural confrontations and conflicts and compromises. Some of her stories are also based on the interesting problem of the combined minority culture representatives confronting the common other, the white hegemony. Italians, Filipinos, Arabs, Latin Americans, Sri Lankans, Indians, and Blacks, to name a few, interact with one another in her stories. The ethnic variety is bewildering and she overcomes the resulting confusion of cultural mixing with sharp use of the techniques of irony, humor, bathos and anticlimax. The unpredictability of behaviour of these various culturally oriented characters also enables her to use surprise endings, non sequiturs, unexpected twists in narrative development and characterisations, quite effectively. She develops an elliptical style in order to represent the split, multiple personalities of the women of multi-cultural inheritance. The narrator's consciousness is also shown as shifting alternatively between the interior monologue and exterior dialogue.

The story called "The Management of Grief" exemplifies several of these characteristics. It deals with the group of Indian Canadians who are the relatives of the victims who had died in a plane crash over Irish seas. The narrator is an Indian mother who has lost her two young sons and her husband, all that she had, in the crash. The attitudes to grief shown in the story are as various as the variety of people involved. The scene shifts to and from Toronto, Ireland, and India. Grief has plunged the young Indian woman in Toronto into a deep depression and she struggles to surface at least to some distracted level of coping with it. She learns to "manage" her grief and even in her distraction she can see the business-like way in which the Canadian social worker tries to teach them the management of grief, as though there is a formula to the method. The conflict in perspectives is not only an inter-cultural one, between the Canadian woman and the Indians, but also an intra-cultural one, between the Indian Punjabi, the Indian Tamilian, etc. But the underlying meaning in the story brings out the humanity of these people in the face of a commonly shared tragedy. The fragmented, shifting voice of the narrator, saves the story from being a sentimental/ insensitive account. Although these Indian Canadians see themselves, and are also seen by the white majority as "marginal people", as "different people," in the event of a shocking tragedy, some of them rise to awesome, unpredictable strength of character. The impressiveness of Mukherjee's story is in her bringing into recognition the unseen depths of these "marginal people," and reacquainting the people of the other culture with the little known individualities of these people who had been living amidst them as strangers.

"A Wife's Story," like "The Management of Grief," is told by a woman narrator. Panna is many persons and she reveals them, one layer after another, as she recounts her experiences as a research scholar in an American university. Her husband, a businessman, comes to visit her for a short period during this time. With Charity Chin, her Chinese American room-mate, she is on a level of female bonding while talking about men, with a Hungarian fellow scholar, Imre, she shares a secret pact as two foreigners against the white hegemony in the U.S. When she goes to the airport to receive her husband, she changes from jeans into a sari and becomes the docile Hindu wife. While they are on a sight-seeing bus trip she becomes a kind of mediator, interpreting and translating the American culture to her newly arrived husband. As they go about discovering New York, Panna also discovers new sides to her husband and even to herself. Their experience of American culture at first hand is for a short while, because ultimately they both have to go back to India. The story reveals the culture shock that both of them feel, her husband as a tourist and she as a more seasoned resident scholar. As the title suggests, the story is Panna's as she tries to discover her deeper, real identity as a woman during her experience in America. At the end of the story she stands naked in front of the bathroom mirror gazing at her own body. She feels "free, afloat, watching somebody else." (40). Panna's release from her fixed roles, stereotyped roles, of foreigner, Indian woman, Hindu wife, is indicated in her standing naked and confronting herself, her "other" self, in the mirror. It is a rare moment for Panna to feel herself as a woman and observe that "the body's beauty amazes." (40). She stands "shameless, in ways he has never seen me." (40). Throughout the story Panna is made to feel that as a woman she is an "object" for the other's gaze, but it is only at the end, when she is alone, that she can see herself in her own body and truly appreciate her own being as woman. But in spite of this self awareness the woman in the story appears to be a split personality. She does not seem to have triumphed in her womanhood as the woman-narrator in another story, "Orbiting," does. The woman gazes at her mirror-image, seeing in the reflection another woman, a new self, but that is distinctly outside, confronting her instead of merging with her. The split is further deepened between the sexual and the intellectual selves of the highly educated narrator. When she tries to be a mediator to her awkward husband amidst the strangeness of the American scene she is rebuffed by him. As an Indian woman she is expected to be obedient to her husband, not to show any superiority or independence. Here there is a conflict between her female intelligence and his male authority. She feels guilty because as a liberated woman she has inevitably become a different person. The story makes it clear that a woman may have to face a conflict within her own culture besides having a confrontation with another culture in order to find her identity. The story seems to be told on two levels of narration, one by Panna in relation to herself within her own consciousness, the other by Panna, the student, the Hindu wife, in relation to the outside world.

Renata, the Italian American narrator in "Orbiting," is also engaged in the same struggle as Panna. But she faces it differently as a feisty, Italian American young woman of a second generation. She is openly rebelling against the dominance of her own culture as well as that of the master race. Throughout there is the actively protesting, examining, criticizing, attitude in her, whereas in Panna all this is only internally verbalised. In the story, Mukherjee relentlessly dwells on the awkward, seemingly incompatible differences among people of different cultural backgrounds. This she does by depicting reactions to love, marriage, and people's social behaviour in relation to food.

During Renata's Thanksgiving dinner party her parents and her sister's family meet her lover, Ro, who has arrived just three months before from Afgahanistan as an illegal immigrant. He has orbited for six days between airports in Seoul, Bombay, Geneva, and Frankfurt, waiting for an illegal visa to enter America. "Orbiting" is one of Mukherjee's best stories, dealing with characters from cross cultural angles, but above all revealing them as complex human beings. Renata expresses this deeper bond of humanity when she says: "I realized all in a rush how much I love this man with his blemished, tortured body. I will give him citizenship if he asks. Vic was beautiful, but Vic was self-sufficient. Ro's my chance to heal the world . . . I shall teach him how to walk like an American . . . instead of melting and blending but still sticking out in an Afghan way." (pp. 74-75). That is Renata's way of handling her true love in a cross-cultural situation, with a mixture of the humorous and the serious. Just as the headily aromatic nutmeg from Pakistan has to go into the stuffing of a frozen turkey from Little Italy, her fun-loving Italian American family has to accept her Afghan lover who comes from a "Culture of pain".

As in "The Management of Grief," even in another story called "Fathering," Mukherjee deals with the tragic consequences of ethnic mixing. Confusion rather than fusion may be the result, leading to the disintegration or the cracking up of the individual. A feeling of rootlessness and lack of identity drive the person to the brink of insanity. This most often happens when the person has to face a tragic situation rather than a comic one. "Fathering" has a male narrator involving a Vietnamese veteran who has to take care of his illegimate, five-year old Vietnamese daughter in America. Hiw wife, Sharon, himself, and the child, all end up as psychotics in their efforts to live as a family. The story is interesting in that it is the little girl and Sharon who are driven mad, whereas the male narrator keeps some semblance of balance. The girl's way of reacting to her situation is to torture her young body, by deeply pressing and twisting a quarter-coin into her flesh, secretly. Multilating her own body is one way of expressing herself to this girl who has been cast out by two cultures.

With the advantage of her own multicultural background, Mukherjee, a first generation Indian American, more than any other writer considered in this article, has dealt with problems of ethnic confrontations in a variety of situations. As someone considered as being in the margin of American society, she appears to be looking at America "through the wrong end of the telescope," as she puts it in "Orbiting." As Werner Sollors has pointed out in his *Beyond Ethnicity*, this kind of unusual perspective might bring forth new possibilities in literary form. (237). For instance, the ethnic writers' frequent use of the autobiographical form has led to a kind of writing that is called "faction," which is a combination of fiction and fact, as in Alex Haley's *Roots*.

Writers like Mukherjee, Mori, etc. belonging to different cultures and coming to the English language in a fresh way appear to be writing for a double audience, one that understands the work linguistically, and the other through content. The writer is thus under great pressure to reconcile her own double consciousness as well as her double audience in creating her work. Some of these successful writers have shown that one way of doing it is by depending on the technique of irony, of exploring the nature of the absurd and the irrelevant. Another is to depend on the communicative power of humour. Still another is to use skillfully the imagistic and stylistic features that link the worlds contextually, for instance, as in the description of the memorial ritual for the dead mother in Mori's "Yellow Mittens," or the references to food and eating in Mukherjee's "Orbiting."

The writers' double consciousness enables them to turn narrative development in unexpected directions. Shocks of recognition and surprises in expectation may be employed especially in situations which involve characters from different cultural backgrounds. For instance, in Mukherjee's "Buried Lives," towards the end of the story Mr. Venkatesan is in a fix when the German fellow-boarder in Queenie's Boarding House confronts him with his illegal, transient status in Hamburg and threatens police action against him. Suddenly, Queenie, whose grandfather was born in a Sinhalese village and had later moved to the Caribbean and Suriname, bursts through the kitchen door and yells: "You are harassing my fiance! He's a future German citizen. He will become my husband!" (176). This is indeed a surpriise to Mr. Venkatesan, let alone to the German or to the reader.

The ethnic women writers' works especially focus attention on the complexities of female discourse in the modern context. Not only must they bring to light the nature of their lives which have been considered as being merely incidental or minimal, but they must also find a language in which to express this. Ethnic women writers struggle against a subtle "colonial discourse" of nationality, race, gender, as well as language. Their writing is a powerful way of breaking this oppressive discourse. It is the first step in overcoming the barrier of silence.

Their writings give textuality to their lives which are otherwise spent in endless household activities, unhistoric and unsung. These ethnic women writers draw upon their multicultural inheritance and put together their variegated responses in their stories. Their art has been compared to quilting, an activity famílar to women. Maxine Hong Kingston compares it to embroidery. Lim quotes the relevant passage in her Introduction in order to explain what the "forbidden stitch is":

> Long ago, in China, knot-makers tied strings into buttons and frogs, and rope into bell-pulls. There was one knot so complicated that it blinded the knot-maker. Finally an emperor outlawed this cruel knot, and the nobles could not order it anymore. (11).

Tsutakawa takes the explanation further:

> Women in traditional China, even those of the higher classes who escaped daily toil in the fields, were assigned to, and judged by, the fine embroidery patterns they created. Indeed, the finest stitchery was not worn by women, but reserved for the emperor's costume. The expert costume creator stood anonymously by, not even allowed to gaze on her breath taking handwork as the emperor passed. (13).

Further, critics like Carolyn Durham and Roland Barthes have analyzed the activities of knitting, embroidery, stitching as being close to women's lives, a part of them. Barthes describes them as semiotic coding and freely uses the common critical terminology of braid, weave, fabric, text, texture, etc. to analyze writing with words. It may be pointed out that the word 'text' comes from the French term, 'texere,' meaning to weave.

Embroidery and quilting may be familiar to these ethnic women from their background of female culture but the language that they use belongs to the other. Language has a male voice when women are relegated to the margin and to silence. These women have to find a language for themselves if they have to empower themselves and express their own discourse. Such a language has to be formed by them by valorising their so far limited worlds of home,. family, housecrafts, household activities, etc. In addition to this they have to break down these limitations, and reach out to appropriate the other's discourse, and find a discourse for themselves in such a combination. That the ethnic women ariters are doing just this may be seen in their stories. For instance, there is a remarkanble similarity in the themes and situations in many of the stories considered in this article. Women working in the garden, or women talking about families and friends around the dinner table or in the kitchen, women living in the past and recollecting their memories, women fighting against father, husband, neighbour, in order to retain their identity, these are the repeated features. The difference may only be in the regional or geographical backgrounds. This repetition itself is an indication of the nature of women's discourse, it shows the limited worlds to which they were doomed and from which they have to free themselves by this initial step of writing.

Reading these stories of the multiethnic writers from their background of female culture is a challenge to the hitherto held social and literary biases of the reader. Are they worth knowing? The answer is in President Bill Clinton inviting Maya Angelou to recite her poem during the Inauguration ceremony. His gesture well recognized the need of the moment in present day America. Angelou, in her poem, "On the Pulse of Morning," has responded in a magnificent composition that celebrates the ethnic beginnings of the U.S. and shows that America is still "a nation of natiions". The Japanese, Chinese, Hispanic, Indian, etc. American women writers in the present context, stand testimony to that Whitmanesque prophecy.

WORKS CITED

Barthes, Roland, *The Fashion System*, Farrar, Straus, and Giroux: New York, 1983.

Durham, Carolyn, *The Contexture of Feminism*, Univ. of Chicago Press, Illinois, 1992.

Glazer, Nathan and Daniel Patrick Moynihan, *Beyond the Melting Pot*, MIT: Cambridge, 1963.

Lim, Shirley Geok-lin, Mayumi Tsutakawa, and Margaret Donnelly, *The Forbidden Stitch: An Asian American Women's Anthology*, Calyx Books: Corvallis, OR, 1989.

MELUS, *The Journal of the Society for the Study of the Multi-Ethnic Literature of the U.S.*, Amherst, Massachusetts.

Mukherjee, Bharati, *The Middleman and Other Stories*, Penguin Books: New Delhi, 1990.

Sollors, Werner, *Beyond Ethnicity*, Oxford University Press: New York, 1986.

13

Patterns of Colonialism in the New Zealand Stories of Katherine Mansfield

Colonial attitudes in Commonwealth writers are nearly of as many varieties as there are writers. Although the colonial burden is one of the main experiences that binds the Commonwealth countries together, it also happens to be an experience that keeps them apart because of the widely differing nature of the experience. The implications of colonialism for a writer from New Zealand are obviously different from those implications to writers from Africa, India, or the West Indies. The emphasis may be on class distinction in one society, and on race or colour in another society. The intensity of the colonial response is surely determined by whether the emphasis is on the latter or the former. One may have social significance, the other political and the importance of the writer is ironically enough determined by the priority that social and political problems attract in particular contexts. Protest, rage, satire, aggressive exposure, these tones are familiar in Commonwealth writers dealing with colonial societies where the political implications are dominant. Writers like Wole Soyinka and V.S. Naipaul represent this tone. Irony, humour, subtle descriptions of the incongruities of the colonial life resulting from the social problems- these are the milder characteristics of colonial writing that one can trace in a writer like Katherine Mansfield.

Not merely the social and political problems but the context of the writer is also important in determining the intensity of the colonial attitude. Nadine Gordimer and Katherine Mansfield, although similar in many respects as short story writers, react very differently to the society they are observing, for there is a basic difference in their situations. Gordimer, and even Doris Lessing, happen to be white women who find themselves in a country of blacks, whereas Mansfield is in a background which is similar to her native country racially and socially. Whether a writer is from a minority group that is superior or a majority group that is inferior is also important.

Moreover, the shades of colonialism have deepened with the increasing political awareness of Third World countries. Wole Soyinka and V.S. Naipaul came to the full awareness as writers at a time when the Empire was crumbling and the Third World societies were coming into their own. This major political confrontation has obviously given colonialism a nastier turn. But at the time that Mansfield was writing, in the 1920s, there was no such feeling of confrontation, hence the subdued, oblique colonial attitudes in her stories. To this is added the fact that she was a woman who experienced and recorder her impressions in an indirect, suggestive fashion. And also the fact that she left the colonial society to which she belonged as a child, and migrated to the main land, "Home" as she calls it, and wrote about her early colonial experience from memory. As a result, the treatment of colonial problems in her short stories is indeed subtle and indirect, but nevertheless it is significant, for she portrays the colonial background in especially satisfying aesthetic patterns.

In this article my purpose is to highlight some of these aesthetic patterns that have enhanced Mansfield's art as a short story writer. Experience of colonialism has meant disaster and bitterness for some writers but for some others it has symbolised memories of a good world gone by, an old order vanished, taking with it a familiar milieu which formed their past, their childhood, their innocence. Mansfield's experience is of the latter type. These are the two interfaces of colonialism. From one results the literature of protest and anger, from the other the literature of nostalgia, exile, and of course, at its worst, the colonial cringe. The latter can also be termed as the literature of Anglophilia. The Anglo-philes have an inordinate love of all that is white, all that is arrogant and autocratic, all that is "Home." Writers like Nirad Chaudhury display this all-too familiar attitude. In her recent book called *Karma-Cola* the writer Geeta Mehta describes this colonial mentality, of especially the Indians, and says: "To many Indians the sun rises and sets in an Englishman's arse." It is such Indians who perpetuate the "white cringe."

Although Mansfied was not an extreme Anglophile, it was her love of London life that made her reject her homeland decisively. Kathrine Mansfield Beauchamp belonged to a pioneering colonial family originally settled in Australia. Her great grandfather had left England and gone to Australia by the middle of the 19th century to seek his fortune as a goldsmith. One of his sons, Arthur, emigrated to New Zealand in 1848. The new land was rough and offered no easy prosperity. He shifted from the lawless mining communities to the quickly growing towns around these areas. His son Harold, Katherine's father, built up his own successful financial business in New Zealand eventually, and his fortunes grew along with the expansion of the land.

The daughter, however, was not willing to settle down in that small island. When she came back to New Zealand after three years at Queen's College, London, she had become a sort of inverted colonial. She had written to her sister on her return to New Zealand: "I am ashamed of young

New Zealand, but what is to be done. All the firm fat framework of their brains must be demolished before they can begin to learn. They want a purifying influence—a mad wave of Pre-Raphaelitism, of super-aestheticism should intoxicate the country. They must go to excess in the direction of culture, become almost decadent in their tendencies for a year or two and then find balance and proportion. We want two or three persons gathered to discuss line and form and atmosphere and sit at the street corners, in the shops, in the houses at the Teas. People who would quote William Morris and Catulle Mandes... These people have not learned their alphabet yet." (Katherine Mansfield: *Letters*, ed. Middleton Murry: New York, 1929; vol. II, p. 4). In 1908 she set sail for London a second time, never to return to New Zealand.

But almost all the stories that she has written are about New Zealand. Ian Gordon lists at least 59 stories in his *Undiscovered Country: The New Zealand Stories of Katherine Mansfield.* All her spiritual and artistic satisfaction as a short story writer appears to have been derived from her remembrance of her homeland.

To her colonialism had presented the picture of a divided world—the division being between classes rather than races. If the racial differences were also there, they had not yet assumed such magnified proportions as in Third World colonies. Nevertheless the awareness, the upheaval had started and the fixed social order of colonial dominance was shifting. Emancipation, revolution, reform were in the air and the artistic perception of Katherine Mansfield was undoubtedly disturbed by all these disruptions. Her observations of these problems find oblique presence in her stories. She was no political or social reformer but was only interested in holding these transitional moments in the crucible of her stories. One has to look for evidence of this awareness in the structuring of the stories, the confrontation between characters, the importance of the setting, etc.

Dominance of one over another, feelings of condescension and social superiority, the disgruntled, suppressed attitudes in lesser characters like women or weak men, the obsequious attitudes of cast out figures, it is in these patterns that one recognises the characteristic elements that would inevitably be present in a colonial set-up.

In his edition of the New Zealand stories Ian Gordon specifically groups ten stories as "Scenes from Colonial Life." During her intensely self-tormented adolescent life, in 1907, her father had arranged for her a caravan trip through the New Zealand countryside. She had observed here the real native landscape where the Maoris lived in their pahs untouched by the outside world. She absorbed the natural atmosphere of the rugged background, observing with an artist's eye the easy life of the Maori settlements, watching the change of daylight hours over the sulphur baths of Rotorua or noticing other impressive elemental scenes. The ten stories recall these experiences vividly. Stories like "Old Tar", "Ole Underwood", or "The woman at the Store" deal with the native inhabitants i.e. old Maori tribe individuals or off-springs of Maori and white mixing. These stories depict the raw, violent, antagonistic elements present in a colonial society. Murder, killings, rape, robbery etc. are common in this neglected, back-of-beyond, impoverished colonial background and Mansfield deals with them in a Faulknerian style, suggesting social and psychological insights into her characters and the society in which they live.

"Ole Underwood" is the study of a native with "rings in his ears" who has slowly descended into madness after a lifeterm in a prison for killing a man who had raped or seduced his wife. In "Old Tar" we have the short, poignant story of a man who is bent upon building a house for himself to symbolise his rootedness in a new land—something in the nature of the house Mr. Biswas wanted to build for himself in V.S. Naipaul's novel *A House for Mr. Biswas.* Old Tar's grandfather had bought a piece of land from the Maoris on top of Makara Hill and had handed it down to his father who in turn gave it to him with the advice to build the house. The story depicts a typical colonial settler's attitude with his sentimentality coupled with greed and ruthlessness in trying to make something of the land his very own property and in the end feeling the despair and futility of it. After the house is completed Old Tar wanders around the rooms with the howling wind for company and wonders "Wot's it doing there-wot's it for? ...Oh, Lord, wot'ave I done-wot'ave I done, Lord?" (Ian Gordon: *Undiscovered Country;* Longman Group Limited, London: 1974; p.303). Old Tar's wife has no idea of the anguish that her husband is feeling and she in her turn displays the smug, class feelings of the colonial woman who imagines herself "turned into a fine lady." The short piece is noteworthy for its fine way of depicting the feelings of a man finding his roots, a problem Mansfield herself faced throughout her life.

Similarly, "The Woman at the Store" vividly describes the situation of settlers' in a sparsely inhabited mining countryside. The heat, the dust, the loneliness have made the woman brutish. There is a trashiness about her, far from the superiority of fine ladies like Old Tar's wife. And the strangeness of the landscape has entered into the bones of the woman and the child, who between them hold the secret of the shooting of her husband out of spite. Without much elaboration Mansfield describes the gradual deterioration that has entered into white blood in a native, Maori landscape. The savagery, the primitivism of the land have taken over even human nature, somewhat in the style of Conrad's Kurtz. The urbane, humorous way in which the situation is described belies the violence underlining the whole story andthe macabre ending of the story suddenly brings this to the surface, when the kid draws thé picture of a woman shooting a man and also draws a hole in which the man was buried. And even more thanthe macabre the poignancy of the lonely and lost colonial woman is brought out in the character of the woman, who was pretty as a wax doll once but is now turned into a crazy hag.

"Millie" is another story of a pioneering, colonial woman brought to the edge of sanity by the harshness and loneliness of the colonial background. The rawness, the roughness that will touch even a good woman in such a make-shift frontier society is exposed in the character of Millie. Once again, the simple technique of Mansfield, pared to the bones to suit the elemental back ground in the story is in sharp contrast to the frightening, cruel events that are described of a young man on the run after he has killed a farm owner, and his pursuit by Millie's husband with his hunting-dog.

Further reading her stories like "Kezia and Tui" and "Maata" one realizes that colonialism is a theme rather than an attitude or issue in the art of Mansfield. Her vignettes of colonial life as seen in the ten stories came mostly in the early part of her career. Hence there is direct exposure of the rawness and cruelty attendant upon such a narrow colonial set-up. It was out of hatred for this kind of life that she had left New Zealand and chosen to settle in London and this antagonism is evident in these stories.

But as happens inevitably she started discovering that life in the Bohemian world of London society was also rough and raw in its own way. The refinedly cruel, calculatedly childish perversities of the Bohemian set, someof whom like Middleton Murry and W.W. Gibson were also indisputably gifted, quickly brought bruises to her physical and emotional being. The reaction was to withdraw into her former world of childhood and innocence. Her admiration for everything English started waning with the growing disillusion and frustration attendant upon the choice of the exile and at least in her imagination she went back to the refuge of her child's world and the small, colonial community that she had known in New Zealand.

The loneliness and purposelessness of her life in London brought home to her the beauties of her well ordered colonial background, of life in a small, close-knit, struggling community, where values were strictly arranged in proper priorities, just as neatly as the classes andthe social distinctions, and these values were just as strictly adhered to. Her vision has matured, and her art also developed towards greater perfection. Her nostalgia for the colonial community was indeed there, but this did not mean that she wrote in favour of it entirely in her period of reaction. Despite her nostalgic love for her childhood world, as an adult looking at it from a distant angle, and as an artist, she could not but see the inherent rot in even the best colonial memories. Her naturally sharp and satirical mind reflected that those colonial values were perhaps a little too strict, a little too rotten to be of advantage to a progressive community. Her objective portrayal of the subsurface discriminations of class, wealth, social and cultural difference are subtly brought out in some of her best stories of this later period. "At the Bay" "The Doll's House", "The Garden-Party" and "The Prelude" belong to this group. In these stories the split personality of the exile provides the dynamic tension. The artist in her was quick to perceive that the reassurances of a colonial community were rather shallow. For the child and the young woman it spelt security, with its easily recognized and automatically accepted divisions and separations but for the artist there was something debased and corrupt in such an unfair set-up. Harmony was simply not made to last in a world where such unnecessary differences could prevail.

In her story "The Doll's House" these problems are subtly depicted. Kezia belongs to the upper class whereas Lil and Our Else come from the dregs of suburban Karori society being the daughters of the washerwoman Mrs. Mackelvey. The Karori Primary School, which forms the fictional background in the story was a hot-bed of colonial distinctions imposed even upon the half-aware children, somewhat in the fashion of the school Lamming describes in his *The Castle of My Skin*. The class distinctions operating between the Mackelvey children and the rest are humiliating and crude as they can only be in a colonial society. Yet Mansfield does not expose the situation in a biased or militant manner. But by repeating the picture of discriminations that the children have learnt from their adults and practice even in their childish world, Mansfield mocks at the very gestures of aping and mimicking that she had seen even in the adults in the youthful New Zealand world and which is a characteristic of colonial manners. This surface reality of social discriminations might later even turn into serious, hampering deeper psychological idiosyncrasies as we see in same of the grown-up characters like Aunt Beryl in "The Doll's House" and "At the Bay" and her sister Linda in "The Prelude". Beryl appears to be a domineering, arrogant, condescending, mixed-up kind of young woman who harms her own chances for love by these split feelings. Similarly, Linda in "The Prelude" hates any kind of dominance and is always in a state of antagonism and protest against her husband Stanley Burnell who flaunts his male superiority.

Even in "The Garden-Party" there is no indication of any specific colonial background forming an issue, but nevertheless, one can feel the social classification of the colonised society suffusing the meaning of the story. The Scotts, in whose house a violent, accidental death has occured, live at the lower end of the lane and appear socially inferior to the Sheridans, who are having a garden-party on the lawns of their house at the upper end of the lane. The class differences are suggested through the descriptions of their houses, mainly. Here, the slightly older youth figure Laura, unlike the other children in "The Doll's House", does not approve of the class distinctions that her mother and sister take for granted and certainly does not want to imitate them. To her mind the complexities of colonial and social contrast cannot be so neatly arranged as in a doll's house, and an event like a death can seriously underline the inhumanities in such an artifically ordered society.

"At the Bay", running into 12 short sections, is one of the best stories bringing out the cross-sections of colonial life in Wellington, depicting in an episodic style that is reminiscent of Virginia Woolf, the momentariness, the shifting moods in a small colonial community. The VIII section dealing with the fancy outing of Alice, the servant girl in the Burnell household, and her friend Mrs. Stubbs, provides an interesting contrast to some of the other sections where the family of the master and Mrs. Burnell is described. Alice and Mr. Stubbs and Linda andBeryl and the others are playing a game in the social world just like the children "playing house" like adults with their diminutive dolls and dinner-sets in the VIII section of "The Prelude". The sharp contrasts of the colonial world are all there without becoming confrontations in these stories of Mansfield.

It is needless to emphasise that her preoccupation with the colonial world of her childhood has deeply influenced the style of Mansfield's short stories. For instance, the choice of the child-heroines like Fenella or Kezia, or Laura in some of her best stories has necessitated the use of the short story rather than longer fiction. This preoccupation has also introduced the patterns of nostalgia, dream-sequences, fantasy and temporal shifts of memory for which her technique is famous. Her choice of a young girl as the centre of consciousness is as significant as Mark Twain's choice of

Huck Finn as the hero of an American classic dealing with a frontier, pioneer background. The child figure symbolises the youthfulness and innocence of the new, growing, country, standing for the primordial, natural background of an almost Edenic, Pre-Lapsarian paradise.

While seeking to go back to New Zealand in her imagination Mansfield was also involved in the act of seeking an identity for herself, through establishing an identity for her "undiscovered country". The result of this self-probing as exile, artist, woman, has been the creation of such complex characters as Linda, her old mother Mrs. Fairfield and Laura.

Even with regard to the surface characteristics of technique it is interesting to notice the difference that New Zealand has made to her art. An exotic regional interest and local colour have enhanced the descriptive style of her stories. The New Zealand colonial usage of English with Alice's term of "kitching" for "kitchen" in "At the Bay" and words like "larrikin" for a boy-friend and "paddocks" and "gully" for landscape features have added to the interest of the tone. It is also natural that some of her best stories are set out-doors, as though to make the most of the picturesque, colonial background. "The Prelude" is set in the garden of what was obviously their Karori home. "The Prelude" was earlier significantly called "The Aloe". The aloe, a hard-stemmed, prickly plant specifically of New Zealand vegetation becomes a central meaningful, expanding symbol for human relationships and for life itself in the consciousness of one of the prominent characters, Linda Burnell. Similarly "At the Bay" has mainly an out-door setting as the story covers a day at the Bay. The background comes alive with references to the "manuka tree", "the picotees", etc. Even the setting in "The Garden-Party" contrasts the beautiful, bedecked lawns of the Sheridan's house with the run-down, poky atmosphere of the Scott's house.

Her famous rejection of New Zealand, like Joyce's rejection of Dublin, introduced the theme of being an exile and an alien into all her writing. And this theme further extended into the existential concerns of loss, negation, rejection and death. David Daiches bases a comparison of Joyce's "The Dead" with Mansfield's "The Stranger" in an interpretation of the similar sense of alienation and rejection in the two exiled writers. (David Daiches: *New Literary Values*, Edinburgh & London, 1936, p. 89).

Her rejection of New Zealand was also similar to Naipaul's rejectionof West Indies. The same horrors of narrow colonial education that had driven away Naipaul and Lamming from the West Indies operated in her case also. Antony Alpers in his biography of Mansfield amusingly records that one of the primers that the children in the Karori Primary School where Katherine, and much later he, studied had as its central lesson story with the refrain: "Run, boy, run." (Anthony Alpens: *Katherine Mansfield—A Biography*: London Jonathan Cape, 1954, p. 5). Katherine did run, but her country also went with her.

Thus, one recognizes the pressing need Katherine Mansfield had to speak about New Zealand in order to shape herself as a writer. Her life in New Zealand was short, but like the leavening in bread, it was New Zealand that made her rise to her full proportion as writer. One wonders if she could have been a writer at all if it were not for her colonial complex.

14

Theme in Patrick White's *A Fringe of Leaves*

Patrick White belongs to the group of Commonwealth writers who present their material from the perspective of the coloniser rather than the colonised. His novels are set in the background of the all-white colonial society of provincial Australia, or the native, aboriginal bush-country landscape; his main interest in his novels is revelation of the complexities of human nature rather than description of a way of life or creation of a new sensibility for the scope of English fiction. He is a profoundly moral writer and is not a novelist who can be called a social mannerist in the convention of Jane Austen or Henry James, nor an innovative formalist in the style of James Joyce or Virginia Woolf. From first to last he is deeply involved in clarifying some truth of human existence. Among the modern writers of fiction he is surprisingly traditional and conventional in both his vision and his art. His philosophy is of the old world, where simple goodness and kindness in human nature are still considered to be of the highest value. His novels have such a powerful, organic flow and rhythm that they seem to derive from the elemental background of the Australian landscape. In plot construction and narrative structure there is a dynamic growth that seems to stem from the interplay of human nature and organic nature that forms the substance of his novels. Each of his well-known novels also has an intricate story pattern and narrative suspense; but in spite of these obviously traditional and conventional qualities of fictional art, White presents a complex moral vision through a peculiarly rich and original prose style.

In *A Fringe of Leaves* (1976), which is one of his later novels, White excels himself as a powerful narrative artist and moral visionary. It is a novel setting up contrasts between opposing elements in human nature and organic nature. Ellen and Austin Roxburgh are a married couple, never separated except at the moment of death. Throughout the depiction of this relationship between a man and woman bound within the institution of marriage, White studies the true natures of Ellen and Austin, as though to see how their marriage was successful in spite of such tremendous differences. He analyses the polarities between male-female, rich-poor, plebeian-noble, healthy-sickly, civilised-savage, educated-uneducated, good-evil, etcetera, in order to unravel the mystery that is at the heart of human relationships. Increasing the mystery is the contrasts in the Australian landscape itself, between developed underdeveloped, beautiful-ugly, fertile-barren, and so on.

In this article I analyse all the important aspects of *A Fringe of Leaves* in an attempt to bring out the essential, unified significance of these polarised themes.

A Fringe of Leaves is set in the Australia of the 1840's. On one level it is a historical novel and is based on the experiences of Eliza Frązer, a nineteenth century Englishwoman who accompanied her husband to Van Diemen's Land to visit his renegade brother, and who was shipwrecked off the Queensland coast in May 1839. Shewas then taken captive by the Aborigines. White makes useof the history and legend associated with her story; the novel is a rich combination of a historian's and an anthropologist's knowledge of the human race, a poet's understanding of human experience, and a philosopher's wisdom about life's essential meaning. It is also an adventure story and a suspense tale in the Conradian style. It deals with the wreck of the ship *Bristol Maid* off the coast of Queensland and brings to light the aboriginal tribal life and the bush country landscape of the Australia of early colonialism. The action of the story actually starts around 1835.

Austin Roxburgh and Ellen, his wife, have visited Garnet Roxburgh, the younger brother of Austin, on his farm in Van Diemen's Land. As the novel opens, they are on their way back to England in the brig *Bristol Maid.* Their friends, Mr. and Mrs. Merrivale and Miss Scrimshaw, have just seen them off at the port of Sydney. These friends act as a kind of chorus in the opening scene, introducing us to the main characters through their suggestive prologue. In the very next chapter the novel travels backwards, taking us to the events happening in Dulcet, the farmhouse in which Garnet has settled in Van Diemen's Land. Flashing in between the immediate narrative sections are scenes from the private lives of Mr. and Mrs. Roxburgh before and after their marriage. Ellen Gluyas was a farmer's daughter in a small village in Cornwall before Austin Roxburgh went there as a paying guest and courted her and married her. It was not passion that prompted this gentleman from the upper class to marry and do the right thing by this farm girl: it was his own need and innate sense of propriety that guided him. Austin was a rich man, and his one love was books. Throughout the novel we find that a copy of Virgil's *Bucolics* is a closer companion to him than even his wife. Ellen Gluyas is exactly the opposite of Austin Roxburgh. She is uneducated, simple, and bursting with health; she is twenty years younger than her husband and is genuinely in love with him.

From the beginning the reader notices the opposing but complementary characters of Austin and Ellen. They mutually strive to adjust to each other in spite of the tremendous class and social differences between them and have nearly succeeded in establishing a smoothly working relationship within the difficult institution of marriage. White treats their relationship on a primarily human plane rather than on a social or intellectual one, though all these aspects are inevitably involved in such an unlikely match as Austin and Ellen. The essential meaning of the novel comes out in White's probing of their capacity to hold on to a deep, individual morality that is the only factor that can make their marriage meaningful.

Van Diemen's Land was a penal colony, and Garnet Roxburgh had retreated to that settlement under duress. There is a question of unproved dishonesty is his case, for he has been involved in a forgery episode in Cheltenham. Now, we learn that in Van Diemen's Land he has been involved in a gig accident as a result of which his elderly wife's neck has been broken. He automatically inherits all her wealth as a result of her death. Austin and his brother are shown as being poles apart in their natures. Ellen, as a foil standing between them, shares a little of the qualities of both of them; she suffers her moral slip in the company of Garnet but works herself away from his corrupting influence by cultivating a scrupulous sense of duty similar to her husband's. It is as though White is presenting the different scales of honesty and personal morality in this juxtaposition of the rich young man who has fallen and turned into a farmer (Garnet), the poor farm girl who, as a rich woman, is a fallen woman but manages to rise above material circumstances in every way (Ellen), and the sickly young man who is neither rich nor poor in material and moral circumstances. (Austin)

Ellen takes an instinctive dislike to her husband's younger brother, Garnet; she feels disturbed when she perceives a similarity between her brother-in-law's present and her own past situations, for she too had been on a farm in the rugged regions of Cornwall, leading a rough life tending cows and sheep and taking care of her alcoholic father. But in her case the coarseness was only in external circumstances, not in her nature, whereas Garnet has fallenfrom an upper class society into a criminal class because of the crudity and criminality of his inner nature. White has set up a moral contrast between Ellen and Garnet. Individual merit and innate goodness on the one hand and evil and corruption on the other are mainly responsible for the making or marring of character but nevertheless biological factors have great influence in shaping one's character, in White's vision. When Ellen succumbs to Garnet's seduction in a forest clearing, she hates herself for it and immediately acts to remove herself from him emotionally — and even physically — by leaving Dulcet, whereas Garnet wallows in his sensuality and persists in pursuing her.

Ellen and Garnet are attracted to each other in an animal fashion, although Ellen inwardly is repelled by her brother-in-law. Like a genuinely good woman and a true wife, she resists this attraction constantly throughout their stay at Dulcet. When Garnet opens his arms for her as she steps down from the carriage on their arrival, common courtesy (if not willingness) would have required her to accept his invitation, but she risks an unsocial response and waits for her husband to descend and hand her his arm, however weak it might be. She keeps a journal in which she truthfully writes down her antipathy towards him and attempts to correct her response, to be neither loving nor hateful but to be correct.

The climax of the visit to Dulcet occurs on the day when Ellen goes out riding alone in the clearing in the woods: she falls from the mare and sprains her ankle. Garnet has followed her into the woods, and the latent attraction between them is let loose, and they succumb to the temptation of their own passionate natures. White's depiction of this climactic scene is reminiscent of Thomas Hardy's description of a nearly similar situation in *Tess of the D'Urbervilles*. Amidst the sylvan surroundings there is the coupling of Ellen Roxburgh and Garnet and all nature gives in to this wild abandon. The reader notices the peculiarly indirect, symbolic way in which White describes the scene. Ellen is in a green riding habit as she lies on the lush green grass; she has a violent waking dream that she is like a great, green, obscene bird on whose heart Garnet is preying. Even in her moment of undoing she is conscious of the evil that she has committed, but she cannot stop herself.

Ellen's character is a deep and complex one; she is a perplexing combination of her past Cornish blood and her present, painfully cultivated, upper-class manners. Her passionate nature, which she had learned to curb to a great extent after her marriage to a sickly man twenty years older than herself, had never quite been suppressed. Like the creatures of nature that had kept her company on their farm in Cornwall, she too gives in to nature unyieldingly; but this yielding is also a strength in her, as we find later in the novel when she is taken captive by the Aborigines, and she has to live for a couple of months amidst them. Her closeness to nature and her familiarity with the elemental background with which she was faced on the Cornish coast have added indestructible strength to her character.

At the same time it is her yielding to this natural urge in her that causes her downfall and introduces a sign of degeneration in her. Her cultivated social manners cannot save her, for there is a rawness and rot in her that is part of the baser side of her nature. In the seduction scene we notice how she is lying on a bed of rotting leaves and mould, signifying this rot and decay that nature is capable of. In the novel White deals with both these aspects of nature — the beautiful, good side on the one hand and the debased, rotting side on the other. Australia in the nineteenth century was under colonisation. Some parts of it were still beautiful, virgin land, and others were rugged and harsh. Van Diemen's Land itself, for instance, was half a penal colony, with convicts working in stone quarries. On the other hand we have the lush, abundantly fruitful farm of Garnet, appropriately named Dulcet. Even later in the novel, White shows the evil side that can be in nature when he depicts the aboriginal tribal way of life.

After her single, moral slip Ellen is more careful than ever when she is with Garnet, and her adulterous mistake draws her closer to her invalid husband — as though she is making reparation for her health and sensuality which were responsible for carrying her away from her husband.

As a consequence of this shameful incident, Ellen persuades her husband to leave Dulcet under the excuse that they would move to Hobart Town and wait for a boat there to take them "Home". Austin, who also has not been too well towards the end of their visit, gladly agrees and they leave Garnet's farm for Hobart Town. After a few days there they have the good news that the *Bristol Maid* will shortly be sailing for England. They find berths (although it is not a passenger vessel) and their journey to Sydney is uneventful; in Sydney they meet the Merrivales and Miss Scrimshaw, as already mentioned.

During the voyage from Sydney, Austin Roxburgh blossoms into anoter being altogether: he appears to be discovering himself anew and comes into his own when they experience the isolation of the sea. White devotes nearly the whole of Chapter Four to Austin and his latent personality, and the contrast between the natures of the husband and the wife are clearly revealed here.

There was something creative about Austin Roxburgh, but this has been curbed because of his perpetual sickliness; he turned into a peevish invalid living in a world of books and medicines. "Waste knowledge and moral inhibitions" (129) had killed the good, natural side of him. He was a "slanted stick of a gentleman...scattering a dust of dictionary words and useless knowledge" (51). His marrying the Cornish farm girl was beneficial to him: he had used his creative urge in transforming her into a finer creature, in the manner of Pygmalion transforming Galatea. His personality and Ellen's are truly opposite and complementary, and their marriage works because of this. He is weak and she is healthy physically, but morally he is the strong one and Ellen is the one who is indebted to him. During the voyage, which symbolically becomes a voyage into self, both of them discover their hidden natures.

The setting on board the ship is an expedient one for White to explore the depths of human nature and human relationships. This background is used to unfold the moral drama that develops out of close proximity of people with diverse natures. This isolated atmosphere heightens the meaning of human actions and thoughts, and the deepest consciousness of the individuals are exposed. Conrad had already explored the meaning of waterscape exclusively in works like *Lord Jim, The Nigger of the "Narcissus",* and *The Secret Sharer*. We find that later on, the background of the isolated aboriginal island serves the same purpose and heightens the significance of the developing human drama in White's novel also.

The disastrous incident of the wreck of *Bristol Maid*, when it hits a reef, starts off a new chain of events in the lives of the Roxburghs. The boat is stuck on a reef-bed, and those on board can do nothing more than launch out in two longboats in search of land. Mr. and Mrs. Roxburgh are too shocked to understand the situation fully; nevertheless, they respond to the crisis admirably and help each other in facing the crisis. Ironically enough, Mrs. Roxburgh takes her rings, her jewellery, and her journal as indispensable items, while Austin chooses to preserve his copy of *Virgil* next to his skin as his most valuable possession.

On the fifth morning, the occupants of the two boats land on what had deceptively seemed like the coast; it was only a coral island, a kind of scrubland, far from the pastoral island that Austin was looking forward to after his constant reading of Virgil's *Bucolics.*

The members scatter themselves around the island, seeking some kind of renewal after the terrible confinement of the tiny boats. For the first time, Austin and Ellen are separated for a while.

Austin heads towards the southernmost tip of the island to explore what might be there. In such a situation of isolation White describes the true nature of this man who had never been stripped down to such physical and spiritual loneliness as now. In a significant passage White brings out one of the main themes of the novel, which is to examine human nature in its barest state without the props of society or external accretions of social and economic status. White points out:

> a white light threatened to expose the more protected corners of human personality. Mr. Roxburgh was fully exposed. In advancing towards this land's end, he felt the trappings of wealth and station, the pride in ethical and intellectual aspirations, stripped from him with a ruthlessness reserved for those who accept their importance or who have remained unaware of their pretentiousness. (185)

Austin Roxburgh, like Ellen a little later when she is among the aborigines, is about to confront himself either in a state of pure being - or nothingness. The incident which is to expose the truth of his situation is his sudden discovery that Spurgeon, the steward of the ship, has beaten him to this land's end and now lies there in misery, for he has realised that he is afflicted with sea-boils — a sure way for a seaman to die.

Austin, with his Virgil still secretly clutched to his breast under his shirt, is made to face an extraordinary situation. Until now his "experience of life, like his attitude to death, had been of a predominantly literary nature" (186), but his bookish, sickly, hypochondriac nature is face to face with a living situation, and he has to get through it all by himself, without either his mother or his wife by his side.

In a fleeting vision, Austin sees what his life has been —

and he sees it mainly in relationship to his wife Ellen — in the institution of marriage. He has been selfish, he realises, and suddenly a sense of guilt strikes him in this moment of vision: "it was on account of a sense of guilt he was nursing, for the many occasions on which he had abandoned someone else drowning by clambering aboard the raft of his own negative abstractions. Her hair floated out behind her as though on the surface of actual water instead of in the depths of his thoughts" (187).

But it is to his credit that slowly, without even his being conscious of it, he rises to the occasion and takes charge of the situation; he completely forgets himself and concentrates on helping Spurgeon. He suggests that sea water will help, and proceeds to administer the simple medicine to Spurgeon's boils. Grimacing at the repulsiveness of it, he rubs the froth on to the boils and, strangely enough, it is he who is being healed rather than Spurgeon, by the beauty of his new-found faith.

The coral reef offers no shelter, and the two small boats are ready to launch out again in search of land. As they proceed, the master boat and the longboat following it drift away from each other. Mr. and Mrs. Roxburgh, who are in the longboat, realise that they are heading towards some part of land, and what appears at first to be paradise itself turns out to be the land of the aboriginal savages. The white people are soon taken captive by the hostile aborigines. Captain Purdew and Austin are speared to death; Ellen Roxburgh, alone and in helpless mourning for her dead husband, is surrounded by a group of savage women.

The savages are in no way noble: they prod her and jeer at her and soon methodically strip her. Leaving her alone after sometime, they run back into the bush with her clothes. Mrs. Roxburgh, with a civilised sense of modesty overcoming her, plucks the vines of convulvulus growing around and winds them around herself, draping her nakedness with that fringe of leaves.

As we have noticed in the opening pages of the novel, White has been drawing out attention to the beautiful shawl, a green leaf-patterned one, that Ellen Roxburgh is wearing when she meets the Merrivales and Miss Scrimshaw.

The symbolic nature of the change from a leaf-patterned shawl to a fringe of leaves vivifies the predicament of Ellen Roxburgh: she is now stripped down to her essential personality and must now be reborn as her true, if changed, self. The green shawl has already shown the earlier change in Ellen from being a Cornish farm girl to becoming an upper-class lady in Cheltenham. Now the shedding of the shawl and assuming of the covering of the fringe of leaves must show her transformation into her real self amidst the savages. But as a link and symbol of her former life as Mrs. Roxburgh, she retains her wedding ring, hiding it by stringing it to an inner layer of the vine.

Attitudes of civilisation and savagery are juxtaposed in the episode concerning Ellen and the Aborigines. Savagery is mostly cruelty, and the aborigines are cruel even among themselves, not just towards the white intruders. One girl is killed in the jealous entanglement of love. They make a ritual of devouring her body. And out of necessity, Ellen joins in the ritual feast and partakes of the flesh. She is now no more than a creature of circumstances, although she very much remembers her past.

Her meeting the escaped convict Jack Chance puts her back on the road to civilisation. She keeps company with Chance with the same simple and unpretentious attitude that she had shown with Austin Roxburgh earlier. The underlying theme that White emphasizes in showing all these changes in Ellen is one of belief in moral values. Although her external positions might change, Ellen remains changeless in her inner nature, which is constituted of simple goodness. Her character during her companionship with the convict becomes more complex than ever. She learns to love this man, and once again the hunger that she has always felt to assuage her need for love obsesses her. One of the disturbing features of this woman (disturbing to her genteel mother-in-law and learned husband as well as to the reader), is her excessive sensuality. Perhaps, it was her closeness to nature on the Cornwall farm, or, perhaps, it is because of her woman's need, but Ellen feels a sexual drive that is part of the attractiveness of her character. Her husband, being twenty years older than she is and living in his world of books, is shocked at the manifestation of his own need in the beginning of their marriage; as a consequence, her need was frustrated. When Garnet comes into her life, he rouses this dormant drive and, against her better nature, she gives into his demand on the fateful occasion in the forest clearing. That was the only lapse of her will, and it is once again the strength of her goodness and better character that asserts itself after that, although there are many importunities later from Garnet. Even she recognises that this was lust; this was not what she wanted. There is a finer, healthier nature in this Cornish farm girl that even her aristocratic mother-in-law and Austin, her own husband, did not possess.

Even before she meets her husband, White has drawn attention to the peculiar, problematic proportions that sensuality and sexuality have assumed in Ellen's nature. Pa,her father, who lived alone with her after the death of her mother, is much too dependent on her and attached to her: he shows incestuous leanings when he is in a drunken state. White suggests phallic imagery in the description of the horn-like thumb with which Pa strokes Ellen's cheeks when he is drunk. Ellen herself is disgusted at Pa's behaviour as much as she is disgusted with her brother-in-law Garnet's behaviour later on. Even this latter relationship is an incestuous one, strictly speaking. Just as Ellen earlier had been fascinated by Pa's horny thumb, she is also repeatedly drawn by the sight of the back of Garnet's hand, with its gash and streak of blood. One of the main themes that White draws attention to is the theme of sexual relationships. Ellen's life long quest for her spiritual identity is closely related to her sexual relationships with people.

That her feeling of love is stronger than her sexuality is suggsted by the secret dream that she has nursed within herself from girlhood — that a lover would come out of the sea and that she would sail away with him to Tintagel. (The reference is to the story of Tristan and Iseult and their romantic, tragic episode of love.) But neither her love nor her sexuality had found a proper outlet during her life with her husband, Austin.

During the latter part of the novel, when her companionship with the convict Jack Chance is well established, Ellen is freer to express some of her dormant feelings of love and sexuality. Like two creatures of the woods, they make a pact with each other, physically as well as spiritually. Unlike Garnet, the convict speaks to her of love and asks, "Can you love me, Ellen?" Ellen is elated in his company and experiences a full blossoming in her contact with him; in a way, she is reborn at this stage into her real self; she is neither the drudge of her father nor the nursemaid of her sickly husband but lives on her own terms on a natural plane with the convict.

In a manner reminiscent of D.H. Lawrence, White expresses his belief in the organic and biological side of human personality influencing the feeling towards regeneration, a spirit of renewal in an individual. The elemental, natural background of the forest contributes to a primordial friendship between Ellen and Jack Chance. The nature of their friendship contrasts with the behaviour of the Aborigines, who also live in an elemental background. The civilisation that backs both Ellen and Chance does help them at this stage. In the polarities that White sets up between savagery andcivilisation, there is no doubt as to where his belief swings. In depicting the difference in Ellen's own life, between her brutish background during girlhood and her refined life during her maturity, White demonstrates his faith in civilisation contributing towards an improvement of human nature. But even in this there must be balance rather than polarisation towards one extreme or the other. Unlike her husband Austin, who has made himself effete and peevish by his over-fastidious and over-refined bookishness, Ellen retains a healthy rustic directness and strength and resilience as a woman until the very end. She is the balanced middle between the two extremes of Austin and Garnet in this respect.

When she parts from Chance at the edge of the forest after their escape from the captivity of the Aborigines, Ellen once again enters a civilised background as she steps (or collapses) onto the Oakes' farm. She comes back to life likea newborn babe, literally and Mr. and Mrs. Oakes slowly coax her into a normal kind of existence. Ellen rehabilitates herself once again, but she must come to some reconciliation between her past and her present. The past was the forest as well as Cheltenham society and the Cornish coast; the present is her loneliness and the company of strangers (Mr. and Mrs. Lovell and their two young children, Tom and Kate). Gradually, painfully, she grows away from her past and learns to accept the present. The novel, set in the past, ends on a significant note: the acceptance of the present is the only reality.

One of the main themes that *A Fringe of Leaves* explores is the possibility of living as a simple, whole, human individual in a world made complex by the divisions of class, social distinctions, biological inheritances, and so on. As Miss Scrimshaw puts it, "life is a series of blunders rather than any clear design, from which we may come out whole if we are lucky" (354). Although she is a minor character in the novel, it is with Miss Scrimshaw's vision that the novel ends — and has begun. At the end, she has succeeded in bringing together

Ellen and Mr. George Jevons, a merchant and widower, travelling in their boat to Sydney and then onward "Home". She envisions a settled, happy future for her disturbed and ravaged friend Mrs. Roxburgh. Throughout the novel White emphasizes this urge, this instinctual thrust in a human being towards a wholeness, a naturalness in behaviour. In spite of all the scars remaining with her from a devastating past, Ellen is still vulnerable, still solidly concerned with what is right and what is wrong, what is her own duty, and so forth, and she still retains that hunger to love and to be loved. In these things lies one's humanness, according to White. It is this utopia of wholesome human nature that White believes in, as we see in *A Fringe of Leaves*.To quote his last words in the novel, "for however much crypto-eagles aspire to soar, and do in fact, through thoughtscape and dream, their human nature cannot but grasp at any circumstantial straw which may indicate an ordered universe" (366).

A major theme of the novel, underlying all the polarities of dialectical processes, is the theme of how Ellen arrives at this life of order. Her character grows and shapes itself into that of an essentially good human being. White's belief in the goodness of the human heart is extraordinarily optimistic in this novel of his maturity.

As *A Fringe of Leaves* is a historical novel ofcolonial times, one of the themes in the novel is about the clash of cultures; European culture and the native, aboriginal culture are juxtaposed. Europeanism is presented in all its refined form in characters like Austin and his mother. Austin is in possession ofthe best symbol of European classicism, Virgil's *Georgics*. The elder Mrs. Roxburgh, with her kid-gloved hands holding a beautiful China vase, as Ellem remembers, symbolises the actual living culture of the European background.

And there is the culture of the new colony also, symbolised by Mrs. Merrivale, Miss Scrimshaw, and Captain Lovell, for example. Europeanism cannot survive on its own terms in a new land; colonialism is a culture of adjustment of compromises, not extreme polarisations. Garnet Roxburgh has practised this adjustment and compromise to an extreme extent, and this is not right either.

The contrasts and the significances of the several themes in the novel are enhanced by the four meaningful epigraphs that White provides. The first one, from Ibsen's play *Little Eyolf,* draws our attention to some of the problems present in the play and the novel. Almers, the father of Little Eyolf (who is drowned) is (like Austin) consumed by a sense of guilt about being an inadequate husband; he also feels guilty about his incestuous feelings towards his sister and about being responsible for the drowning of his son. We find that in White's novel both Austin and Ellen share some of these guilt feelings. Ellen has a consciousness of the incestuous feelings between her father and herself, feels responsible for her miscarriage and the death of her infants, and has a sexual involvement with the brother of her husband. And just as the mother of Little Eyolf offsets her guilt by taking care of the children of other people, Ellen also does the same at the end of the novel with the Lovell children, as earlier with the tribal children.

The second epigraph, containing lines from Wordsworth's poem "She was a Phantom of Delight", a poem about his wife, draws our attention to the ardent wish that Austin Roxburgh has of transforming Ellen into a finer creature. He wants to be a Pygmalion to his Galatea-Ellen and wishes to shape her into "A perfect Woman, nobly planned/To warn, to comfort, and command." He wants to transform Ellen into a gentleman's ladylike wife. The third epigraph to the novel consists of a quotation from Simone Weil, "If there is some true good in a man, it can only be unknown to himself." And Louis Aragon's words that constitute the final epigraph ("Love is your last chance. There is really nothing else on earth to keep you there") further emphasizes the theme of love. Ellen's one aim in life as seen throughout the novel, is to be a woman, true and good. Her great capacity for love is the "true good". She herself is not aware of the depth of goodness in her, but we find that consistently she retains this quality of loving others, even when the others are cruel to her. Starting with her Pa and ending with her cultivating a feeling of love towards Mr. Jevons in the last part of the novel, we find that Ellen has sustained her own spirit on this spirit of love.

Austin discovers the hidden true good in himself in a moving way in the episode on the island involving Spurgeon. He leaves his world of books and miraculously emerges out of himself to grapple with the challenge of the very real sea-boils on Spurgeon's neck and redeems his hitherto selfish existence by ministering tothe needs of another. He realises that only in love is one reborn or made to attain one's full stature. Even the desiccated Austin Roxburgh realises this during his strange and unlikely friendship with Spurgeon. The quotation from Simone Weil is quite relevant to the unfolding of Austin's character.

The convict Jack Chance also believes in the need for love—in his own confused way. When his girlfriend, Mab, was unfaithful to him, he killed her in a mad fit of jealousy, and that was the reason he was convicted. Later, when he meets Ellen, he shows his love towards her in his own fashion and in turn wants to know whether she loves him.

Besides these epigraphs, which highlight some of the themes in the novel, we have the repeated references to Austin's copy of Virgil. In the beginning we find Austin concentrating on Virgil's fourth *Georgic,* where there is a suggestion of the celebration of the personal life, the country life. Ironically enough, Austin is hardly suited to put his love of Virgil into practice, as we see during his foray into country life when he is staying as a paying guest on the Gluyas's farm in Cornwall. He is anything but a countryman: he lives in a world of art, not ina world of nature. And the Gluyas farm is hardly idyllic: a pig is having its throat slit when Austin is standing nearby discussing his "crib" on Virgil with Ellen. He has given her his crib so that she too can become another admirer of Virgil, and this is his way of "creating" a new character out of this farm creature.

The underlying philosophy of Virgil in his *Georgics* is that the image of disorder is rooted in man's mind, and that order, the idyllic pastoral world that he seeks, is only a momentary escape. This is a rather pessimistic suggestion in Virgil's concept of human nature, but in *A Fringe of Leaves* White himself does not seem to subscribe to this belief.

Although in the chapters where the Aborigines are described he shows the incipient cruelty and inhumanity of the tribals, in characters like Mrs. Roxburgh and Ellen he appears to be expressing his faith in the inherent goodness in human nature that can be a redeeming factor.

Besides all else, *A Fringe of Leaves* is also a novel about a developing female consciousness. It is significant that White has a young woman as the central figure of his novel. He probes the consciousness of Ellen as a woman placed in a man's world. In the very beginning it may be noticed that Ellen Gluyas has a hard time adjusting to a man's world — here mainly her father's farm. She is hardy and healthy, and her father expects her to do a man's job on the farm. It is to her credit that she rises up to those expectations; she is stronger than her father, and it is to her that his care calls. Her father clearly exploits her. Her desire to be a woman, loved and cherished, is confined only to her dreams, as she dreams of being an Iseult who waits for her Tristan to come and carry her off to Tintagel.

But what does happen in actuality is that Austin Roxburgh comes on the scene next and becomes equally dependent on her. He is hardly her Tristan: he is sickly and in failing health and spirits, and she is the stronger of the two in every way. In spite of her moral slip later, she remains the stronger of the two. But even though he is exploiting her, Austin is also condescending and patronising to her, and his whole attitude is somewhat unfair. In this smug, unjustified feeling of social and intellectual superiority, he accepts Ellen as his wife so that she can serve "not only as his wife, but also his work of art. This could be a project which might ease the frustration gnawing at him: to create a beautiful but socially acceptable companion..."(54) Even personally, Ellen is frustrated and cheated in her marriage, but she learns to accept this because of the social conditioning that beats her down and suppresses her. She learns to hide her natural sensuality and sexuality because of the discipline her mother-in-law the old and genteel Mrs. Ropxburgh, subtly instils in her — and also because of Austin's inadequacy. And when Garnet shows his lust towards her after her own fateful slip, her natural good instincts as a woman make her turn away from him, even if she has to repress her sexual urges.

When she comes to share her companionship with Jack Chance, Ellen seems to be at her happiest. Significantly enough, she loses her wedding rise at this point. In the primordial background of the forest she is neither patronised nor exploited as a woman. Both of them take each other on their own terms in spite of relating their past histories for each other's benefit. Needless to say, even this relationship is a far cry from her romantic dreams of sailing off with her lover, Tristan, to Tintagel.

The last reality that Ellen has to accept is the relationship with Mr. Jevons and the expectation that love might be possible between them. The Dickensian, Mr. Jevons, in spite of his bullfrog-like appearance, claims her attention, and Miss Scrimshaw believes that order will once again be restored in Ellen's life. Ellen, with her resilience and her continued attention to another human being accepts the attentions of this awkward man.

Louis Aragon's words that White has quoted as this final epigraph, "Love is your last chance. There is really nothing else on earth to keep you there." serve very well to express the final meaning of the novel. Ellen's development through all these phases of sexuality and love is one of the important themes in the novel.

WORK CITED

White,Patrick. *A Fringe of Leaves*. Harmondsworth: Penguin, 1977.

15

Parallel Symmetries: Seepersad Naipaul's *The Adventures of Gurudeva* and V.S. Naipaul's *Miguel Street*

The writers of an article in *Modern Fiction Studies* point out that generally the Short Story still remains an unexploited genre[1]. Although most of the best known novelists like Poe, Hawthrone, Hardy, Joyce, Lawrence, and James have used the form in a variety of ways, many times their skill as short story writers surpassing their skill as novelists, it is at best considered as a secondary kind of fiction-writing. The inherent delicate nature of the form is no doubt responsible for this view. Secondly, the lateness of the flowering of the genre historically is another factor contributing to this view. Yet, at this point of time, it must be admitted that neither reason is justifiable enough for the casual treatment meted out to the short story in academic circles.

With the increasing use of the short story form by writers in different languages of the Commonwealth cultures, it must now be considered as a separate, independent form and not as being merely fall-out or residual material thrown off the novelistic tradition, as being but a chip of the big block. Indeed, it has been treated so independently as a form by many writers that they have written nothing but short stories during a good part of their writing lives — Poe, Mansfield, and Prem Chand come to mind in this connection. Even writers like Conrad and Hardy have proved that instead of appearing as fall-out material from their novelistic extravaganza, some of their short stories have actually preceded the novels and have thus acted as spring boards for the development of the idea later into longer novels. Conrad's *Lord Jim* and Hardy's *Tess* are famous examples of such instances.

The popularity of the short story with Commonwealth writers like Katherine Mansfield, Nadine Gordimer, Shirley Hazzard, and Raja Rao, to name a few, is a curious phenomenon. Is it for lack of sustained vision and artistic endeavour that some of these writers have mainly confined themselves to the short story? Or is it the nature of the society that they depict that is reflected in this phenomenon — a society which is fragmented, perhaps, or which is polymorphous in its set-up, defying confinement into a whole even in a novelistic genre?

The one basic reason for the Commonwealth writers' extensive use of the form appears to be its rootedness in oral, mythological tales and grandmother's stories. Especially in African and Indian backgrounds, after-dinner story-telling by the elders to an audience of youngsters is a familiar activity. Stories of the family or clan, or of ancient mythology were constantly being repeated from generation to generation. The short story is thus the oldest form of narrative, although it has only recently gained respectability as a literary genre. To the Western writers the attraction of the short story was there because of its potentiality for adaptation into radio, television, or magazine serial purposes.

But though recent as a literary genre, the short story has changed its form rapidly in the hands of a variety of writers. The most important growth that one observes between the 19th century and the 20th century is the change in depth and complexity. Stories of similar length have become infinitely richer in recent times. From a developmentally structured, climactically moralistic, linear form, they have become multi-surfaced, symbolically deep, open-structured units with significant dimension. To study the two collections of the Naipauls, father and son, is to trace many of these changes in the short story.

As East Indians living in West Indies both Seepersad Naipaul and his son, V.S. Naipaul found the form especially pliable for dealing with the cross-cultural patterns amidst which they lived. The form itself was symbolic of the disjointed, fragmented kind of life on the islands. The colonised people of the West Indies had little historical substantiality and less social continuity. Both the Naipauls were quick to observe the nature of these lives lived in moments. Between their two collections of short stories, a reader can not only trace on exchange of reciprocal identities between the father and son as writers but can also observe the full development of the East Indian immigrant life in the Caribbean islands, and further note the development of the short story in West Indian literature.

Seepersad Naipaul had written his stories as early as 1940 and they were published in a modest local edition for the first time in 1943 in Trinidad under the title *Gurudeva and Other Indian Tales*. In 1976, V.S. Naipaul put together several of his father's stories written after 1943 and published the whole volume again in England as *The Adventures of Gurudeva and Other Stories*. There are ten stories in this later volume. The last three stories namely, "In the Village," "The Engagement," and "The Gratuity," as also parts of "The Adventures of Gurudeva," are the later additions included by V.S. Naipaul.

The central story in the volume is "The Adventures of Gurudeva" consisting of seventeen segments. Each segment describes an adventure, or misadventure of Gurudeva.

Stylistically no attempt is made by the narrator to hold them together and each segment is almost a short story in itself, as indicated by the subtitles in each segment. But Gurudeva is the central character and his growth and development into an adult and a middle-aged man is chronicled through the story and it is the theme of his growth that provides the unity.

The adventures are recorded by a narrator who is no doubt in sympathy with the character he is creating, but he does not have much sympathy for the personality of that character. Gurudeva is the son of Jaimungal, a first generation East Indian Brahmin who has come to the rice-lands and cane-fields of rural Trinidad as a migrant labourer. His son Gurudeva, who is an infant at the time of the migration, develops into a wayward, irresponsible, devil-may-care, yet an orthodox, rigid Brahmin in the background of Trinidad. The development of Gurudeva is symbolic of the larger transformation that was taking place in the phenomenon of the migrant labourers' life in the Trinidad of the late twenties and thirties. Jaimungal, the semi-literate, simple Hindu belonging to a village in Eastern U.P. carries his India with him and remains with it till his death. Although he has learnt to read and write a little English, he does not become Westernized in his dress and continues to wear his dhoti and koortah to the very end.

But the son Gurudeva, who was only a child when the family migration took place, is without a first hand knowledge of the Hindu background. The Trinidadian society turns his head as he is not rooted in it. As a result he grows up in the midst of a chaos of ideas and values. He gives up schooling and takes up life as a vagabond as his father is always there to support him. He turns out to be the village bully and coward by turns, gets into a series of scrapes, including incidents of violence, jail-term, and local girls. His escapades throw his own family into confusion and unhappiness and even destruction when he at last attempts to turn into a Guru, a devout pundit defending the Sanatan Dharma against the onslaughts of reformism, which is brought into Trinidad by a man called Pundit Biswas, a free-thinking man who opposes the caste system, idol worship, the concept of many gods, of Hinduism in general. A good part of the story deals with the struggle of Gurudeva to find an identity for himself as a practising Hindu Pundit. He then comes into confrontation with his former schoolteacher, Mr. Sohun, who is a "Christian". In the long harangue delivered by Mr. Sohun, Seepersad centralises the religious issue plaguing the East Indian community in the West Indies. The moot point of their argument is over the question as to who is a Brahmin.

> "Pundit Biswas condemning caste, too," Gurudeva said. "Man saying anybody who can read and write canbe a Brahmin. He saying he can be a Brahmin even if the father is a chamar. [A low caste sweeper or worker in leather.]" "What you think of that?"
>
> Mr. Sohun chuckled.
>
> "I suppose that must be hard on you," he said. "But a Brahmin should be a man of knowledge and piety; yet ninety-nine in every hundred of you who pride yourselves on your being called Pundit or Maharaj, are in fact neither the one or the other. Caste, thank goodness, is non-existent in the West Indies. No body really keeps caste-rules, yet, ridiculously enough, most of you keep quarreling over caste — as though you were still in some remote village in India ... Not caste, but the shadow of caste remains in the West Indies. Its only use here is to inflate some people's ego."[2]

The passage serves well to illustrate Seepersad Naipaul's style as well as his theme. The writer is apparently himself caught in the changing, conflicting values of Trinidad society. He forgets even to throw a veil of fiction over the discussions of some of the ideas in the story and presents them in long-winded comments of elaborate descriptions. The style of such passages is quite markedly different from the dialogue that he puts into the mouths of some of the women characters. The authorial voice and the charcters utterances are many times not so well-blended in the elder Naipaul's fictional style. The patois Hindi or English that the characters use is different from the chaste literary style of the authorial voice.

Themataically, the writer's preoccupation with the deeper problems of the East Indian's adjustment to a colonial society is very strongly presented in this main story. The account records the passing away of the East Indian past and the struggle to come to terms with the West Indian present that the immigrant settlers had to face. Each generation has its own set of problems and the story records the struggles of the two generations, namely, of Jaimungal and Jhulani, the parents, and Gurudeva and Ratni, the son and daughter-in-law.

The story records with remarkable clarity the day to day life of Jaimungal's family. Seepersad Naipaul is deeply interested in pointing out the intriguing way in which rituals and customs of a native land continues to be practised in the new "home". It is a concrete visualization in fiction of the way in which colonising and the process of changing countries can erode one set of values leaving place for gradual replacement of a new set in the course of acclimatization. Acculturization is an inevitable corollary of colonising. The struggle for retention of proper values is consciously or unconsciously carried out in both the process of giving up and taking on of the old and the new. This is the hard struggle of individuals as well as communities in the context of colonialism. Seepersad painstakingly records this struggle on both planes in his short stories, so much so that they are unique, well-preserved documents about the East Indian settlers inWest Indies. They are revealing social histories of the West Indies, in a nutshell.

The remarkable feature stylistically is the stance of the writer iin depicting this life. Although the authorial tone is distinct and separate, it cannot be mistaken as being that of an "outsider" or observer. He definitely stands inside the community for he is a part of it, yet he sees it detachedly. (There is no irony or criticism implied in the tone — it is, on the contrary, sympathetic and amused at the comedy of the moving life around him). One is frequently reminded of the irony of R.K. Narayan while reading these stories. In fact, in his Introduction to an edition of *The Adventures of Gurudeva*, V.S. Naipaul says that around 1950 he had sent his father some works of R.K. Narayan from London. And his father wrote back to him: "You were right about Narayan. I like his short stories....he seems gifted and has made a go of his talent, which in my own case I haven't even spotted."[3]

Seepersad Naipaul had already written most of his stories when he made that observation. Although there may be some affinity between the Senior Naipaul and Narayan in their comic sense, one cannot miss the basic difference in the two writers' visions. The older man saw his world from a mood of quiet desperation regarding the uprooting and uprootedness that was behind all these comic incidents. The colonised, trapped, closed-in feeling of the writer is the very inspiration behind this comic vision. Whereas, in Narayan, that concealed thrust is totally absent, understandably enough, as his predicament and the predicament of the characters in his fiction are quite different. As a writer Seepersad has imbibed the Western writers' attitude of characterization without giving up his East Indian sympathy. His heaviness of detail, care and concern about description and explanation invest his stories with a substantial quality that is lacking in Narayan.

V.S. Naipaul learned many things from his father as a short story writer. Although he lived in a totally different world than Seepersad Naipaul's and developed a radically different vision of the world, he looked up to his father's achievement for inspiration from the very beginning.

Miguel Street, which is Naipaul's first book although it comes third in the line of his publications, is in every way a unique kind of sequel to Seepersad's *Adventures of Gurudeva*. The world that it depicts, the time of action that it covers, the people that it introduces — they are all historical continuations of similar features that figured in *The Adventures*. Such an effect, needless to say, was not intended by the writer himself. It merely happens to be the reality of historical necessity both in terms of the West Indian society and its growth and the two generations of writers and their development.

Soon after Naipaul left for London in 1950 for higher studies, he started writing. The very first result was a classic achievement of an exile's effort, his *Miguel Street*. In this book with the significant title Naipaul recreated the life that he had left behind in Trinidad. There are seven short pieces in *Miguel Street*. One does not know whether to call them stories or vignettes or sketches. They are separate accounts of different episodes involving different characters and each piece has a separate title. Yet they are all as closely interlinked as several chapters in a novel.

The interlinking is established by the intermixing of the characters. It is the same crowd in all the stories and Miguel Street keeps them together. And more than that the boy narrator keeps them together, for it is through his eyes that we see the action in all the stories. Yet the book cannot be called a novel for the pieces are too fragmented and separate, and also too short and episodic in nature. Life on Miguel Street is a medley of disparate experiences and the boy-narrator is not fully conscious or fully aware of his role as narrator and observer, hence the lack of proper focus for the pieces to substantiate themselves into a novel. Some of the pieces were apparently placed in the book much later at the time of publication, for they are not obviously among Naipaul's first writing. For instance, Ganesh Pundit in the last story called "How I left Miguel Street" is referred to as being in an expensive-looking lounge suit, not in a dhoti and koortah as in his mystic days, i.e., as hero of Naipaul's second novel *The Mystic Masseur*.

Naipaul's style in the stories is very different from the style of his father, Seepersad. Recounting the experiences through the boy-narrator has eliminated the straight, almost reportage kind of detailing of event and action that one finds in *The Adventures*. The narrative tone is a personal, unifying one in *Miguel Street*. It is closely autobiographical in effect because of this first-person narrator's voice. Fact is more finely transformed — almost by the skin of its teeth — into fiction in Naipaul's stories.

The East Indian world is not so exclusively and insularly presented in Naipaul's book as it has been in Seepersad's. The closed society of the immigrant world of *The Adventures* has given place to the open society of *Miguel Street*. From the rural part of Trinidad one has advanced to the urban Port of Spain of Trinidad between the two books. Miguel Street is a multi-racial street, with negroes, poor whites, creoles, and East Indians mingling together. Hence the East Indians' predicament also has changed. No longer is it possible for them to reproduce the living conditions in Indian villages in distant Trinidad in a quaint, dead way as in *The Adventures*. In their home in Miguel Street the boy and his mother are left to fend for themselves without even their multifarious family gods as were found in the stories in *The Adventures*. Unlike Jaimungal and Jhulani and Guru in *The Adventures*, all of whom can arrange even a harikatha or a Muharam celebration in a remote village of Trinidad just as it is done in their ancestral land, United Provinces or Uttar Pradesh, all that the Mother in Miguel Street can do is to consult Ganesh Pundit about her son going abroad. To the young boy on Miguel Street, Uncle and Aunt Bhakcu are the only Hindu relataives that he knows in the vicinity, all his other close associates are negroes or creoles, like Hat, Eddoes, Bogart, and B. Wordsworth. Both the theme and technique of V.S. Naipaul have indeed become more universalised than the special, ethnic theme and style of Seepersad. For instance, a story like "B. Wordsworth" where Naipaul uses a boy-narrator to introduce to us an unsung, unappreciated poet calling himself "Black Wordsworth", in a touching, lyrical tone, is much more subtle and imaginative as a composition than Seepersad's "My Uncle Daloo", where we meet an eccentric, busybody through a short, quaint episode involving a bit of sham crystal-gazing. Seepersad mostly reports the incident.

In every way *Miguel Street* is an advance on Seepersad Naipaul's *The Adventures.* West Indian fiction has taken a new turn of development passing from Naipaul Senior to Naipaul Junior. If Seepersad had attempted to write a long short story in a fragmented, episodic style, as he did in *The Adventures,* Naipaul has succeeded in stringing together short, episodic, fragmented short stories into a fictive whole like a novel in *Miguel Street.* The distanced, reportage style of the father has developed into the personal, involved style of the son.

To look at the two volumes closely is to realize that a great deal has happened to the West Indian society as well as to the West Indian short story in the course of the lives of the two writers. The passage from the village to the city, and then from the urban ghetto to the further freedom of the cosmopolitan world, from the narrow, immigrant, closed society to the multi-racial mixture of the colonial city street, and from there directly to what is considered "Home" by the colonial majority, can be clearly traced. If Seepersad Naipaul's "grats". Sanyasi in his story "The Gratuity" has to depend upon a donkey as a mode of travel, V.S. Naipaul's Uncle Bhakcu in his story "The Mechanical Genius" has progressed into being the proud possessor of a second hand lorry. If Seepersad Naipaul's Kanhiah has to wed Kamli only after going through the

Hindu ceremony of "seeing of the bride" by the families, Dolly of Miguel Street can go from man to man just as she pleases.

Seepersad's stories follow a conservative trend, tending to be descriptions of village life that the Indian community experiences in a West Indian background. It is a peculiarly isolated community closed in upon itself in the midst of that island. Stories like "The Panchayat" or "The Engagement" for instance, record events that could very well be taking place in a village in India. To addto the conservative element, Seepersad's style of writing is quite often Biblical.

The Indian community in Miguel Street is only part of a larger society, and is not so isolated as in the earlier work of Seepersad. They live in the midst of a fast growing colonial society of negroes, creoles and other floating population like the garrisoned American soldiers on the outskirts of the city. The change, or growth, from the village to the city has been responsible for the mixed, multi-racial society. From the youthful narrator's point of view, the change has been good for himself. It has enabled him to grow out of an insular background. For instance, his friendship with Hat was one of the formative influences of his life. The happy-go-lucky negro helped the fatherless boy to develop into an independent spirit.

Between Seepersad's "The Panchayat" and V.S. Naipaul's "The Maternal Instinct," for example, many changes had taken place in the Indian community amidst the West Indians. The West Indian society had evolved into new patterns of life style befitting a colonised society. In the atmosphere of the earlier story, "The Panchayat", it was considered totally wrong for a woman even to leave a husband, let alone go ahead and take another man. Moonia, the young wife, although deserted by her husband three times, wishes nothing more than to return to him. She only pleads that he swear an oath by the Ganga that he will not desert her again. On the other hand, the society in V.S. Naipaul's "The Maternal Instinct" is much more advanced.

Laura, the woman in this mixed society, has eight children that she has begotten by seven different men. Her daughter Lorna is also as promiscuous as she is. And Miguel Street is not too critical of them, unlike as in the village community sitting in panchayat.

Miguel Street is Naipaul's first work. It served as an exercise in literary apprenticeship to the ambitious writer. The loosely strung, fragmentary collection gathered strength and unity in its evolution into novel forms like *The Mystic Masseur* and *A House for Mr. Biswas* which also go back to the same colonised society for setting and atmosphere, *Miguel Street* provided Naipaul with a chance for technical experiment in the process of his quest for a novel in which to embody his vision of his colonial background. To go from *Miguel Street* to *The Mystic Masseur* and tahen on to *A House for Mr. Biswas* is to see the full development of Naipaul's art as a writer of fiction. Substantiating casual observations, fleshing out characters, filling out the story line, unifying them all into a broadened vision of a man's predicament in society — Naipaul was thus able to establish his hold over the novel form. As a result, the Commonwealth novel in West Indies emerges as a unique blend of various elements — social history, social documentation, autobiography, and cultural chronicle, using for its medium the varying tones of irony, comedy, tragedy, and symbolic effects. It combines a journalistic style with a fictional style. It envolves from a fragment into a story. The development that one finds in the finished product of *The Mystic Masseur* and *A House for Mr. Biswas* is not only from the younger Naipaul to the more mature one, but it is also from Naipaul Sr. to Naipaul Jr. A study of the two collections clarifies many points regarding the coming into maturity of West Indian fiction.

Both the Naipauls demonstrate the dramatic rather than the lyrical or poetic elements of the short story. The unities that Aristotle recommended for drama, namely, of time, place and action, are significantly made use of in *The Adventures* and *Miguel Street*. The dramatic tension, giving an effect of the whole meaning more than the parts, is skilfully made use of, especially by V.S. Naipaul in *Miguel Street*. The narrative device made use of in this novel works on a double plane, wherein the stories appear to be fragments and yet are integrated into one long account of life in Miguel Street.

Generally, the short story is described as being closer to a poem than a novel or fiction as a genre. Suggestiveness, implying a purely metaphorical or figurative language, and lyrical tone, implying a subjective angle, are the critical terms most used in analysing the qualities of a short story. Individual phrases and lines, paragraphing, the end-line finality, — all these details are stylistically as important in a short story as metrics and prosody in versification. The short stories of Joyce, Lawrence, Mansfield, O. Henry, etc., can best be analysed within the frame of reference of poetic composition.

But the short stories of many Commonwealth writers like R.K. Narayan, V.S. Naipaul and Seepersad, do not have much affinity with poetic composition. Their style in the short stories is closer to the newspaper style in that the detached, detailed, almost laconic tone is more commonly used. The dialogue style is more often used than the lyrical or suggestive style. The spoken idiom is more important than the metaphorical or figurative language, R.K. Narayan's "The Cobbler and the God," for instance, or V.S. Naipaul's "Hat" derive their appeal mostly from the skilful use of the dialogic tone.

Miguel Street presents the picture of a colonised world as few stories do. The burden of a colonised society, ridden with problems like multi-racialism, negro slavery, acculturisation, lies heavy on life in Miguel Street. Although life in Miguel Street is as rich as that in Joyce's Eccles Street or Narayan's Lawley Road, it progressively ends in being a cul de sac by the time we arrive at the end of the collection of stories. The growth of the young narrator himself into an adult, and his outgrowing of the wanderings on Miguel Street inversely shrink the small street into a narrow area with no exit. The boy has become a man and must cut himself adrift from the vagabonding life on Miguel Street. The last scene inthe book is significantly enough the one in which we find the young man walking across the airport tarmac towards the plane that will take him out into the world.

The unity of the stories in the book is remarkably achieved by developing these inter-faced themes of the narrator's growth and the inverse shrinking of the colonial background. Colonialism has defeated itself in the world of Miguel Street, and the grown-up man rejects this defeatist world. It is for this gesture of repudiation of colonialism that Naipaul's *Miguel Street* is most significant.

In his autobiographical account, *The Middle Passage*, Naipaul has written: "The history of the islands can never be satisfactorily told. Brutality is not the only difficulty. History is built around achievement and creation; and nothing was created in the West Indies."[4] But this is not true. The fiction of Seepersad and V.S. Naipaul himself was created in the West Indies and this stands as a fine achievement in Commonwealth literature.

NOTES

1. Mary Rohrberger and Dan E. Burns, *Modern Fiction Studies*, 28, No. 1 (Spring 1982), pp. 5-12.

2. Seepersad Naipaul, *The Adventures of Gurudeva* (JLondon: Andre Deutsch, 1976), p. 48.

3. Seepersad Naipaul, *The Adventures of Gurudeva*, p. 7.

4. *The Middle Passage* (Penguin Books, 1968), p.29.

16

Gandhi and Ruskin on Education

As one progresses with the study of John Ruskin's and Mahatma Gandhi's views on Education, one is amazed by the discovery of the ever-widening and deepening percolation of the influence of Ruskin on Gandhi in a variety of aspects. Thanks to Chapter XVIII 'The Magic Spell of a Book', in Mahatma Gandhi's *Autobiography* the influence of Ruskin on Gandhi is no surmise with regard to the philosophy of social economics. But he says: "This was the first book of Ruskin I had ever read". He does not mention whether he read his other works and felt their influence equally. But the similarity of unusual and original ideas of education, e.g. that the least intellectual method of education, learning through manual labour is better than book-learning in a modern, scientific age, makes us realize that Gandhi may have deliberately exposed himself to the influence of Ruskin in a wider field after his first reading of *Unto This Last*. Gandhi's conception of the Phoenix Settlement in South Africa and the Sabarmati Ashram in India are very much on the lines of Ruskin's St. George's Guild. Though St. George's Guild was to concern itself mainly with art activity, Ruskin intended to start schools for the children of the workmen there as we come to know through some of his letters in *Fors Clavigera*. *Fors Clavigera* itself, the periodic journal in the form of letters, associated with the affairs of St. George's Guild may perhaps have been the model for Gandhi's *Navajivan* and *Young India*. Apart from this surmise, one can with surely trace Ruskin's influence on Gandhi in is one of his most important educational beliefs, that of Basic Education, for the idea was expressed by Ruskin in his preface to *Unto This Last* where he says: "That there should be training schools for youth established at Government cost, and under Government discipline, over the whole country; that every child born in the country should, at the parents' wish, be permitted (and, in certain cases, be under penalty required) to pass through them; and that, in these schools, the child should (with other minor pieces of knowledge hereafter to be considered) imperatively be taught, with the best skill of teaching that the country could produce: (a) the laws of health and the exercise enjoined by them; next (b) habits of gentleness and justice and last, (c) the calling by which he is to live. The order of emphasis in the 3-fold formula is significant and Gandhi was to take up only the last idea on which to build his elaborate structure of Basic Education. In this, the visionary and the practical philosopher drew the inspiration for their concepts from the needs of their own respective societies. Perhaps they were also influenced in their bias by their own early upbringing and educational training. And this was as different as that of two people could be.

Ruskin, in his early life was mainly educated at home by his parents. His father, a prosperous sherry merchant, put before him the best models in Literature and Art. His mother, an austere woman, tried to neutralise this effect by instilling him with her own stern Scotch Puritanism. The Bible was the book that he read first with the help of his mother, strictly corrected in the pronunciation of every word to the last syllable with a proper accent by the iron will of his mother. He records in his autobiography, *Practerita* that his was a toyless childhood when he had to be satisfied with a bunch of keys or a ball if he wanted to amuse himself, if he did not want to stare incessantly on the figure in the carpet or at the arrangements of bricks in the opposite house. Apparently this was the unconscious early training for his later studies in Art and Architecture. He gratefully acknowledges his mother's influence in the annual readings of the Authorised Version and says that these readings established his soul in life and were the one essential part in all his education.

Another equally important aspect of his early education was the annual tours that the family took to the continent to shrewdly combine the business of sherry selling and buying with the study of the Art and Architecture of the stones of Venice, Rome, Florence, the cathedral cities of France. Later all this self-education was supplemented by his scholastic training at Oxford and one realises that this later period was not at all as important as the earlier one, for Ruskin, till the end reflects the conflict and the contradictions of his parents' training. He could never resolve the tension between the sensual and the spiritual strains that his home/life engendered in him and perhaps this was the reason why he attempted to sublimate his conflict by advocating an Utopian concept of education where the body, mind and spirit were to be wholesomely and harmoniously educated. It is interesting that he stresses one important need if education is to become meaningful, i.e. manual labour, what he himself had never to undertake in his indulgent and luxury-soaked lif. In letter 47 in *Fors Clavigera* he says: "you don't know how to make a brick, a tile, or a pot; or how to build a dyke, or drive a stake that will stand. No more do I. Our education has to begin". Perhaps it was for this reason that he felt all his early education was towards a negative effect. Was it, really?

Gandhi's *Autobiography* contains his earliest views on education. With his extra-ordinary clarity and directness of thinking and expression he tells the story of his own early education, at the same time giving us a glimpse of the background to his later theories. Routine school education started for him at a very early age in the primary and high schools at

Porbander and Rajkot. Unlike Tagore he does not seem to have rebelled against the system of education, but speaks of the affection of his teachers for him and how he more or less took the routine for granted. Even on Gandhi this part of his education seems to have had a negative effect. He owned to this phase just a few of his later beliefs, that physical training was as important as mental training, though he had not realized it then and a love of the Indian languages inspired by the affection of the Sanskrit teacher for him. The lessons that he was learning were in the more important school of experiment and experience and it was in this kind of education that he was to have faith in later life. His account of his escapades with his friend in meat-eating and smoking and with his brother in stealing a bit of gold show in what strong and deep ways his later belief in Truth and Ahimsa were striking root. Even at an early age Gandhi had no belief in the learning of the three R's through books for he himself says that he had a "distaste for any reading beyond school books".[1] It is significant that the chapter on his marriage is sandwiched between the II chapter on childhood education and IV chapter on High School education. His marriage appears to have been the most profound lesson in his life, for that afforded him the maximum scope to learn through experiment and experience. Further, there are the chapters on his exposure to English education. He went to England to study Law, but there is very little account of this aspect of his education in England. Even here, he was learning in the wider school of society and talks of his learning the art of knotting his tie, learning to dance, to speak. If his school education at Rajkot was passively negative, the lessons that he learnt in England were violently so and shaped his character decisively. Salt's *Plea for Vegetarianism* had more influence on him than Bentham's *Theory of Utility*. In the chapters where he does speak about his education in Law, he strikes one as an extra-ordinarily diligent and hard-working student. He would not spare himself in reading the prescribed text-books even when he knew that other students were managing by reading notes and summaries. As he declares, all this careful readings of Law stood him in good stead in South Africa. It is this same diligence and hard-work that Gandhi demands from the students of India too, for, as in everything else, he felt that what was possible for him, an ordinary person, should be possible for others.

So it was from these vastly different backgrounds that Ruskin and Gandhi emerged as self-appointed educationists. Necessity was the mother of their inventive ideas on education, especially Gandhi's. They were neither of them academicians, though Ruskin did occupy the position of the first Slade Professor of Art at Oxford University for a number of years, and they were not interested in writing treatises on learning and education like Newman and Dewey. But like Plato and Socrates, they chiefly concerned themselves with enlightening the masses in a simple, practical way, or rather, it all started in a simple, practical way but developed into the most radical and complex views on education.

Ruskin's views are expressed in a desultory fashion in just a few of his works— some letters of *Fors Clavigera* and the two more popular lectures in *Sesame and Lilies*. The first of these lectures, "Of King's Treasuries" deals with the education of the workers in cities like Manchester. Ruskin teaches them no other subject than how to fit themselves for life, throughout the lecture. The lecture illustrates eloquently the reason why Ruskin was inspired to become a teacher. He deplores the industrialisation and materialism that was creeping into England and turning them into a nation of barbarians incapable of sensitive feelings even when faced by shocking incidents of death of the poor from starvation. In his caustic way he observes: "My friends, I do not know why any of us should talk about reading. We want some sharper discipline than that of reading; but at all events, be assured, we cannot read. No reading is possible for a people with its mind in this state. No sentence of any great writer is intelligible to them. It is simply and sternly impossible for the English public, at this moment, to understand any thoughtful writing,—so incapable of thought has it become in its insanity of avarice"[2]. He accuses the English society of having despised Literature, Art, Nature, Compassion and humanity. We notice that as a raesult he himself passionately attempted to remedy all this omission and advocated the study of music, dancing, painting and the history of rocks and stones in his suggestions for a wholesome education.[3] This was not just idealistic enthusiasm for in his essay "A Joy For ever" he explains himself: "We shall not succeed in making a peasant's opinion good evidence on the merits of the Elgin marbles: yet I believe we may make art a means of giving him helpful and happy pleasure and of gaining for him serviceable knowledge." In the lecture he emphasises his belief that to become `mighty of heart, mighty of mind' is truly to be educated, not learning a utilitarian profession to advance in life.

The second lecture, concerning itself with the education of younger minds especially that of young girls, highlights another of his important beliefs, that it is not only necessary to teach them how to read, but also what to read and why to read.

Both these lectures bring out the salient features of Ruskin's concept of education, that it is not merely intellectual training but it must help towards a moral and spiritual development.

Gandhi has written and spoken copiously about his views on education. Most of the discussions were published in *Young India* and *Harijan*. Gandhi appears to have carried on an extended dialogue with the students all over India through these publications. He taught and advised them more as a father than as a teacher, inviting them to correspond with him, encouraging them to seek his advice and guidance, publishing their letters and discussing them publicly if the problems were of general interest. Besides these lectures and addresses, there is, of course his manifesto of Basic Education.

As already pointed out, he appears to have developed his theory from the suggestion made by Ruskin in his *Preface to Unto This Last*. Thus the whole theory is based onthe question of social economics. It was apparently inspired by the need of the moment of the country, mainly embodying two of his beliefs: (1) Gandhi was resolutely opposed to the British system of educating Indian youth through a foreign language in a pseudo-literary manner chiefly to produce clerks for the Government and (2) he was strongly disapproving of the incursions of the machine into the Indian rural economy. Thus he meant to use his system of Basic Education to eradicate the evils in both the urban and the rural worlds.This as we see now, was too idealistic and ambitious a project to succeed. Ruskin too, was agitated by the second problem, the ugliness and sordidness that increasing mechanisation brought in its wake in England. It dehumanised the worker. It also affected the agricultural economy of England. Yet, he appears to have realized that he could not close his eyes to the fact that the machines had come to stay. So, reckoning with the machines one had to find an antidote in order not to be complete slaves to it. Hence his insistence on acquainting the present and the factory worker with the Elgin marbles and Shakespeare, so that the dehumanisation could be arrested by the aesthetic and moral development of the ordinary individual. His starting of the working Men's College, St. George's Guild, 'Ruskin's Tea-Shop' and cleaning the slums of St. Giles are important from this point of view. It was better to educate the taste of the people in aesthetic and moral concerns and teach them to transcend the evils of a mechanised society for they could not escape the inevitability of scientific progress. If the men had to work in offices and factories in the mornings, they could at least neutralise it by taking lessons in draughtsmanship leading to a knowledge of art in the evening. They had to and would drink tea, so it was better to make them drink pure good tea. Slums would inevitably spring up in an industrialised area, but one should at least attempt to keep the roads and pavements clean. The difference between Ruskin and Gandhi appears to be like the difference that existed between Tagore and Gandhi. One remembers the criticism that Tagore makes of Gandhi for thinking of the mundane matters of food, clothing and shelter for the masses all the time and not thinking of their artistic and aesthetic needs and in his inimitable way saying that the urge of the bird when it wakes up in the morning is to soar towards the sky and sing before it starts looking for its worm and Gandhi's replying that may be Tagore was thinking of birds which were well-fed the previous night and so could afford to sing and soar but he was thinking of the starving millions in front of him.

So we see that Gandhi out-Puritans the Puritan Ruskin in his advocating the Basic Education theory without qualifications. He is extra-ordinarily idealistic in his desire to do away with all kinds of inevitable divisions, i.e., between urban and rural, young and old, men and women. In a talk which C.F. Andrews records in his book *Mahatma Gandhi* he quotes the Mahatma as saying that he was not totally against machines for he was aware that his own body was a machine and the spinning wheel was also one[4] but one wonders how far he made this concession in practice while advocating the Basic Education theory. Ruskin would have his children taught lessons of health, then gentleness and justice and last, a craft by which they are to live, but Gandhi would have all the "lessons in history, geography, arithmetic related to the craft"[5] which they are to learn.

It is this insistence on a handicraft based education and merging of the urban and rural population that perhaps makes Gandhi place an emphasis on the Indian languages as the medium of instruction. Within the limits of the applicability of his theory of Basic Education in present times, his emphasis on the Indian languages is also correct. The question is about the applicability of the scheme itself.

It is significant that Ruskin describes the third requirement as training the child in the "calling by which he is to live", whereas Gandhi insists on a handicraft and especially spinning, as the only vocation. Is it so easy as all that for everyone to learn and live by a handicraft even if they are taught from early stages? It is apparent that Gandhi was looking at the problem mainly from the point of view of economics and it was but natural in the context of the country. It is true that the handi-craft brought out the whole man and was an education in itself but could not some kind of manual labour along with the learning of the three R's also develop the man? Ruskin believed in this idea, so he would have the under-graduates at Oxford, Toynbee and Oscar Wilde among them, continue at Oxford with their History and Literature but mend the roads of a slum in their vacation. It is true that some of Ruskin's educational schemes which he himself tried to put into practice were failures, but they appear to have failed because of the impulsive enthusiasm insufficiently backed by sustained effort, not because of the impracticability of the theory. For example the Working Men's College which he had started in Red Lion Square, London and which had at first attracted people like Dante Gabriel Rossetti and Burne Jones as teachers, vanished into thin air for the workmen were too tired in the evenings and the artist-teachers were too impatient to continue thus. The model schools and museums which were to be started as part of the St. George's Guild Scheme never came into being due to lack of effort. The difference between Ruskin and Gandhi comes out even in this feature. If, Gandhi by the very triumph of his integrated personality illustrated the practicability of an unusual idea in the setting up of his Satyagraha Ashrama,

Ruskin on the other hand demonstrated the failure of a practical theory by that very lack of integration in the collapse of his St. George's Guild. But then Ruskin had to shake the complacency of the Victorian public whereas Gandhi had a nation in ferment to listen to him.

It is interesting to note the impact of their ideas on people around them. E.T. Cook in his biography of Ruskin discusses the point and says the present British Education Code of 1894 and the "Memorandum of Courses of Work in Rural Evening Schools (July 1906) read like a practical commentary upon Ruskin's *Letters* of a quarter of a century ago". We have Gandhi's own comments on his experiments in education on his own children. Looking back upon the experiment in his *Autobiography*.[7] Gandhi justifies it to himself saying that his three younger sons have not done so badly after all and that if only they had imbibed an amount of literary training in them, he would have given them an ideal education. Gandhi does not seem to realise that there is all the difference in that 'if only' and that 'an amount of literary training' may have proved to be more explosive material than he thought it to be. About his eldest son Harilal, he explains that he was a product of his early, indulgent life and grew up even when Gandhi himself was not sure of his ideas.

The collection of his addresses to students gives a wider perspective of Gandhi's views on education. The recurring topics of the talks are, as elsewhere, what is Ahimsa and how can students practise it, what are the duties and obligations of students' to their parents and their communities which support them to lead a carefree life, students and strikes, students and politics etc. His attacks and demands on the students are many times relentless and harsh, for he too had known the weakness of indulgence and had not sprared himself in mortifying himself out of it. According to his high -minded ideology, true education means self-control and self-discipline to such an extent that it goes against the nature of youth, e.g.

the rules he lays down for a student to observe to belong to his Satyagraha Ashrama are, to mention a few, "the vow of Truth, Doctrine of Ahimsa, the vow of celibacy, the vow of control of the palate, the vow of non-thieving, the vow of Swadeshi, the vow of Fearlessness, the vow regarding the untouchables, Hand-Weaving" etc.[8] Not for thim the study of books, Nature, Art which Ruskin advocates. In his violently anti-Western mood, Gandhi imposes a Spartan simplicity on the youth. According to him, the schools and colleges, especially on the India of the 1920s were "citadels of slavery" and he advises the youth "it was far better to remain unlettered and break stones for the sake of liberty than to go in for a literary education in the chains of slaves"[9] Seen from contextual relevance, there was no other way in which the youth of the country could be exhorted. One invaluable suggestion that he offers that is of universal applicability is the great importance of a disciplined home education for children in preference to an artificial school education. To him the Teacher-Father image were one, as he himself symbolised. When one comes across such sound and simple ideas, one just cannot dismiss his educational ideas as "fads" as he himself describes them to be in his *Autobiography*.

Of course, there cannot, and need not I think, be a systematic study of the exact extent of Ruskin's influence on Gandhi or the parallelism in their ideas of education. After all, they were both highly individualistic thinkers, expressive of the genius of their own age and upbringing. The very way in which they express the same idea in different styles is characteristic of them. Here is Gandhi, speaking of the importance of physical training: "I then had the false notion that gymnastics had nothing to do with education. To-day I know that physical training should have as much place in the curriculum as mental training".[10] Ruskin, in his *Crown of Wild Olive* (1869) had, observed: "The true 'compulsory education' is not teaching the youths of England the shapes of letters and the tricks of numbers, and then leaving them to turn their arithmetic to roguery and their literature to lust.

It is, on the contrary, training them into the perfect exercise and kingly continuence of their bodies and souls".

Yet another significant difference is in their views on women's education. Ruskin is staid and Victorian in his outlook and would have the woman reign over her own garden like a lily after undergoing an education that would not set her at naught with her own natural propensities. Gandhi, on the other hand, under pressure of the need, was thinking of the young women as the reserves of almost half the resources of the country and would have them undergo the same training and discipline as the youths to shape their lives towards independence and service. In a "Letter to a Modern Girl" he exhorts some girl students who had complained about the behaviour of their men classmates "to initiate a crusade against the rude behaviour of students... and learn the art of protecting themselves against ruffianly behaviour (for)...God helps only those who help themselves".[11]

Yet, in spite of such differences their principles illustrate the essential oneness of their views, reinforcing in our minds the idea that great men think alike. Both of them had the highest conception of education, realizing that it was a moral and spiritual question. Thus they were concerned with the fundamentals of education; not for them the superficialities and artificialities of an education for a living and knowledge for its own sake. Whatever their failures or successes might have been, what strikes one is their touching, common concern for their fellow-men, disturbingly termed "the masses", and how they rose to the occasion of the moment and gave unsparingly of themselves to the welfare of these "masses". No subject interested them for its own sake, but all that they had to say upon various topics like Art, Nature, Politics, Religion, Education, work etc., were logical extensions of the theme of man's welfare in society. Though their ideas on education do not form a very prominent part in the body of their work, it is for this reason that their study is rewarding.

REFERENCES

1. *Autobiography*: Part I, Chapter II, p. 4. Navajivan Publishing House.

2. *Sesame and Lilies*, pp. 28-9, Modern Library Edition.

3. *Fors Clavigera*, Letters 9 and 5.

4. C.F. Andrews: *Mahatma Gandhi's Ideas*, p. 335, George Allen & Unwin.

5. *Basic Education*, Chapter II, p. 10, Navajivan Publishing House.

6. E.T. Cook: *The Life of Ruskin*, Vol. II, pp. 365-66.

7. *Autobiography*: Part III, Chapters, XXIII, XXXII, XXXIII and XXXIV.

8. Address delivered at the Y.M.C.A. auditorium, Madras on 10th February 1917. In *To the Students*, Navajivan Publishing House.

9. *Autobiography*, Chapter V, p. 15.

10. *Autobiography*, Part I, Chap. V, p.10.

11. *To the Students*, p. 40, Navajivan Publishing House.

17

Love and Marriage in Raja Rao's *The Serpent and the Rope*

One of the main themes, ever-fascinating and inescapable, for an Indo-Anglian novelist is the problem of East-West confrontation. The cross-cultural complications arising from the meeting of the East and West have a built-in ambiguity, complexity, and teasing interest that enable the novelist to handle the dynamics ofthe plot, story, characterisation and philosophical depth effortlessly if he concerns himself with this particular theme. The novelist can work within these inherent complexities and bring out the dramatic patterns as naturally and meaning fully as an artist working within the inlaid grains of a beautiful piece of wood to expose the deep rhythms of the lines.

A basically important level of this confrontation is on the plane of personal relationships. And of these relationships none seems to be more interesting than that between man and woman. The question of love between a man and woman belonging diversely to East and West, and the institution of marriage enshrining this love, is a perpetually disturbing problem involved in East-West confrontation. Kamala Markandaya in *Some Inner Fury*, R.K. Narayan in *The Vendor of Sweets* and Raja Rao in *The Serpent and the Rope*, to mention a few significant Indo-Anglian writers, have engaged themselves with this problem. Even ordinarily, a love relationship or marriage demands infinite adjustments from the individuals involved. And if the individuals happen to belong to two different cultures as the East and West, the ramifications of the adjustments are geometrically multiplied. The novelist can treat the theme on the sociological, psychological, or existential plane and considerably deepen the implications of his narration dealing with developing individual and national identities and consciousness. Thus the love relationship or marriage becomes a thematic and technical strategy maintaining the artistic tension in the work.

In Raja Rao's *The Serpent and the Rope* this theme of the love relationship between man andwoman is explored in all its complications in the attitudes that exist between Ramaswamy and Madeleine, the two main characters in the novel. The other ancillary themes of the narrator's quest for identity, and the problem of East-West confrontation that is so familiar to readers of Indo-Anglian writing are closely related to this theme of love. Rama's obsessive feeling of alienation and lack of identity springs from his heartfelt realisation that he is an orphan, with neither the love of a mother nor the shelter of a homeland. In this very beginning of the novel he speaks about this growing realisation that has made him weep unaccountably in lonely hotel rooms amidst the far-off Pyrenees.[1] Agape symbolising motherly love is absent from his life; Eros symbolising romantic love has eluded his grasp. Hence this total lack of love lends a feeling of melancholy and loneliness to the figure of Rama the narrator. It also contributes to an overwhelmingly futile and sad ending that goes beyond the tragic overtones in the development of the two main characters, Ramaswamy and Madeleine, Rama's quest for identity and Madeleine's striving after a selfless identity are doomed to negativism because of this failure at the very root of their existence-in the equisite love-relationship that had miraculously sprung up between them.

In the course of the novel Raja Rao draws upon a number

of love stories from myth and legend, history and mundane reality, culled from Oriental and Occidental sources, against which to explore the relationship between Rama and his wife Madeleine. To mention a few, we have the Oriental mythological references to Siva and Parvati, Radha and Krishna, Rama and Sita, Mirabai and Krishna, and Yagnavalkya and Maitreyi. We have the references to Lakshmi and Shyam Sundar, and Saroja and her husband in the world of mundane reality. Besides these there are the Occidental echoes in the stories of Penelope and Ulyssees, Dante and Beatrice, and Tristan and Isuelt. There is also the parallel reality in the affair between Lezo and Catherine and the seamstrees and Lezo, and the marriage between Georges and Catherine. By implication in the title there is above all the story of that legendary Indian saint, Vamana, who blinded by lust one night slid into the room of his beloved by the help of a snake hanging down from the tiled ceiling which he in darkness thought was a rope. Legend has it that this man became a poet and worshipper of God after realising in self-disgust his mistake of intense attachment to this world.

The references in *The Serpent and the Rope* cover the whole gamut of romantic love-relationships in marriage, out of marriage, idealised love, spiritual love, lust, etc. Indeed, the nuances of the theme are so well illustrated in the stories of the different characters that the novel may well be considered a finctionalised exploration of Denis de Rougemont's discussion of the topic in his *Love in the Western World.*

In the main story, at the heart of Ramaswamy's and Madeleine's quest is the need to understand the true nature of love. Whether they achieve this understanding or not is the main question. A discussion of this problem is so closely related to the theme of realising one's self that it is dangerous to separate the two in this novel. Critics who have attempted to explain these separately have not been very convincing. For instance, speaking about the theme of love and divorce in the novel. Narsingh Srivastava believes that Madeleine obtains a "...self-willed divorce from her most beloved husband simply for attaining perfection in her spiritual development."[2] In an attempt to read Madeleine's obsessive leaning towards Buddhism as a justification for the idea of self-less love, Srivastava maintains "...by taking a divorce from her husband she was not denying the social and moral virtues of marriage but transcending them for total liberation of the self from the bondages of the self. She might not have attained perfection, but she was on the way to it all right. Her knowledge of Buddhism and the wisdom she gained from Ramaswamy prepared her to comprehend the truth which is neither social nor moral but only metaphysical.That is why she wanted to make herself completely free from all social and moral commitments. Marriage is nothing but a social commitment and it involves bondage for those who do not love as well as for those who realise the truthof love. Madeleine has grasped the truth of existence and she is on the wayto become love, hence the divorce."

Such a view of Madeleine's divorce glaringly ignores the part that Savitri plays in the relationship between Rama and Madeleine. In order to read even Savitri's love in terms of Advaita philosophy Srivastava comments: "Savitri could successfully detach herself from the claims of the body, but mentally she is so profoundly attached to Rama that she is content to accept him even as a spiritual husband before she goes to marry Pratap. Her love, no doubt showsa progression but it rises only to the level of spirituality where physical marriage with one and spiritual love for the other can go together without violating the claims of either."[4]

On the other hand, referring to Ramaswamy's quest for self-identity, Brij. M. Bhalla observes: "So this divorce is also a discovery. The obvious tragedy is the enrichment and affirmation in the sense that identity crisis has been successfully resolved."[5] Further Bhalla once again justifies Rama's choice of going to a

Guru by maintaining that this is in the Advaitic tradition. Just as Rama himself has acted as the Guru for Savitri, he now surrenders his ego to a Guru. Bhalla also totally ignores the part played by Savitri in the relationship between Rama and Madeleine and concludes in a lofty, Advaitic tone: "Hence Savitri goes back to Pratap and marries him. She realises that she is getting married to the eternal in him and there Rama's and Pratap's truth become one 'Absolute', and all contradictions are resolved."[6]

Explanations such as the above are obviously one-sided and thus lose themselves in a justification of the metaphysical principles of the Advaita philosophy that pervade the novel, and ignore the reality principle of a human situation in which Rama and Madeleine are primarily involved. Although the novel is heavily loaded with metaphysical argumentation, it would be misleading to read the story of Rama and Madeleine in the light of these reflections. On the contrary, the tone and validity of these meta-physical arguments must be interpreted in the light of the failed relationship which stands there as a prelude to the whole narration, and stares us in the face at the end of the novel. It would not do for the critics to be simply as much the fools of philosophy as the fictive narrator Ramaswamy is.

To believe in an exalted Madeleine who obtains the divorce in order to realise the ecstasy of spiritual love, and what is more, to believe that she realises it, is to callously close one's eyes to the loss, the pain, and the suffering that she undergoes as a human being. It is simply to ignore the part that Rama plays in forcing her to that shattering decision.

Tracing the very root of Madeleine's decision, one realises that she finally ordains a divorce because she becomes aware, when Rama returns from India, that she has lost her husband to someone. "Mado, something has happened," Rama himself says on the first day of his return. He has just come back after seeing Savitri in her own house in Allahabad. Rama himself believes that it is India that has come between them but that is Rama, characteristically mystifying a fact. Application of metaphysics to simple, everyday things can be dangerously misleading.

Although Madeleine has kept up her study of Buddhism even during the absence of Rama, it is after the incident of his return that she strangely starts practising it. It is obvious that she turns to Catholicism with an intense fervour when her child Pierre dies, and to Buddhism increasingly when her marriage cracks. The divorce is plainly a result of the failure of their marriage, of the pure love that had existed between them before Rama came under the spell of Savitri. And what kind of spiritual love can Madeleine achieve when there has been this failure at the very heart of simple, human love? Human love has to be transcended, not denied or rejected, in order to attain spiritual love.

Similarly, her practising of Buddhism is not originally for the noble purpose of self-realisation. At first her interest in that religion was academic. It enabled her to find a common ground between hers and Rama's interests and backgrounds. But when she finds her hopes of love shattered and her world emptied, she frenziedly clings to Buddhism as a refuge and resorts to self-mortification. In a bitterness that she does not wish to show, she attempts to annhiliate the self, for she cannot transcend it after such a failure in her life. It is interesting that she chooses to be a Buddhist and does not fall back upon her original Catholicism, for Catholicism, with its emphasis on the love of a deity and the distracting elaborateness of ritualism, would not allow for the detachment of the self, the mortification of the flesh, as itself the main religious practice. Although she herself says about her acquaintance with Buddhism: "Beloved it's you who have brought me this," (p. 314), her statement can be seen to be ironical. She might very well have said: "Beloved, it's you who have brought me to this."

To maintain merely that Madeleine's interest in Buddhism starts as a result of her love for Rama is once again to ignore the way in which she pracatises it. She is working herself away from Rama. She recoils from his touch. She is covering up a distate for life that has crept into her because of the strained relationship between herself and her husband. Not to acknowledge this is to overlook the behaviour of Ramaswamy.

Thus a clue to the failure of their relationship is in Ramaswamy, the narrator. Although he represents himself as a student, a young man interested in ideas, one who possesses an objective analytical mind, he is hopelessly irrational and sentimental-qualities that throw a man's personality into confusion. He himself attributes this to being a mystic son of India, but his sentimentality and immaturity run deeper than that. He entirely lacks a sense of self-irony. He is a curious type of sincere scholar-hero like Edward Casaubon in George Eliot's *Middlemarch*, who takes himself much too seriously to realise his own inauthenticity. He is scholar-manque rather than a true scholar. But the reader is all the more aware that this scholar-hero who is divorced from reality is an unreliable narrator.

A man who tells his own story at length must either be supremely sure of himself or so unsure of himself as to need the articulation of his innermost thoughts and doubts to formulate his own identity to himself. Rama belongs to the latter category. He lacks a sense of identity not because he is a Hindu Brahmin living away from the mainstream of his tradition, in the geographically and culturally distant Westrn world, but because he has no understanding of even the instinct of love. Having lost his own mother early, he has not known mother-love. Being a man he admits that he never was much involved with his father. Little Mother, whom he regards as his own mother, is too young and close to himin age to supply the want of mother-love. As a consequence of this basic lack, he looks for maternal love in

Madeleine, his wife. Curiously enough, Madeleine is older than he is—she is twenty-six, the same age as Little Mother. In one instance, he identifies her with Little mother and says: "They had both the same shy presence, both rather silent and remembering everything; they loved, too, more than is customary. Both knew by birth that life is no song but a brave suffering, and at best there are moments of bridal joy with occasionally a drive over a bridge-and then the return to the earth and may be to widowhood." (p. 20). There is constant glorification of Madeleine as mother (pp. 37, 38, 133, 143, 146). He further points out: "Hinduism glorifies the Mother." (p. 117). Madeleine's name also suggests the figure of Mary Magdaleen, the mother-surrogate for crucified Jesus.

The love between Rama and Madeleine was bound to fail because Rama was looking for the wrong kind of love in their marriage. The death of their infant son Pierre is significant in this context. Madeleine fails to achieve the mother-status, Pierre could have been a bridge between them, Rama observes, but this bridge broke down and could never be crossed. Speaking of himself, Little Mother and her son Sridhara on the other hand, Rama observes that Sridhara was a bridge between them. (p. 34).

Rama's relationship with Savitri is also a complicated one. One might believe that his marriage with Madeleine failed because East and West could never meet, and so he turned towards Savitri to find the kind of love he wanted. Madeleine herself feels this and hence her strenuous efforts to Indianise her life. But even here Rama is not sure of what he wants. He has not known any Indian woman except his sisters and Little Mother. His living away from the country, from the reality of Indian womanhood, contributes to this idealisation of the Indian feminine principle. So when Savitri appears on the scene he visualises her as the embodiment of noble Indian womanhood. Being a student of Cathar history and living in Provence the land of the Troubadours, he cannot but idealise

Savitri. Their wooing proceeds on the pattern of courtly love simultaneously as it proceeds on the lines of Indian mythical love. It is love outside of marriage and needs the support of legend and myth. So Savitri the Rajput woman becomes like another Rajput princess, Meera, and Rama becomes Krishna. Rama with his Gnostic intellectual background, idealises Savitri and turns her into an abstracation as the courtly lover does the beloved. Savitri, like the saintly Meera, worships Rama, spiritualises him and turns him into an abstraction. Not surprisingly, she is specialising in Metaphysical poetry at Cambridge (p. 175).

In both Rama and Savitri there is confusion rather than conflicts between human and divine love. If Madeleine rejects human love altogether as inadequate or unreliable and turns her face towards divine love, Rama and Savitri attempt to combine sacred and profane love in their relationship. All their attempts are bound to end in sterile love. One cannot ignore love on the human plane with impunity. Human love involves the physical, the carnal, and only after coming to terms with it can one transcend that to achieve divine love—to rise on the ladder of love, to express it in Gnostic terms. If love is to be considerd a mere abstract quality, a mere mystification of feelings, then the love between Rama and Savitri can be said to be "fulfilled", despite Savitri's marriage to Pratap and Madeleine's terrible breakdown— both of which are hard, existential, negative phenomena difficult to reconcile with the argument of successful self-realisation or achieving of a self-possessed identity.

By the side of this spirituala, colossal, "fulfilled," abstract relationship between Rama and Savitri, we have the sad fact of the shattered love between Rama and Madeleine. To Madeleine marriage and love are inseparable. She respects the institution of marriage more than Savitri does. She is the Savitri of the novel more than the cigarette-smoking Indian girl is. When Rama falls ill she undertakes a fast in all devoutness to pray for the well being of Rama, her husband. (p. 322). Like another Madeleine who undertakes penance on St. Agnes' Eve so that her lover may be made known to her, she constantly prays for the welfare of Rama.

But both her marriage and her love break down irrevocably. As a consequence she turns away from the world itself. Her treatment of her own body when she becomes a Buddhist sadhaka is another way of attempting to spiritualise the body—by negation rather than by idealisation. This self-mortification can only lead to a very limited self-realisation if one counts it in her effort to reach a level of spiritual love.

Even the most ingenious of metaphysics is inadequate to disprove the fact that Rama fails Madeleine and hence the crack-up of her marriage. He has failed because of his own weakness, not because East and West could never meet. Implied in the name Rama, the husband of Sita in the Indian epic *Ramayana,* is a priggishness, a self-righteousness, a feeling of superiority. With half-pride and half-humility that turn him sometimes into a spurious Brahmin and at others into a decadent one, we find him constantly referring to his Brahmanic superiority. He repeatedly melts into self-mystification as an Indian—either individually or collectively. In a revealing passage, rhapsodising over the spiritual pilgrimage he undertakes with Little Mother, he says:

> If there were no barbarian beyond our borders the Hindu would have melted into his nature, grown white as some woman in the zenana, and his eyes would have seen the splendour of himself everywhere. He might have grown emasculated, but he would have played in the garden of the Ganga (p. 36).

He thinks that a fitting mood in which to read Madeleine's letter. (p.36). In another context he admits: "I knew I could not love: that I did not love even Pierre." (p. 24).

Notwithstanding the heavily sentimental and emotional tone that runs throughout the novel, Rama's Brahminism and intellectualism have resulted in a curious aridity of heart that he himself is not aware of. It is this Madeleine his wife cannot contend with. His metaphysical preoccupations result in his becoming an anomaly incapable of being simply Madeleine's husband. His cough, a Byronic defect that he repeatedly refers to invites more than necessary attention to himself. It represents him as a weak man. Curiously true to the Oscar Wildean aesthetics, he wants life to imitate art, and is constantly losing himself in his metaphysical disquisitions, his poses. The telling of his own story is not much more than a catharsis to him, an askesis that he attempts to find his own true identity.

And then, has he at least succeded in finding himself, his true identity at the end of the novel? According to Bhalla's view: "The quest does not end with the end of the book, the dissolution of Rama's marriage with Madeleine does not signify any shrinking of Rama's spirit.... The obvious tragedy is actually an enrichment and affirmation in the sense that identity crisis has been successfully resolved."[7]

But one cannot agree with Bhalla's view. It is no doubt true that understanding the question of one's identity is a never-ending process, a constantly changing, developing phenomenon. Endless becoming is the nature of being. But notwithstanding this dynamic process in human identity, there is an awareness of the essential self-hood that is at the root of developing and realising one's identity. Rama has not grasped this self-hood with any confidence, for we find that at the end of the novel he surprisingly decides to go to a Guru. This implies that he is still not sure of his own moral maturity and unity of being. He shifts the burden of finding the answers to the Guru and prepares to start his quest all over again. His decision to go to the ashram suggests that he is still hedging a confrontation with the outside world and its problems. Firsthe is a student burying himself in his research to find connections, now he is a disciple still looking outside himself for solutions. The crutch of myth is replaced by the crutch of religion. He does not depend on his own heart for answers even after such experiences. And we note that he himself had maintained: "... the going inward is the true birth." (p. 15). At the end of the novel he is still denied this true birth, this essential identity— consciousness.

So we must look at the crisis in the novel, i.e., the divorce, as what it truly is—a negation, a heart-cutting denial. Madeleine's attempt at self-realisation and Rama's quest for the achieving of his self-hood are defeated by this negation at the heart of their lives. Neither of them can achieve any kind of true success after the divorce.

Yet one must concede that a sense of fulfilment pervades the novel. This lies chiefly in the love that once existed between Ramaswamy and Madeleine. Raja Rao has created a supreme value for their love while it lasted and this stands above all the negations and failures, giving the illusion that the story ends with spiritual self-realisation for Madeleine and successful achievement of an identity-consciousnessfor Ramaswamy.

REFERENCES

1. Raja Rao, *The Serpent and the Rope* (Delhi: Hind Pocket Books, 1968), p. 6. (Further references to this edition of the novel will be in brackets in the article.)

2. Narsingh Srivastava, "Love and Divorce in *The Serpent and the Rope*," Quest, 9 (Sept.-Oct., 1975), 61.

3. *Ibid.*, 62.

4. *Ibid.*

5. Brij. M. Bhalla, "Quest for Identity in Raja Rao's *The Serpent and the Rope*," *Ariel*, IV, no. 4 (Oct. 1973), 105.

6. *Ibid.*, 104.

18

R.K. Narayan's Fictional Vision

After all critics and readers of Indian English fiction have to conclude that of the three major practitioners of the genre of the novel, namely, R.K. Narayan, Raja Rao and Mulk Raj Anand, it is R.K. Narayan who has shown a continuous, sustained creative energy and a significant development as a novelist. He has steadily kept adding to his creative output and as each new work comes out, the already existing ones have to be seen in a fresh perspective. It is now possible to see his novels as parts and also as a whole cluster adding up to an impressive creative canon of fictional design. The depth and breadth of his vision emerges more fully after one considers such different perspectives possible at this point. The vision itself takes on greater significance when one realizes the novelist's persistent and unswerving dedication to his art. And a study of his technical development also becomes imperative upon this realization.

Why is it that Indo-Anglian writing still has to depend on fiction and not on poetry or drama to display its excellence? Is there something in the language or is there something in the genre of the novel or is it the nature of the life that is depicted that has caused this situation to occur? Despite the increasing number of people who write poetry and despite poets like Jayanta Mahapatra and G.S. Sharat Chandra adding new volumes to their earlier output and in their own way building up a tradition for Indo-Anglian poetry, the poet has never had it as good as the novelist in the field of Indo-English letters.

This particular phenomenon of the fiction-writer being at the forefront of literary achievement can be observed in the instances of other Commonwealth societies as well. Patrick White in Australia, Chinua Achebe in Africa, V.S. Naipaul in West Indies, Kataherine Mansfield in New Zealand stand out as examples. Dwelling upon the topic both Naipaul and Wilson Harris have observed that the novel is the obvious form that the West Indies writer has to choose almost compulsively in order to express the feelings of his newly awakened psyche. It is as though the restructuring of the economic and social patterns of living that were inevitable in a post-colonial society could best be represented in the miniature patterned world of the novel. The writer could make himself and re-make the world around him in terms of fictional themes and structures. In an essay called "Tradition and the West Indian Novel" Wilson Harris comments upon the West Indian writer's need to handle the genre in new forms. He justifies his own rejection of the conventional novelistic patterns like time, character, plot, social realism, etc., and says that what he and other West Indian writers like himself like to depict in the novel is "..... a sense of subtle links, the series of subtle links which are latent within him, the latent ground of old and new personalities."

Although Narayan has certainly not discarded the conventional patterns of story, plot, character, etc., in his novels he too tries to depict the sense of subtle links between the old and the new personalities, the old and the new worlds. Indeed, his not dispensing with the conventional novelistic patterns is itself certainly significant in this connection. The transition from the colonial to the post-colonial and neo-colonial set-up in the world that he knew was never as dramatic or radical as, say, in the African or

West Indian community. The old structures of society continued unobtrusively all along and only ripples and nuances of colonial influence were felt in the daily contingencies of life in the middle-class world that Narayan is mostly concerned with. There was no drastic racial or social dislocation in this world attendant upon the colonial atmosphere. The changes from the old to the new were imperceptible, subtle. Consequently Narayan has no compulsion to change the form of the novel radically. Into the old form of the novel he introduces his own typically Indian— English idiom and vision and without any flourish moulds it and transforms it to suit his purpose. As far as Narayan's form and theme are concerned, the medium is the message.

The transformation from the old to the new is as imperceptible and subtle as the passage of time itself in Narayan's world. And it is with the advantage of having nearly all of Narayan's work in front of him that the persevering critic can observe the change and growth at the present point. And this perspective now makes it clear that a re-appraisal is called for in the evaluation of Narayan as a comic ironist.

One of Narayan's last novels to date, namely, *The Painter of Signs*, and one of the rather long short stories, called "The Second Opinion" indeed make a second look and a second opinion imperative on the part of the critic. The characterisation of Daisy and Raman in the *Painter* and those of Sambu and his mother in "The Second Opinion" and the relationships that exist between them respectively, are disturbing elements upsetting one's idea of the novelist as a comic ironist. It is disconcerting to see that Narayan's hero has become more ambivalent, showing a deeper incertitude, and a greater propensity for drifting and indecisiveness than the hero in *The Bachelor of Arts* or *Waiting for the Mahatma*, and the woman character has become more strong-willed, harsher, and more hardened. It is with dismay that the reader takes the negative ending of the *Painter*, when after the close relationship Daisy and Raman part company. And this has not been necessitated by any external obstacle, but only by Daisy's character, her decisiveness. The equilibrium that one had automatically expected is seriously upset. Malgudi is being shocked out of its more or less peaceful atmosphere by this uncomfortably purposeful woman. And the dependent Raman is left with his lonely self by this independent new woman.

In "The Second Opinion" too the same kind of drifting hero and determined woman are depicted. The comic spirit of Narayan is even less at play here than in the *Painter*. The widowed mother, who at least has the backing of convention and tradition to give her strength and support her in the daily routine of existence, is at her wit's end when she sees the drifting, evasive development of her son. Sambu's ambivalent attitude and mood of incertitude are not comic at all. His indifference to the question of his own marriage cannot even be dismissed as something usual and expected in an Indian youth, for they are hardly the attitudes of an Indian youth in truth. As in Raman, even in Sambu Narayan shows the lack of purpose and determination in a man who has not loved or married a woman. He is like a man without a centre to relate to. He has not enough will to make any decision about one of the most important events in his life. Even at the end of "The Second Opinion" one is not sure about Sambu, as to what he will decide about his marriage, although he has agreed to go to the bus-stand to meet his relative just to please his mother. Such indecision surely cannot be called as mere comic failure.

In the "Second Opinion" Narayan's vision is more that of an absurdist than of a comic ironist. The suffering of the widowed mother in her illness, her anguish at the awareness of the longely prospects for her son are serious elements in the story that go beyond the comic spirit. The underlying theme of loneliness depicted in the lives of Raman and Daisy in the *Painter* and in the mother and the son in "The Second Opinion" is morf cutting than acceptable. These are prolonged echoes of the loneliness of the English teacher after the untimely death of his wife Sushila in the earlier novel *The English Teacher*. Only, the echo has become the more authentic voice in the later novels. Loneliness almost becomes a main theme in these later works.

The illness of Sambu's mother invests the story with more of a tragic than a comic spirit in "The Second Opinion." It at least shakes Sambu otu of his inertia and makes him less selfish, if not more determined. Just as the vision of the disheveled hair of her small daughter Kamala had made the mother Savitri return to her home in the earlier novel *The Dark Room*, it is the disheveled hair and unkempt appearance of his hitherto neat and self-possessed mother that disturbs Sambu out of his indifference. The quotidian of daily existence is disturbed and this subtly but inexorably indicates the underlying tragedy of chaos and disintegration in human existence. Although Sambu takes the question of his marriage lightly, his mother does not. Narayan balances the tragic and the comic aspects in these two characters. And significantly enough, in the end it is the mother's attitude that wins. The serious element at least begins to enter into the mind of Sambu.

Indisputably, Narayan has shown a steady and constant development in the growing canon of his work. If the critic still labels him as a comic ironist and finds it difficult to reconcile the comic and the tragic elements in his works, it is the critic who is lagging behind, it is not a fault of the writer's vision. Malgudi has grown, for better or for worse.

Thus one has to observe more carefully Narayan's continuing concern for presenting the predicament of the middle-class individual in a changing, growing society, his ironic but tolerant vision of the absurdities, the foibles, but nevertheless touchingly human urges of such individuals that he has consistently developed in the growing body of his works. What

Saul Bellow has done for his Jewish-urban families in the changing background of the ever-shifting milieu of Chicago, what William Faulkner has done for class and race divided families in the transitional South of the United States, the same creative service Narayan has done for the middle-class Indian family and individual life in India in the middle decades of a post-Independent India.

It must, however, also be observed that Narayan's novels are not so complex or dense or verbose as the novels of Bellow and Faulkner. There is a thinness in the fabric of Narayan's works. Perhaps this is because the kind of life that he deals with is also thin. But this, of course, is not a sufficient explanation, for this defence only leads to the fallacy of imitative form. More likely, it is the comic-ironic style of Narayan that has invested his stories with seeming thinness. The style of necessity has to be one of indirection, oblique angles, hinted thrusts, in order to succeed as ironic tone. V.S. Naipaul attributes this thinness and insubstantiality of Narayan's novels to the typical Hindu philosophy of quietism and equilibrium that he finds embodied in Narayan's philosophical outlook. Naipaul is there confirming the faulty assessment by jumping into the pitfall of the fallacy of imitative form. The critic must also remember how much the handling of a "foreign" language has contributed to this reticence of articulation in Narayan as a novelist. Even after all that is said and done, one has to conclude that Narayan's novelistic vision has emerged as a substantial, major vision of a modern novelist seriously concerned with the problems of individual existence in a modern society.

And after such a conclusion one is left to wonder whether Narayan's novels are really so thin, so comic. The question of the nature of good and evil in his novel *The Maneater of Malgudi*, the implications of a relationship of the individual to society and between a man and woman in *The Guide*, the responsibilities of a growing adult in *The Painter of Signs* and "The Second Opinion", etc. all these are serious issues with unseen reverberations of their own that Narayan deals with in work after work. Reader-response and critical focus need to dwell adequately on these issues. Savitri's choice of suicide in *The Dark Room,* Rosie's quiet determination to go on alone after the failure of the two men in her life in *The Guide,* Daisy's hard choice of dedicating herself to her chosen mission which, she feels, will hardly be promoted by her association with a man, in the *Painter,* and the widowed mother's distracted, selfless anxiety for the welfare of her indifferent son in "The Second Opinion"—all these are extremely serious issues in a seemingly quiescent set-up of Narayan's world. It would not do to miss these deepening concerns in Narayan's vision and label him rigidly as a comic-ironist.

19

The Woman Question in R.K. Narayan's Novels

Without doubt R.K. Narayan justifiably occupies a major place in the world of not only Indo-Anglian fiction but also of Commonwealth fiction. He has earned the discerning, expert critical acclaim of writers like Graham Greene and William Walsh as well as the more difficult acceptance of general readers of fiction in his own country. When his latest novel *The Painter of Signs* was recently serialised in the popular *Illustrated Weekly of India,* it elicited the most favourable appreciation from both North Indian and South Indian readers.

The general consensus of critical opinion about Narayan is that he is a tyupical South Indian novelist, a regional writer in whose novels is reflected the subtle, delicate, near-inexpressible nuances of daily life in a small town in the South. His Malgudi is taken to be a fictionalised version of Mysore, a small place in Karnataka where he has spent the major part of his writing life. The South Indian flavour of his writings has been commented upon by writers like V.Y. Kantak and Meenakshi Mukherjee. The latter observes: "R.K. Narayan's novels are so satisfingly Indian perhaps because they are authentically South Indian. This means not only that he depicts the customs and manners of Tamil people accuretely, which he does, but what is more important, through skilful use of the English language he delineates people whose actions, behaviour and responses are shaped by a language different from English."[1]

But to narrow down Narayan's concerns as above may be dangerous. For instance, it would be wrong to specify that he depicts the life of the Tamil people. Although Narayan is a Tamilian by birth, he has lived in the Kannada speaking region most of his life, and his vision as a writer appears to be shaped by life in Karnataka. If one is going to distinguish between Bengali and Hindu and Punjabi and Tamil, one also has to extend the distinction between Kannada and Tamil although they are both "South-Indian." And such distinctions may add to unnecessary sophistry when, as in Narayan's case, one may have to speak about Tamil-Kannada rather than just Tamil or Kannada.

Thus in our anxiety to find a typical or authentic South Indian novelist in Narayan, we might miss the larger, more universal, more disturbing elements in his writing. The surface realism and comicality that has come to be recognised as Narayan's chief charm has elicited comparison with a writer like Gogol. Commenting on Narayan's chief strength, V.Y. Kantak observes that his "...gift lies in perceiving the comicality of men with that subtle blend of South Indian realism and irony indulged without any rancour whatever..."

Yet two of Narayan's most significant novels, his earlier *The Dark Room* and later *The Painter of Signs*, defy categorisation as novels of comicality. Meenakshi Mukherjee dismisses the uneasy disturbing quality of *The Dark Room* by saying: "Even in *The Dark Room*, where the pattern has an unhappy colouring, the norm is set at the beginning: the lopsided family life of Ramani, where there is little understanding between husband and wife, but life goes on. The wife makes an unsuccessful attempt to run away and live a life of her own, but ultimately comes back to the life she had left behind— and we comes back full circle to where the novel had begun."[2]

V.Y. Kantak makes a more worthwhile attempt to look at the novel in a better perspective when he observes; "Early in his development as novelist the temptation did come to him perhaps— the desire to attempt a serious probing of the tragical consequences of passion as in *The Dark Room*. But Ramani and Shanta Bai remain shrouded figures: and the truth of their passion escapes us. Savitri's spirited protest appears to end up in a gratuitious home-coming, simply deepening the bizarreness of the surface world."[3]

The early attempt at probing the tragical side of human nature has once again been taken up with greater seriousness by Narayan in his latest novel, *The Painter of Signs*, Although the typical Narayan realism and comicality are strongly present even in this novel, the personal predicament of Raman and Daisy are shown to be in a more complex state than that of Ramani and Savitri in *The Dark Room*. Daisy's plight is a logical development of Savitri's via the character of Rosie in *The Guide*. Thus to trace the development of Savitri in *The Dark Room* (1939), Rosie in *The Guide* (1958), and Daisy in *The Painter of Signs* (1976) is to trace the progress of the social set-up of the small town Malgudi and to emphasise the growing seriousness of Narayan as a writer. The common concern of the woman in a man's world that emerges as the main theme in all these three novels is one of the few "themes" that can be attributed to Narayan as a writer. His treatment of it with detachment but nevertheless wise awareness makes him a truly realistic modern writer with a widening vision.

Although Narayan's fictional world is comprised of domestic backgrounds where family relationships are dealt with in their varying forms—like the affections between parents and children, nephew and aunt, friends and cousins, grandparents and grand-children, one should not allow his depiction of these to dilute or conceal the man-woman relationship that is ever present in his novels. In his earlier novels *The Dark Room* and *The English Teacher* he considers this relationship in the marital state and in his later novels *The Guide, The Vendor of Sweets* and *The Painter of Signs*, outside marriage. Speaking of this subject Narayan himself has observed that the man-woman relationship in Western society is based on a "...totally different conception of man-woman relationship than ours."[4] He points out the irrelevance of the eternal triangle in the relationship in the Indian context.

Narayan is partly right in his observations, for one finds that in the Indian context the nature of the relationship varies onlyin intensity and depth, not in kind essentially. For instance, in *Waiting for the Mahatma* he himself has treated the love theme between Sriram and Bharati quite elaborately. Despite the title, the novel is mostly concerned with the growing attraction of the girl Bharati for Sriram, rather than with his awareness of the Mahatma. It is a subtle, gentle, highly individual love between a young man and a woman rather than the turbulent, physical, sexual love that Narayan depicts in this novel.

Similarly, there may be the absence ofthe triangle in the relationship in the Indian context but when it is there, the situation is more complex than in the Western background. In *The Dark Room* the action is mainly triggered off because of the development of this triangle. Before the advent of Shanta Bai, even if the relationship between Ramani and Savitri was not romantically ideal, it could hardly be called "lopsided". Theirs was an ordinary Hindu, orthodex marital understanding, for better or for worse. Ramani is egotistical and domineering and Savitri as her legendary namesake, is the woman devoted to her husband and children unquestioningly without being especially unhappy. Theirs is not the norm of individual happiness so much as the quiet continuity of traditional family existence. When the eternal triangle takes shape with the stepping in of Shanta Bai into this world it is then that Savitri leaves home in a tortured state—she does not... "run away and live a life of her own." She leaves home with the intention of committing suicide. The poignant part of the situation is that she cannot live a life of her own. The helplessness of her predicament is emphasised when she is forced to live with Mari and Ponni and later, in the precincts of the temple. Ironically enough being from a "cultured" background she is not even as free as Ponni to express herself. Her endeavour to stand on her own feet are brave but pathetic attempts of a spirited woman who is going to be defeated by social conditioning. Although Savitri comes back to her home at the end of the novel and restores the order and stability outwardly, it is obvious that her return is not completely self-willed. It is such a small thing as the sudden memory of the dis-sheveled hair of Kamala, her small daughter, that pulls at her mother's heart-strings and brings herback. Individually, one cannot deny that she is a changed Savitri, containing her quiet despair—"A part of me is dead," she herself reflects at the end.[5]

The next step of Savitri's development is in Rosie, the heroine of *The Guide*. Even in *The Guide* the eternal triangle is there between Marco, and Raju. When both the men in her life fail her. Rosie succeeds in standing on her own feet—or rather dancing on her own feet—and acquires an independent, more satisfying life of her own. Her full development from being merely a dancing girl pandering to the tastes of all and sundry men, into being a superior artist, is as much the theme of the novel as the development of Raju from being a railway guide into becoming a spiritual guide. Hers is the conscious, hard-won achievement against odds just as Raju's is an unconscious, accidental but lucky achievement against equal odds.

In *The Guide*, Narayan has succeeded in revealing the complex tensions of three people involved in the man-woman relationship. The tensions are not merely of the romantic feelings. The question of fulfilment of individual identities on a social, emotional and spiritual context is fully treated in the lives of Marco, Rosie, and Raju.

One of the charges of the critics against Narayan is that he does not treat the question of sex openly in the man-woman relationship in his novels. Speaking about *The Guide* one critic observes: "If Narayan baulked anywhere in the sphere of art in this novel it is where the question of sex arises. He dismisses things hastily. Since he is much of a realist in it it is expected of him that he would touch sex intensely but it does not happen. A curtain is immediately drawn by the essentially puritanical artist".[6]

Applied to Narayan's earlier novels like *The Dark Room* and *The English Teacher*, Som Deva's statement is correct. But one cannot deny that there is a progressive inclusion of the subject in his later novels, *The Guide* and *The Painter of Signs.*

In *The Painter of Signs* one may well describe this as the main theme. The novel deals with the alarming problem of a rapid growth of population in the smalltown of Malgudi. There is, indeed, the question of sex behind this problem. There are also the bold scenes in the later development of the relationship between Raman and Daisy. But ironically enough, as Daisy advocates Family Planning and stands as a denier of sex, Narayan has not much scope to dealwith the explicit sexual implications of the free-love relationship between Daisy and Raman. Conservative Malgudi is reluctant to accept this disturbing element of the sex business, and Narayan deals with the theme obliquely—through an eaves-dropper:

> "H'sh, don't be childish, let go, you are hurting me; behave like an adult." The eavesdropper applying his

> eye to the key hole athis point would see nothing.
> A stillness followed before the light went up again the female voice saying. 'If you must stay, please bring the bicycle in...'
> And as the door bolt is heard drawn, the eavesdropper vanishes, leaving Daisy's food at the threshold.[7]

The introduction of the sex theme in his latest novel is a measure of the growth of the writer's theme as well as his art. By 1976 Malgudi has grown not only physically but also socially and culturally. It has become part of a "money-mad world" and Raman paints signs demanding "strictly cash." And according to Freudian terms the observe side of the money-drive is the sex-drive.

The most controversial point about contemporary literature is the overwhelming treatment of the sex theme. The trends that were observed in British and American literature of the fifties and sixties are inevitably being reflected in recent Indian literature. The one area in which the break from the traditional to the modern can be palpably felt is in the realm of changed sexual morality. No novelist worth the name can afford to ignore the topic if he remains in tune with his world. And Narayan,like the sharp observer that he is of the society around him has not fallen behindthe need of the times in *The Painter of Signs*.

Speaking of the world of Narayan, V.S. Naipaul in his *India: A Wounded Civilization* observes:

> We lived within our lesser world; and we could even pretend it was whole because we had forgotten that it had been shattered. Disturbance, instability, development lay elsewhere, we, who had lost our wars and were removed from great events, were at peace... But Narayan's novels did not prepare me for the distress of India. As a writer he had succeeded almost too well. His comedies were of the sort that requires a restricted setting with well-defined rules;...[8]

Naipaul's statements are understandable because he sees Narayan's world mostly through *Mr. Sampath* and *The Vendor of Sweets*. Even if Malguidi is a small town in size and represents a select fictional society, in *The Painter of Signs* it has advanced into being a respectable,microcosmic reflector of the macrocosmic changes. The older is giving place to new and the Hindu equilibrum which Naipaul finds unacceptable, is definitely being eroded.

And this erosion is most obviously measured in Narayan's depiction of the women characters in *The Painter*. Raman—the name of the hero is significant both when connected with Ramani in *The Dark Room* and Rama in the Indian epic—gets as companion not a Savitri or a Sita but a Daisy. Daisy is the "new woman" just as Raman's aunt is the "old woman," Raman himself is torn between the two and in the end we find that he belongs to neither.

V.N. Chibber comments on *The Painter*: "The novelist's focus is not on family planning. Neither is it an attempt to clarify the moral or political values implicit in this particular campaign. The centre of the novel is Raman who being already much of an alien meets with a punishment eminently deserving."[9]

The ambivalence with which Raman is treated in the novel makes one wonder whether he really is the centre of the story. On the other hand, the bold treatment given to Daisy and the strength of her conviction irresistibly draw the reader's attention. In an interview published in *Span* (New Delhi) three years ago, Narayan observed that his daughter, after reading the manuscript of *The Painter* expressed the opinion that he had been harsh on Daisy's character. Another reader, Shyamala A. Narayan in a discussion observed that she did not find Daisy's character credible in the Indian context. I should simply say that I felt her under my skin.

According to Chibber "Daisy is the logical culmination of his (Raman's) rationality as though a one-track mind meets with its formidable match!"[10] The varying opinions testify to the unorthodox treatment of Daisy. From Savitri to Daisy Narayan has travelled a long way in his portrayal of women. He has shown a man's awareness of their position as women in a changing society. The growth of his Malgudi is to be measured not by the expansion of the railway station or the increasing traffic in Market Street but by the transformation of the woman's identity from a Savitri to a Daisy. Although the transformation at first appears to be far fetched, it is not truly so, Narayan himself connects Daisy with, if not Sita or Savitri, at least Shakuntala or Damayanti when he writes:

> "He had explained to Daisy the five kinds of marriage he had read about and they had come to the conclusion that the system called Gandharva was the most suitable one for them; that was the type of marriage one read about in classical literature."[11] And Daisy characteristically maintains:

> "I won't change my name .... Long ago I broke away for the routine of a woman's life. Thereare millions of women who go through it happily. I am not one of them ... If you want to marry me, you must leave me to my own plans even when I am a wife. On any day you question why or how. I will leave you. It will be an unhappy thing for me, but I will leave you...."[12]

The juxtaposition of the aunt and Daisy in the novel brings out clearly the polarities of characterisation of the Indian woman. And despite the striking surface differences, one realizes that they are women of the same stock. Both of them strain towards a fulfilment of their identity, the right to follow their own faith. There is no display of ego or selfishness in their striving. In fact, their desire is for extreme self-sacrifice. The widowed aunt wishes to go to Benaras at the end of her life of devotion to Raman and the unmarried Daisy wishes to return to society to devote herself to her work.

In both Rosie and Daisy, Narayan has shown the individual potential of the Indian woman just as he has shown the

In both Rosie and Daisy, Narayan has shown the individual potential of the Indian woman just as he has shown the ambivalence and incertitude of the man in Raju and Raman. But though the realisation of the potential is admirable in the women, it is also unfortunately accompanied with a denial, for they are forced to make a choice between their men or their work. One wonders whether their choice is a happier one than Savitri's who had no alternative in *The Dark Room*. But perhaps the question of happiness does not arise in the Woman Question.

REFERENCES

1. Meenakshi Mukherjee, *The Twice Born Fiction* (Heineman Educational Books, New Delhi; 1971); p. 174.
2. Mukherjee, *op. cit.,* pp. 154-155.
3. V.Y. Kantak, *The Achievement of R.K. Narayan, Indian Literature of the Past Fifty Years* ed. C.D. Narasimhaiah (Prasaranga, University of Mysore; 1970); p. 136.
4. R.K. Narayan, "English in India," *The Times of India,* December 2, 1964.
5. R.K. Narayan, *The Dark Room* (Hind Pocket Books, New Delhi, 1972); p. 177.
6. Som Deva, *R.K. Narayan's The Guide* (Prakash Book Depot, Bareilly; 1974), p. 95.
7. R.K. Narayan, *The Painter of Signs* (Indian Thought Publications, Mysore; 1977); p. 144.
8. V.S. Naipaul, *India: A Wonded Civilization* (Andre Deutsch, London; 1977); p. 21.
9. V.N. Chibber, "R.K. Narayan: The Burden of Stability", *The Sunday Statesman* (January 1, 1978), p. III.
10. V.N. Chibber, *op. cit.*
11. Narayan, *The Painter,* p. 158.
12. *Ibid.,* pp. 158-159.

20

Indian Expatriates: Kamala Markandaya's *The Nowhere Man*

A recent trend for some Indian novelists in English has been to deal with problems of Indian immigrants in England. At least three novels on this topic have appeared in India in recent years: Anita Desai's *Bye Bye, Blackbird* (Delhi, 1971), Reginald and Jamila Massey's *The Immigrants* (Delhi, 1972), and Kamala Markandaya's *The Nowhere Man*. The latter is an ambitious work, spanning the development and progress of India and Indians during the period 1918-1968. It tries to deal with the problems of Indians as strangers in their own land under British rule, and as strangers in a strange land in post-Empire days. There is a heightened awareness of the delicate situation that existed for Indians in their own country during and after British rule, and there is even some poignancy in the predicament of the main character, Srinivas, who, as persona non grata with the British, has to leave India in the early parts of the novel. But the novelist overplays her hand by developing Srinivas into a total martyr duringthe latter partof the narrative.

No one is better qualified to deal with this theme than Kamala Markandaya, who is herself married to an Englishman and has chosen to live in England and even bring up a child there. Yet *The Nowhere Man* lacks the power and ring of authenticity that one would expect from a writer in her situation, and only rarely rises to being an impressive work. Unlike her earlier novels, *Nectar in a Sieve, Some Inner Fury, Silence of Desire*, and *Possession*, where a woman is the main character. *The Nowhere Man* is dominated by an elderly male character, Srinivas. Nevertheless, one can discern many autobiographical elements in the novel. The author's ancestral home in Southern India, 'Purnaprasad', becomes the 'Chandraprasad' of the novel and the names of members of her family in India (Srinivas, Seshu, Nirmala) figure in the story. Srinivas could very well have been modelled on her father. He is drawn with care, understanding and tenderness, perhaps even sentimentality. Though Srinivas had to flee the displeasure of the British in India, and live in England for a time as an emigre, he is more an immigrant than an expatriate. He was not forced out of the country, like a jew out of Russia or Germany. Hence it is difficult to understand Markandaya's portrayal of him as more sinned against than sinning. The point is clarified when one compares the predicament of Srinivas with that of the old couple in W.H. Auden's poem, 'Refugee Blues'. Auden's picture of the old people who are reduced to a 'nowhere couple' because they technically do not belong to any country, is genuinely moving. The personal, emotional, and political feelings involved in the situation of 'Refugee Blues' is obviously intrinsically complex. Without being frivolous, one can say that the Indian immigrants' life abroad is much better suited for comic than tragic portrayal, as V.S. Naipaul has demonstrated in *A House for Mr. Biswas*. Leaving one's country for better prospects is hardly a tragic gesture.

Nevertheless, in *The Nowhere Man* the small irritations and unspoken rejections, imaginary and otherwise, that a foreigner has to face in a country that is not his home are brought out significantly. Minor characters and minor situations are well handled. Dr. Radcliffe and his wife Marjorie and the relationship between them appear more realistic than do Srinivas, his wife Vasantha, and their relationship. The friendship between the lonely Srinivas and the gentle Mrs. Pickering, though unorthodox is entirely credible and is one of the redeeming strokes of the novel. Pictures of Fred and his pub-mates can be better accepted than the unlikely ones of Srinivas wandering around in wintry South London in his thin dhoti and slippers. Unfortunately, Markandaya loads the dice in the main narrative: Srinivas actually contracting leprosy in order to underline the point of his being treated as a leper in a hostile community, is too contrived and artificial. The device loses all credibility when she shrouds the leper in the secrecy and rejection of medieval times, whereas the man is living in 1968 in South London.

In *The Nowhere Man* Markandaya's style, is not as simple and direct as in her earlier books. Words blanket events and characters, so that little significance glimmers through paragraphs like the following:

> Dry husky sobs, on his heels in the middle of the room, that welled up from the deep roots of his being, for what they had the power to do, and he and his people were powerless to prevent: for all that must be relinquished, all the precious frivolities of youth and pursuit of the humanities that must be surrendered to redress the squalid imbalance: and for the dreams he had dreamt, jeweled diadems that had glimmered so brightly over the brows of himself and his bride-elect.

It is difficult to understand either the tone, or the feeling that the novelist wants to convey inso densely-worded a paragraph.

Perhaps of the two sides of the coin of 'Indian identity'—that of the Indian in a changing India and of the Indian in a foreign country—Indian novelists appear better qualified to handle the former. The background at least, with the description of the typical Indian festivals like Holi or Gokul Asthami, the heat, the squalor, and the splendour of Indian cities like Bombay or Calcutta come out appealingly, as in Santha Rama Rau's *Remember the House* or Anita Desai's *Voices in the City*.' That side of the coin at least tells the legendof the mintage, and does not just present the static silhouette of the ex-Emperor.

21

Submission and Revolt:

The Dialectic of Girlhood in Markandaya's *Two Virgins* and Desai's *Fire on the Mountain*

Taking stock of Indian fiction in English, one is surprised to find that very few writers have dealt with the child character as hero/heroine. India, the land of the ancients, is a country for the aged, a country where old people are revered and the young are ignored or neglected. Especially in the typical Indian joint family the elderly are considered useful members while younger persons are looked upon with indifference or taken for granted.

Even where the child is given prominence as a character, significantly the girl child has been ignored. Invariably, it is the male child who gets that attention. The boy's initiation into life is ritualistically observed but the girl's is not given any special consideration. The girl child is thus a shadowy, secondary figure in the Indian family and in the Indian novel. Little Dorrit, Jane Eyre, Maggie Tulliver, Flora of *Little Paul Dombey*, Flora of *The Turn of the Screw*, Pearl of *The Scarlet Letter* and Mick of *The Heart is a Lonely Hunter* have no counterparts in Indian English fiction. Hucklebury Finn and Tom Sawyer have at least, their remote Indian counterparts in Bakha of Anand's *Untouchable* and Swami of Narayan's *Swami and Friends.*

In such a situation, standing out by its unusual treatment of the girl child is Kamala Markandaya's novel *Two Virgins*[1] (1977) where the main characters are the two young sisters, Lalitha and Saroja. Even Anita Desai, who has created memorable women characters has only one girl child in her novels, that is Raka, the great-granddaugher of Nanda Kaul in *Fire on the Mountain*[2] (1976). In this paper an analysis of the treatment of the girl child by these two novelists is attempted. In both her earlier novels, *Nectar in a Sieve* and *Some Inner Fury*, Markandaya had concentrated on the lives of the women characters, Rukmani, and Mirabai. However, they had been introduced at the stage of young womanhood and not girlhood. But in *Two Virgins*, as the title makes it obvious, Lalitha and Saroja are young girls who are on the threshold of that all important phase of adolescent womanhood when sexual awareness first awakens. Saroja is still a child and Lalitha, the elder sister is an adolescent. It is through the eyes of the innocent child, Saroja, that the story of the experience of Lalitha, and of their parents, is narrated in the novel.

Significantly enough, Markandaya has not adopted the first person narrative technique. Hence it is the older writer-woman Markandaya seeing through the eyes of Saroja that we find in the novel. The levels of perception of the writer-woman and the girl character interact perceptibly in the tone of narration. The style of narration is expository, rambling rather than descriptive or dramatic. Despite the authorial presence in the shifting narrative tone, the younger girl Saroja emerges directly as an extraordinarily sensitive, observant, thoughtful, yet extrovert kind of character. Thus, she is well-suited to bear the burden of narration, although the younger of the two girls, for she is a contrast to her sensual, sex-tormented, worldly-wise older sister, Lalitha. Interwoven with Saroja's own musings are snatches and bits of dialogue, family conversations and discussions heard and overheard, and these add to the different levels of perception. By introducing a multiple, internally narrative tone through the consciousness of the young girl, Markandaya maintains the fine balance of tragicomic irony which is an important element in the novel. To miss this tragi comic irony is to miss the true meaning of the novel, *Two Virgins*, and to see only distortions in characterisation or theme.

The growth of a girl's character in Indian society is seen mainly in relation to her attitude towards her family and her duty towards it. In a joint family, children have a special place but at the same time, they are taken for granted. No one believes that they have any individuality. They are not expected to have rights or thoughts of their own.

Coming into sharp conflict with this sense of family duty, however, is the girl's burgeoning feeling of self-identity. It is in the course of this conflict that the full identity of the girl is formed. The successful formation of this identity depends upon the delicate balance that the girl maiantains between submission and revolt. Saroja the younger one maintains this balance, perhaps because of the lessons she learns from Lalitha. In Lalitha, unfortunately, the sense of revolt drags her down. Growth into maturity and selfhood is frequently tested in a family situation in the course of confrontations with the adults. It also gets tested in the adjustments that members can make to the changing biological processes of their own bodies and individual selves. In the course of the interaction of these two main concerns, the identity of the individual character gets defined and firmly established. The intensity of the interaction and the struggle to cope with it is infinitely greater for the young girl than for the young boy, what with the burden of the female body which spells her destiny. Both *Two Virgins* and *Fire on the Mountain* are apparently tense, complex novels for this reason.

Saroja is a child in a joint family. It is an ideal kind of set-up for a child to grow in, as long as she remains in the childhood stage. Saroja learns to forge her values early by listening to the arguments that go on endlessly betweenher parents and Alamelu at home, and among Chingleput, Manikkam, Miss Mendoza and others outside the home. In Saroja, Markandaya has brought out the full personality of a sensitive and intelligent young girl who grows into young womanhood and yet retains the innocence of girlhood. Unlike her older sister, Lalitha, who willingly launches out on a hardened, ruthless existence in a big city, Saroja tastes the temptations of the city in the safe company of her family members and deliberately makes up her mind to return to her family home in the village. In Saroja's development one sees the flowering of a fine girl into a young woman, helped along in her growth by the anchor of the elders in the family and the rituals and traditions of an average, middle class Hindu home. Lalitha, on the other hand, exemplifies the figure of a girl who cuts herself loose from this anchor and pays a heavy price for her rash, independent spirit.

Markandaya's treatment of the characters of the two girls is enlightened and well-informed in the ways of girlhood and its travails. The narrative technique no doubt adds to the depth and authenticity of the treatment. Saroja recognizes early the difference between a boy's and a girl's position in society.Her brothers could leave home,her relative, Anand, and the other menfolk in the family could escape to the coffee shop if there were quarrels at home but the women had to stay where they were and face it Aunt Alamelu boasts that it is her injured feet that keep her from walking out on the quarrelling brother-in-law, but Saroja, with her uncanny insight tells herself, no, "...it wasn't that at all, it was her sex. Appa and Anand could stride off to the coffee shop, Manikkam had his bhang hideout... Women had no boltholes. There was no escape for them, they had to stand where they were and take it." But in the midst of panic'she resolves that she will always have an escape space, symbolised for her by Chingleput's sweet-shop, "For always, she said resolutely: always even when I am awoman" (123-24).

Lalitha and Saroja in *Two Virgins,* unlike Raka in *Fire on the Mountain,* are young sisters absorbed in the numerous problems facing them as adolescent girl children. Although the younger of the two, Saroja is the central figure in the novel, she is also the maturer of the two sisters. Saroja's innocence is associated with the simplicity and uncomplicated routine of village life. Her great friend is the crippled Chingleput, the sweet-vendor. Their friendship is the friendship of the underprivileged, as the novelist seems to suggest. Saroja's love of freedom and independence and her sensible, practical nature render her a better individual when compared to the selfish, glamour-struck older girl, Lalitha.

One important feature of a girl child's growth in her attitude towards her parents, and in turn, the parents' attitude towards her Lalitha is the pampered daughter whereas Saroja is ignored, if not neglected. This is partly because Lalitha is pretty and Saroja is plain-looking.

The burden of the female child is more irksome than that of the male child because aspects of her body, the functions of her femaleness intrude upon the growth of her personality. Not only the parents but also society as a whole is influenced by the physical appearance of the female child. This is a great hindrance to the inner growth of the girl's personality. In a male-oriented society this distortion is inevitable. Markanandaya has emphasised sexual imagery in the novel to underline this point. Although some critics regard the sexual imagery as being in "bad taste", it has a functional purpose in a novel with a young girl as the heroine. It must also be noted that within the novel such imagery has an amoral tone as it is through an as yet "sexless" young girl that it is seen.

By the same token, the opposite sex, the male counterpart, the "Other", is also greatly influenced by the physical aspects, the sex appeal of the girl child even in childhood. her sex-appeal can prove to be a girl's undoing as in the case of Lalitha. Saroja retains her independence to some extent because her simplicity and plainness safeguard her from the advances of the opposite sex. Chingleput, her village friend, and Curly, her pansy acquaintance at the hotel where she is staying with her family when they go to the city in search of Lalitha, treat her as one of themselves, as their equal. When Devraj makes bold to press his advances on her, Saroja is sensible enough to ward him off because she has learnt a hard lesson from Lalitha's experience, even at a young age. Whether she will be able to find a suitable partner later in the opposite sex, who will recognise her independence and her individuality, is a matter for conjucture. At the end of the novel, she recognises that Chingleput and she, friends as they are, can never come together. But she is ready to face anything, because she has learnt so much during her young life. If it is the violent loss of innocence for Lalitha, it is the gentle passing away of it for Saroja, and there is a poignant, nostalgic feelings in this passing away. Markandaya brings this out vividly when she says at the end:

> Saroja wasn't afraid. She knew too much, she had gone through too much to be afraid of anything. But she knew she wasn't for him, she would never be. So she drew away from him. She got up and mounted her bike. She could hardly see for the tears that were cascading down her face, she couldn't have told for whom they were falling, for her, for Chingleput, or for what was ended. After a while she didn't try. She thought instead of when she was older, felt the wind in her face and the tears drying as she skimmed downthe path that led past the fields to the house (250).

Kamala Markandaya's characterisation of Saroja is sympathetic. She shows the development of Saroja's character from girlhood to young womanhood in the context of the joint-family system prevailing in the rural parts of India. Because of the rural background and the choice of a young heroine as protagonist, Two Virgins acquires a poetical narrative quality. The descriptions of village life, despite its mud and dust and buffaloes, follow a lyrical flow.

Margaret P. Joseph's comments in her book on Kamala Markandaya, on the theme, characterisation, and style of *Two Virgins* is a reflection, although indirectly of the sweeping, withering dismissal that the girl child generally receives from society, especially Indian society. Says Joseph, "This novel occupies the lowest position in the order of merit. In fact, it can hardly be called literature..."[3] EndorsingNissim Ezekiel's equally dismissive opinion that the characters are ...puppets manufactured for those who know nothing about India,"[4] Joseph maintains that "the light-weight, synthetic material seems to be woven for the western market."

The misunderstanding regarding *Two Virgins* as a failure, seems to stem from Markandaya's choice of a rare point of view for the whole novel, that of the young girl, Saroja. By accepting the point of view of the girl child, one can see that the main theme in the novel is not the facile one of opposing tradition with modernity or Westernisation with Indian rural life. Saroja's grappling with her struggles which drag her through innocence and experience, ignorance and knowledge, girlhood and adulthood, joy and sorrow, lends the novel an elemental sweep, simple as the surface text appears to be. It is for this reason that Markandaya eschews supplying a name for the village where Saroja lives and uses the village as a paradigmatic background against which to place this extensive, universal story of the passing away of a girl's childhood. It is also for this reason that the story is set against the rhythms of the passing seasons instead of being told in linear, chronological plot-construction.

Similarly, the frequent references to Saroja's awakening consciousness of her own sex, and her preoccupations with the functions of the male and female bodies, are enormously significant in the context. Rather than merely being prurient details of sexual activity interposed to "titillate the reading public,"[5] they from the basic, immediately experienced feelings of female sexuality that are awakened in the little girl. Her sense of identity has to start from her own understanding of the different functions of her bodily existence, passing through puberty, and preparing for motherhood and the creating of another life out of her own body. The elaboration of the scene of Manikkam's wife's childbirth,or the abortion of Lalitha's unborn child serve well to emphasize the recognition of womanhood in the young girl. Markandaya's candid treatment of this important theme was an early sounding of the concerns that now occupy feminist writers and critics, and it shocked readers to such an extent that in 1978, the novel invited a ban, by Madras University when it was withdrawn from the syllabus under public protest. To regard these descriptions as being "in bad taste"is to reflect the popular notion that the female child is an objectionable creature with perverse obsessions. On the contrary, it must be maintained that Markandaya's choice of Saroja, a sensitive and intelligent young girl from an Indian village, is boldly original and sympathetic.

Anita Desai's *Fire on the Mountain,*[6] also published in 1977, begs comparison with *Two Virgins.* Raka, the nine-year old great-granddaughter of Nanda occupiesa central position in the story.

The prominent feature of the novel is the background. The mountain ranges around the hill-town of Kasauli provide a stark and mysterious backdrop to the characterisation of Raka, the moon-child, who is no less mysterious than the mountain ranges themselves. Raka is so unlike achild, and much less a girl child, with her secretive, solitary ways and mysterious wanderings over the hillside. The jagged edges of the crags and cliffs, the violence and destructiveness of the mountainjackal, the vulture, the snake, and the band of monkeys—the langurs—are all reflected in the character of this young girl, Raka. In nature and habits, and even in physical description, Raka appears to be more a boy than a girl. She spends most of her time outdoors either alone or in the company of the servant, Ram Lal. She rejects her great-grandmother totally and prefers to be left to herself. Thus Raka is nearly like a wild creature of the mountains, silent and fiercely lonely. She submits to no socialisation or personal blandishments. Her rebellion is against life itself, its entrapments and alurements. There is no question of submission to any of the limitations imposed on her by girlhood, or society. As a lonely, wild creature she embraces the violence and destructiveness of nature. In her last act of setting the mountain forests on fire she reveals her true nature, of being self-destructively rebellious. Yet Desai's indictment is not against the child; it is against the adults who have driven her to that state.

Raka is seen as a sickly child whose girlhood has apparently been killed long before by the misdeeds of her parents. Her father was a drunkard, driving her mother Tara to abject misery and even insanity. Raka herself appears to be tainted by this insanity and seems to have turned into an abnormal child.

Yet Desai appears to be ambivalent in her novel about abnormality in people. If Nanda and Ila Das find Raka curious and quaint, Raka, in turn, finds adults weird and frightful. The scene of the Fancy Dress Ball at the club is a set piece in the novel marking out the world of difference between the adults and the young girl. To Raka the adults appear as bizarre creatures, more like animals and demons rather than human beings. The difference in the perceptions of the adult and the child establishes the ambivalent nature of reality and the definition of normality or abnormality.

The drastic difference between Markandaya and Desai in the treatment of the girl child testifies to the difficulty of drawing neat conclusions regarding the depiction of the young girl in

Indian English fiction. Social class variations and regional backgrounds have so much to do with the growth of the child that no sterotyping of character is possible. In *Fire on the Mountain* itself this is well-depicted. Besides Raka, there is the passing mention of another seven-year-old girl in the story. This is Preet Singh's daughter a labourer's child who is going to be married off to an old man for his property and lands. Later it turns out that it is Preet Singh who has vengefully raped and killed Miss Ila Das because she has dared to talk to him about social reform and the evils of girl child marrige. Although it is a passing reference it is highly significant in that it shows the contrast between Raka and the labourer's daughter, the difference between the modern, urbanised girl and the orthodox, rustic daughter, and their destinies.

Although the same contrast does not work between Saroja and Raka, still one can perceive the difference between the sweetness of the country-bred girl and the bitterness of the citybred one. Saroja, with all her rebellious nature, passes through the travails of young girlhood and comes out victorious, whereas Raka stands petrified in the self-alienated, self-destructive world of total rejection. Between them, Markandaya and Desai depict the two extremes of normality and abnormality of the Indian girl child.

REFERENCES

1. Markandaya, Kamala, *Two Virgins*, New Delhi: Tarang Paperback, Vikas Publishing House, 1984.

2. Desai, Anita, *Fire on the Mountain*, New Delhi: Allied Publishers, 1977.

3. Margaret, Joseph P., *Kamala Markandaya*, New Delhi: Arnold Heinemann 1980, p. 80.

4. Ezekiel, Nissim, *The Illustrated Weekly of India*, 15 June, 1979.

5. Joseph, *op.cit.*, p. 200.

22

Four Indian Women Novelists and Their Concern with the Indian Element

Perhaps it is unfashionable and what is worse, the mark of a misinformed person to talk of the 'Indian tradition' or the 'Indian spirit' while discussing these women novelists who write in English, especially when one finds that the flaunted photographs on the glossy covers ae those of the authoresses themselves, in slacks and open-necked shirts, with bobbed hair, plucked eye-brows and blank foreheads, sometimes even with a cigarette delicately poised between manicured and lacquered fingers. But I feel that my study is tenable and necessary for there must be something Indian in them for them to be called Indian novelists besides just their being of that nationality. Tenable because one of the novelists herself, Mrs. Sahgal, is solely concerned with exploring the "Indianness" of her main character in her novel *A Time to be Happy*. Like some of the American women novelists, Eudora Welty, Edith Wharton, Sarah Anne Jowett and Katherine Anne Porter, these novelists too have been pioneers in a way but paradoxically, they are also conservatives. Pioneers because they have boldly made use of their political and social emancipation to explore fields of writing, travel, and journalism in an intellectual manner, bringing to bear upon their subjects keen minds which have been sharpened by formal education, instead of confining themselves to domestic tragedies and comedies or personal case histories. National and international politics, the complications in an individual torn between two cultures, the problems of East-West encounter and many such difficult topics are handled by them with extraordinary facility and sophistication and one must grant that they have enriched the scope of the novel even if they do not always stir one's depths as a George Eliot or an Emily Bronte. Side by side with their sophistication which is distinctly westernized, what with knowing, familiar descriptions of cocktail parties and dances at the Gymkhana andthe club, there is an uncanny blend of feeling descriptions of loved Indian scenes and festivals and little ways of life. Even if women are not the strongholds of customs and culture of a country, one can venture to say that the last vestiges of a vanishing civilisation could be found in its women for they instinctively preserve tradition. The Indian women novelists strongly testify to the truth of this statement, at least in their writings. As a point of fact, much too strongly, for they appear to be conservatives and preservers with a vengeance. They anxiously describe the same elements minutely again and again,and many a time the descriptions disconcertingly run almost to pattern in the novels of Santha Rama Rau, Kamala Markandaya, Nayantara Sahgal, Anita Desai—the joint family, residing in a large house with a cool courtyard in Jalnabad, Allahabad, Calcutta, the Indian bazar with its fruit-vendors, bangle-sellers, 'chaat masala and *moodi* wallas' around whom people stand eating out ofpaper cones, the colourful and noisy scenes of bargaining, splendour and squalor, a festival—Deepavali or Dassera or Holi,- a marriage with all its ritualistic and religious significances minutely described, the heat of the plains and the annual exodus of families to the Himalayan hill resorts. The pattern is so familiar and the blend of the westernised self and the Indian consciousness so suspiciously stream-lined that the reader is many times at a loss to know to which world the writer truly belongs, which she genuinely and truly endorses with faith. Especially is this so with a writer like Mrs. Sahgal and to some extent, Santha Rama Rau. Their avid appreciation of Indian ways of life and detailed descriptions of these appear studied and deliberate, many times marring the merit of the book in the eyes of an Indian reader though they may be fascinating accounts to 'foreigners'. It is no mark of powerful narration to linger on unnecessary explanations of even shared assumptions of cultural or social matters. It should be granted that a printer's list of meanings for unfamiliar terms is many a time required at the endof the book, but should the writer be found to sandwich ana explanation for a small matter in an elaborate manner every now and then, for eg., the preparation of kebabs or pan one feels that she is doing so for want of a better subject and more challenging talent to deal with it, for one expects a greater urgency and integrity in a work of art. It is curious that almost all the comments quoted on the covers of the writings of these novelists are by western critics and the tone is even more intersting. One critic, Lord Birdwood, comments on one of Mrs. Sahgal's works: "The blend of Brahman orthodoxy and western sophistication is quiite irresistible." *New York Times* said of Kamala Markandaya"....... *Nectar in a Sieve* has a wonderful, quiet authority over our sympathies because Kamala Markandaya is manifestly an authority on village-life in India." But when the *Sunday Statesman* an Indian paper, commented on the same book, it was to say characteristically: "*Nectar in a Sieve* now deservedly re-issued in a cheap edition, is a well-written story showing intimate knowledge of south Indian life." *The Hindustan Standard* exhibited the typical skeptical tone: "As good as, and in some respects better than the *Good Earth*. *Nectar in a Sieve* has a quiet appeal of its own". May be, after reading these comments, one has to reflect as much upon the state and quality of critical expression in India as on the state and quality of the creative works they criticise. However, after all these above generalizations which, though sweeping are not altogether unjustified, one is reminded that taken individually each one of these novelists has a considerable achievement to her credit.

One important and recurring theme with them is to portray the clash of cultures, in this case, the western and the Indian, in an individual. Fortunately or unfortunately, for most of these women writers, their upbringing in two totally different cultures is a complex reality and the tension that is the outcome is the very substance of their works. The conflict is involved at all levels of life, the trivial not excepted as is seen in the predicament of Pria, a character in *Remember the House* when she tells her head mistress in England that she cannot and will not play hockey because it is not just expected of a girl in an Indian way of life and after all, she will be going back to India. Kamala Markandaya in *Some Inner Fury*, Santha Rama Rau in *Remember the House* and Nayantara Sahgal in *A Time to be Happy* concern themselves with various aspects of this tensiion. In Mirabai, the heroine of *Some Inner Furry*, the tearing apart is in the realm of love, for she, an Indian woman loves Richard an Englishman and can never marry him because of the obvious differences in their two worlds. The most important difference and impossibility of all,that which is due to the political situation is subtly and poignantly worked out at the end of the novel.

In Santha Rama Rau's only novel, the tension is lower-pitched, nevertheless complex, for here the 'foreigner' is American, not English. So the explosive political overtones are not there as in Forster's *Passage to India* and thus the book can interestingly present the clash of cultures and ideals of people brought up in two different cultures. The split is present in Indira or Baba herself, the heroine of *Remember the House*, who feels more at home in the beginning at cocktail parties and races, and with tongue in cheek, dismisses such things as the "tika" as the round 'red spot that most of us wore on our foreheads more for decoration than for any religious significance.' In her western way, she is openly sarcastic about Shalini her sister-in-law, the "perfect Hindu wife" who renounces her own family and is completely absorbed into her husband's family from the day of her marriage and who self-deprecatingly comments, 'I know it's foolish of me to be so old-fashioned' and who found Baba too westernised. Baba analyses her own predicament with great awareness and honesty: "Sometimes I would take the big lamp from the living-room into my room with me and read, late into the night,novels about England or France or Russia. The few novels about India that I had read seemed to concern a different kind of life, almost a different country from mine. It was like visiting a place that you have often heard described, of which you have a clear image, but when you see it you find that you were wrong, the house is much smaller than you expected, the garden only casually cultivated, the pleasant woods that you have imagined where one might picnic with the children are treacherous forests, dark and uninviting. And the people—they aren't welcoming friends, they are hostile strangers, speaking a language you don't understand, making jokes behind your back, wondering when you will go. You know them and recognize them, but they are foreigners". The tone of the passage suggests the disenchantment of a romantic-temperament when it at last confronts reality. And Baba is a highly romantic creature, having been influenced by the western brand of romanticism, but fortunately she is curable, as we see at the end of the book. Even though the novel is written with great charm of style and sensitivity, one has an uneasy feeling throughout the book that the theme of the split and tension has not been tackled in all its depth, for Baba who embodies the spirit of this difference is a very young woman, still an adolescent, in her own words. At sixteen she has left India and gone to study in England. When she comes back at twenty, naturally there is a vast gulf inside her own being which she finds difficult to bridge. When she is recounting the story, even though a couple of years have elapsed after her return from England, she is still an awkward adolescent inwardly. The result is, she cannot resolve in her mind as to where she truly belongs, to the western or to the Indian tradition and finds refuge in the world of her childhood memories of Jalnabad. All that she approves of India are associated with what she has experienced as a child. Hence, there is an element of romanticising in many of her descriptions of Indian scenes and they appear to be woven into the novel in a mood of nostalgia and reminiscence for their own sake. She grows up only at the end of the book, shedding all her wrong ideas of love and romance and at last is prepared to face life on proper terms of duty obedience, routine etc. The conclusion of the book to me has been a frustrating two-sided experience. It is rather disappointing that a chance to develop this important theme of tension in herself and in her surroundings is not fully exploited, cannot be fully exploited, for Baba grows up only at the end of the book; but that she develops at all, casting away her illusions, is the satisfying, significant thing. Without too much high-powered discussion of the merit of the shortcomings of the two cultures which she has known, she grows into adulthood from a confused state of adolescence and gains a proper, mature understanding of love and life. The discussion between her grandmother and herself recalls this development simply. The two represent the two different attitudes to love, her grandmother the Indian and Baba the western, which she has imbibed from Alix, her American friend. Her grandmother tells her: "At first I was only obedient. It was years before I experienced also the glory of loving. It came to me gradually through many days and nights when at last I knew hiim as I know myself, when there were no more discoveries, when there was no longer need for forgiveness or understanding or expression.... When he died I, too, wished to die for I could not find in myself even a love for God except with him". She paused, thinking of the old days, and added after a moment, "you can see that when we talk of love, you and I, we talk of different things."

"Yes, I see that (Baba replies). But the thing I talk of, that love, is it less valuable, less glorious?"

With utter conviction she said, "Of course, just think—what is it this 'love' of yours? A little excitement, a little impatience, much imagination—is that enough to found your life on? Can you base the structure of your feelings, your fulfilment, your children, your whole being on so little?" .... (Baba continues) "I had been moved by her conversation but didn't yet realize that my feelings about love could be undermined by some quality, some toughness in the fibre of her thoughts. It's all very well for her, I thought; she is an old woman, her life is over, she'll die soon. I hadn't yet allowed the idea that it might also be best for me that something incontrovertible in my blood or earliest upbringing responded to her altitudes and convictions. It took Krishnan himself to complete the circle, to show me that the story that began with the Nichols and their effect on mewould never reach an ending that they could approve of that the exoticism they represented, their strange approach to life, their unfamiliar concept of personal relationships would eventually be overruled by the timbre of love in an old woman's voice and the off-hand common sense of an ordinary young man. In the other words my preoccupation with romance began, in my mind, to seem cheap. Or perhaps it was simply that I came to the end of a delayed and fanciful acolescence." The brittle veneer of westernisation in Baba is broken and she has come into her own. But the disappointing factor is, the growth somehow, does not appear to have stature for it has not been a matter of choice. She has just grown from adolescence to maturity. But perhaps the significant point is that it is in Chenur, in the heart of the Indian experience in the book that she learns the lesson of her life. The hold of her Indianness on her has been there always, only it was waiting to break through. The clash had apparently been only on the surface and had only been an interlude in her growth, an accidental one. The gulf has been more between childhood and maturity than between the western or the Indian elements.

The theme of Mrs. Sahgal's work is more impersonal and broadbased than that of *Remember the House*. Even though *Remember the House* also started in the shadow of the year 1947, Santha Rama Rau introducs politics warily and does not lose herself in discussions and debates about political means. The high-powered talk which is kept out of her book floods the passages of *A Time to be happy*. A decade comprising the time just before and after 1947 is the background to the story and no doubt it was the most crowded and interesting time in India's recent history. The book is a fictionalized representation of the history that was being made then so rapidly. Onesuspects that the characters are thinly disguised and the issues not at all. The emotional, romantic, personal tone that one found in *Remember the House* has no place here for it is the heat of politics that one finds everywhere. There are endless intellectual and social debates in the drawing rooms and clubs among people with various attitudes: those who are for independenc for the natives, those who are not, those who are imitators of the English ways and the others who are indignant at this attitude, discussion on prohibition, cottage industries, spinning, non-violence, the Swadeshi movement etc. etc. There is no topic about the Indian Independenc movement that is not discussed. Mrs. Sahgal puts her intimate knowledge of the details to excellent use, and if only for this the book makes interesting reading, reminding the readers about the many sidedness of this crucial period in the nation's history. Mrs. Sahgal discusses the issues at hand most competently. One important feature that stands out in this novel as a proud banner is the author's firm idea of what the staunch Indian is a wise calm soul, loving his independence and his leisure, cultivating his mind without neglecting his body, gaining his own perspective of the world from this mood of calm thoughtfulness. Govind Narayan is a standing example of this as also the narrator. There are little details everywhere to show that this Indian character can never mix with the British variety. Govind Narayan is practical and quick to see the impossibility of serving Indian food in paper containers, but his wife Lakshmi, who is the embodiment of "the sort of Indian woman that is becoming rare in present times, a woman content to be a woman" is not so practical when it concerns her dress in the typical Indian way. While on a picnic, Harish, observing the saris of Lakshmi and Maya ballooning out in the breeze, irritably says "I don't know why you women don't wear slacks, it would be so much more sensible". "Who wants to be sensible when one can be pretty?" Lakshmi asks. Again, at a fancy-dress party in the hills, Veena-Govind Narayan's child is given the second prize in the last minute as she is an Indian child, for the English women there have protested at her being given the first prize earlier. Govind Narayan brushes aside the affront unconcernedly, but the narrator, in patriotic fervour quarrels with Govind Narayan: "In the name of your culture and traditions, if not your own personal pride, doesn't it upset you at all?" Govind Narayan's eyes twinkled: "What are 5000 years of culture if they have not taught one to be polite?" We see that here is no groping for understanding about one's inheritanc and coming to terms with life after an agonized search as in *Some Inner Fury* or *Remember the House*. It is a committed, pitched battle between the "Indianness" and the "Englishness" of things as they were during that particular period in India, with constant, openly ironical referencs to the in-between imitativeness on the part of some Indians. The narrator himself emphasises frequently this constant pull of opposition between the two. He has scrupulously rejected all that is English and is a staunch, patriotic and wise Indian as his observations show: "Here in U.P., the heart of India, where men still greet one another with 'Ram Ram' where the carved images of many-armed gods and goddnesses reign over the country-side on festival days, where Diwali is still a blaze of earthen lamps, the "Englishness" had only seemed fantastic. It had the incongruity of fluffy white lamps painted on a massive, brooding landscape an after thought and an absurd one, on the part of the artist. Still, Saharanpur was an Indian city for all its industrial importance—Indian with an English gloss, as I have said, "like Yorkshire pudding served on a thal". He asserted that he had chosen to cut himself off from the "Englishness" of the life around him though it had been a matter of pride and prestige to others to have an English veneer and gloss. He adds, "I had viewed this life objectively, and for me it had an element of fantasy, with its chota pegs, its dressing for dinner, and its jokes repeated standing at a bar in a voice that must sound British to belong". But Harish,—No. 3 in the British firm of McDermott and James is presented in vivid contrast to this, with his classic phrase, "My dear fellow, to tell you the truth, I'm far more at home in Paris or Rome than in the south", by the south meaning South India, "which vast piece of territory began far him just outside the southerm boundary of Lucknow". Even in the discussions of the Indian philosophical attitude to various aspects of life, the narrator staunchly holds on to his inherted conviction andfaith: "Marriage among us, is for life and those who do not adjust to its ups and downs must for ever remain unhappy. If they were under any compulsion to behave with consideration toward each other, then that compulsion, I am convinced, was a very good thing, and I should like to see more of it to-day". With this quotation one immediately notices the utterly different ways in which the same truth is realized and expressed in *Remember the House* and the novel under discussion. This example is sufficient to set off the difference in the styles of the two novelists. In Mrs. Sahgal's novel problems are thrashed out threadbare through length discussions and there is to much talk in the atmosphere, always at the level of the drawing room or the club invariably. There is an intelligent, brittle liveliness in the whole presentation but one unaccountably misses the depths of an involvement with the subject which one finds in the account of the young narrator in *Remember the House*. One wonders how such passages as these can be expected to find a relevant place in a tightly knit, compelling narration: "I followed her out to her car. She sank back against the green upholstery, the usual look of marble indifference on her face. The car window was an inappropriate frame for the chiselled outline of her profile. Therewas a quality of unmoving and immovable repose about it, the long eye with its clearly traced brow above it, the straight nose, the modelled chin. Her face had the delicate perfection of a pastel. It belonged in the arabesque setting of a Persian miniature, and the hands, tapering and motionless, that lay in her lap should have been curled about a rose". And this is the description of an uninteresting character who does not speak or reveal herself at all but who is forced to become important for the sake of a climax. Such unpardonable preciosity of description definitely mars the integrity of the novelist and Mrs. Sahgal is not the only culprit among the Indian women novelists.

Of the four novelists mentioned in my paper. Anita Desai is perhaps a novelist with a difference. She could be least guilty of the charge of studied, stereotyped descriptions of country or culture. If she describes the loo of the Delhi summer or the rituals of the Durga Puja, it is because they are ineradicably connected with the spirit of her story, the compulsions of her narration. But in *Cry the Peacock*, she appears to carry the difference to incredible lengths. No doubt the story is based on the familiar, typical 'Indian' belief in horoscope and astrology but the theme is strange and different from the Indian scene that one generally knows of. The astrolger who reads the horoscope of the heroine when she was a young girl foretells that after her marriage, one of the couple is to die on unnatural death. This dire prophecy taken hold of the mind of the heroine, gradually unhinging her and since she is the narrator if the story in the first person, of necessity the tone of narratiion is pitched to the hysterical, mad tone which reaches its climax towards the end when one night, she half-deliberately and half-accidentally pushes her husband off the terrace to his death on the pavement below. It is the story of a woman who is entering the "snake-pit", not coming out of it and the whole book is a tour de force, a pervertedly powerful story (or powerfully perverted?). But Anita Desai's second novel, *Voices in the City* is truly a noteworthy achievement by an Indian novelist. Like Kamala Markandaya's novel, *A Handful of Rice,* set in Madras and dealing with the life of Ravi, a village lad who has come to the city to make a living. Anita Desai's book too depends solely on an Indian background and spirit without the contrasting forces of western civilization. The setting is Calcutta, one of the most complex metropolitan cities under the sun and there is immense scope for the novelist to weave this complexity into the fabric of her novel. Yet, in no part of the novel is there any documentation for its own sake. Calcutta is no longer the same city as it was in Mrs. Sahgal's *A Time to be Happy* with its English life set apart from the Indian scene and forever offering contrasts between the two cultures, but by the time Anita Desai writes about it, it has emerged with a new character after all its experiences of the British impact. It has come into its own as an exotic, brooding monster of a city, swallowing up the English memorials and monuments that ardent Sanad had objected to in *A Time to be Happy* and which held sway over the scene a decade earlier, and has now become a city with its own true traditions as much as New York or Moscow and in the same magnitude, where it is as natural for Bengalis to sit at 'Firpo's or the 'Blue Fox' drinking beer late into the night as to eat fried fish with their fingers in smoke-filled Bengali kitchens.

And the character of Nirode, developed in this fitting background, is another remarkable achievement in the novel. Perhaps it is because of the advantage of writing at a period in India which is surer of itself, which has settled into its character more or less, as contrasted with the shifting, political scenes of crisis that one saw in the books of the earlier novelists, when Indian writing has come into its own almost, that Anita Desai never gives the impression that she is writing about India with a western audience in mind. As a result there is a freedom and boldness in her treatment of the cultural idiom. Rejecting the theme of developing the story of Arun, who is sailing to England when the book starts and later marries an English nurse, with admirable nerve she concentrates on Nirode the elder brother, who has never left Calcutta in his adult life. Nirode is a lean and hungry journalist who refuses to make even the necessary compromises that life demands if it means giving up his independence and integrity to the slightest extent, and success, being based on compromise according to him, he appears to seek failure in a strange manner. He is a Kafka-like character whom one is tempted to discuss in the new terms of nihilism, existentialism or fatalism rather than in the hitherto usual terms of an East-West encounter. Anita Desai is apparently gifted with the more difficult talent of probing and understanding and portraying the depths of human nature and character rather than in merely discussing issues. The story of Nirode is the first part, told by the author, Monisha tells her own story in the second part, a non-too appealing part as it deals with a neurotic temperament which ends itself in a suicide (reminding one of the earlier novel, *Cry the Peacock*), the third part deals with Amla, a contrasting character to the nihilist Nirode, with her full acceptance of life onits own terms, and the fourth part is dedicated to their mother, as different as any mother could be from her children, leading her sensual, artistic, trouble-free life in the remote, picturesque hills of Kalimpong. And then there is Calcutta, almost the most important character, introduced every now and then in its various, compelling aspects, as thus in the beginning during an evening: "They wandered away, together, leaving the lake to suck in small waves at the clay bank beneath the rain-tree. But even the lake formed no pocketof solitude and balm, and here came the train, rocking and wailing and warning away all travellers that were fearful. On all sides the city pressed down alight, aglow and stirring with its own monster-life, like an ogre, kept one eye open through sleep and waking. Calcutta, Calcutta—like the rattle of the recklese train: Calcutta, Calcutta, the very pulse beat in its people's veined wrists. The streets where slaughtered sheep hung beside bright tinsel tassels to adorn oiled black braids, and a syphilitic beggar and his entire syphilitic family came rolling down on barrows, like the survivors of an atomic blast, then paused to let a procession of beautifully laundered Bengalis in whiite carry their mari-gold decked Durga—or Lakshmi or Saraswati, or Kali—on their shoulders down to the Ganges amidst drums and fevered chanting. In one shadowy doorway an old cronelit a fire mumbling. Beneath a brief canvas roof a skeletal old gnome with electric white hair served kebabs, first to an urchin who had his days' earnings knotted at his crotch, and next to a party that waited in a long American car drawn up to the pavement. From the balconies above the streets long saris hung limply down, and voices murmed, reciting prayers or lessons. Down below funerals passed by the bearers of the white, flower-laden stretchers vacant—eyed and smooth-browed as they chanted Hari Om, Hari Om. 'Sweet lily, sweet li-ly', cried the flower vendor who carried garlands of jasmine and tuberose strung upon a bamboo frame. Wedding marques shivered in stripes of red and white bunting, and blue neon-tubing, and within them the shehnai wailed of the folly of man in endeavouring to perpetuate his name. Trams and barrows rolled by, klaxon horns honked. Odours of naphtha, gasoline and rotting mangoes, cinders and frangipani, open gutters and temple marigold. Calcutta, Calcutta, prayed its victims, and Calcutta stirred as though in answer as though it were a living spirit. Calcutta was not merely the bazars ringed by cinemas, slaughter houses and pan booths, but also the history of those old Georgian houses that lined still gaslit streets, their sweeping marble staircases and deep pillared verandas, their shuttered windows, that seemed to enclose and hide their memories of the balls and crinolines and horsedrawn carriages a hundred or two hundred years ago—The city was as much atmosphere as odour as much a haunting ghost of the past as a frenzied passage towards early death".

Anita Desai's is the rarer achievement for she has presented the Indian scene and the Indian spirit of life with such compelling force as to inspire with awe even an Indian reader in the same way as a modern Russian or an American novelist would.

23

Anita Desai's *Where Shall We Go This Summer?*: An Analysis

With more than six novels to her credit to date, Anita Desai is by far the most serious Indo-Anglian novelist actively engaged in her work. Her serious dedication to her art is a part of her concern for and involvement in the life that she depicts in her works. She appears to find abundant material in the limited field of urban, middle class life around her to draw upon for her fiction. Unlike the expatriate Kamala Markandaya, who journeyed too fictitiously and sentimentally to an Indian village background in her nostalgic novel *Nectar in a Sieve* and ventured still farther into an exotic historical remoteness in her latest work, *The Golden Honeycomb*, Anita Desai adheres strictly to the contemporary, realistic, urban, Indian background from which she herself draws sustenance as an individual and a writer. She is much too close to the society that she describes to sentimentalise about it. The social and emotional complications in which an educated Indian finds himself caught in a post-Independent India are enough material for her imagination. Unlike Nayantara Sahgal she has not drawn upon the obvious political concerns to find themes and settings for her novels.

What exactly is it that makes her novels be classed as those by a woman? Is there a special feminine sensibility manifest in any particular aspect of her work—in characterisation, plot, story, creation of atmosphere, language? When George Eliot wrote her novels under a man's name, did she do so in order to pass safely as a woman in a purely man's world, or was it because she felt that the novels themselves did not particularly depict a feminine sensibility? Even after her identity has been revealed we cannot with any justification say that her novels are "womanish." On the contrary, critics repeatedly comment on the "masculine quality" of her work... the heavy-weight intellectualism and the discursive, ideological style of novels like *Daniel Deronda* and *Romola*. How shall we resolve this quibble about "masculine" and "feminine" sensibility when we find a critic of the early, anonymous work of Thomas Hardy suggesting that perhaps the work is by George Eliot? One is also reminded of the usual criticism about Jane Austen that she could not create convincing men characters because she was a woman writer. But ironically enough, the most unforgettable characters in her novels are men... Collins and Wickham and Mr. Bennett. The truth is, each writer— man or woman... works within certain limitations. The masculine limitation is just as narrow as the feminine one. A close look at the women in Raja Rao's *The Serpent and the Rope*, for instance, makes it clear that the author has never deeply known an Indian woman. Savitri, Saroja, Little Mother, they are figures without flesh and blood and serve as figurative embodiments of the author's ideals of Indian womanhood. They are successful in so far as they embody these ideals. Thus success or failure in achievement does not really depend upon whether the writer is masculine or feminine.

Published in 1975, *Where shall We go this Summer*? is Desai's fourth novel and perhaps her shortest. The compact form the taut style, and the economy of detail render the work a curious tour de force. Like her heroine Sita, who is a high strung, uptight woman, the author herself never relaxes her hold on the effort of probing and laying bare the inner life of her main character.

The structure of the novel is strinkingly similar to that of Virginia Woolf's *To the Lighthouse*. There are three parts in Desai's novel too: Part one/Monsoon, '67; Part two/ Winter, '47; Part three, Monsoon, '67. Each section is thus concerned with a particular season, time and space. The action of the first section takes place on the island Manori in the present time of Sita's life, that of the second in her past, and the third in what she has accepted as her future. The Manipulation of time and space to depict the extraordinary inner consciousness of Sita is especially reminiscent of Woolf in *To the Lighthouse*.

Manori, like the Island of Skye, is more a symbol than a place. The island concretises the feeling of isolation of Sita. She retreats into it as into a womb, with an obsessive desire to recapture once again her childhood innocence and purity. Her childhood memories are full of the sea, the waves, the sky and the rugged, rustic characters of the little village on the island. She is doubly obsessed by this desire for purity and innocence because she is herself with child and has come to the island in search of this pristine world for the sake of her child. Obviously, her own frustration with her life in Bombay drives her in her desire to provide her unborn infant with a world that is uncorrupt.

Manori also concretises the nostalgic memories of Sita's childhood. The island primarily exists in its full reality only in her mind. The island is no more than a projection of her inner psyche.

Further, Manori surrounded by the waves of the beating sea, symbolises Time—its flux are its fixity. The island thus fuses into one as theme and technique.

Sita's desire to abandon the sweat and turmoil of the urban atmosphere in Bombay where she and her husband Raman live with their four children in a bourgeois neighbourhood is triggered by the subtle incompatibility between husband and wife. Ironically, Raman and Sita are no mythological sterotypes. Sita, especially has left the tradition of her namesake far behind and has taken to smoking and neurotic outbursts as a result of this growing incompatibility. As in her earlier novels *Cry, the Peacock* and *Voices in the City* in which Maya and Monisha, respectively, crack-up eventually under the pressure of urban domesticity, Sita too arrives at a near break-down and this is what brings her to the promised island.

But Moses, the boat-carrier who has now after twenty years grown old anddecrepit is no more capable of leading her to this Promised land than Sita is capable of rejuvenating the innocence and purity of the past. The island, alas, is no prelapsarian Eden. Sita has grown up, she has gradually come to realisethe rottenness and subtle evil that lie under the surface of the exotic atmosphere. The island has also been affected by the passage of time: "...the island on which they had arrived seemed flat, toneless, related to the muddy monsoon sea rather than to the sky and cloudscape which steadily grew more gorgeous and brilliant by the second"[1] "Manori village was an evil mass of overflowing drains, gaping thatched roofs and huts all battered and awry."

The serpent in the garden is none other than Sita's own father. The second section of the novel takes Sita back to memories of this man. Like Prospero on his island. Sita's father presided over Manori like a saint or more exactly like a magician. Whether he was a charlatan or a genuine mystic Sita herself cannot decide. This middle section of the novel is an opaque, fuddled part of the story. Perhaps the befuddled state only serves the purpose of symbolising Sita's inchoate childhood and adolescent experiences. The experiences lie buried in her memory. They are mingled moments of childish enjoyment of the natural scenery around the island and the adolescent bewilderment about the strange relationship between her father and her elder sister Rekha, and her now dead and forgotten mother.

The third section once again picks up the narration from the point of their arrival on the island after twenty years. Will Sita succeed in recapturing the lost innocence or is she to face the inevitable knowledge of decay and death that has taken place?

The conflict is between Sita and her own two children in this section. Menaka and Karan hanker to go back to the highly urbanised life that is real to them. In their opinion, retreat to the island is the madness. Their struggle develops into the vital question of the acceptance of the terms of life. Sita has to make her compromises and the children have to make their adjustments in order to establish proper relationships with the society around them. On the now vastly changed island the two generations learn to face the future. The island after twenty years is half-paradise and half-urban reality. Sita learns to temper her exotic and mysterious memories of her childhood island by reconciling them with the present actuality of a dilapidated and run-down life that she now finds there. She realises that no man is an island. She sheds her obsession with isolation and learns to connect—with Raman especially when he visits them there. Menaka and Karan in turn give up a little of their urban non-entity and narrow-mindedness. They learn to relate to Nature and to the wildness and beauty around them. Their narrow vision of the strip of the Napean Sea near their flat expands into that of the largeness of the real sea around the island. Thus, in the third part the functional background of the island has fully served the purpose of being a metaphor with many meanings.

Speaking of the ending of the novel, Suresh Kohli rightly points out that as compared to her earlier works, there is "one distinct change: Sita neither dies in the end nor kills anyone nor does she become mad. She simply compromises with her destiny."[3] The positive ending is an important feature of the novel. It is now a critical commonplace that Anita Desai is a novelist predominantly depicting the feminine, abnormal sensibility. More often not, her heroines come to a violent end. But in *Where shall we go this Summer*? Sita learns the courage to face life with all its ups and downs. It is after all Raman, whom she despised earlier for his practicality and matter-of-factness, that teachers her that ".....life must be continued and all its business .....Menaka's admission to medical college gained, wife led to hospital, now child safely brought forth. The children reared, the factory seen to, a salary earned, a salary spent."[4]

The triptych structure of the novel neatly forms the pattern of thesis, anti-thesis, and synthesis. Sita's consciousness develops through the process of consideration, rejection, and acceptance of the terms of life within this structure. She makes a new life for herself and is eager to let the new life in her be borninto this world. It is sad that she has to give up her individuality to some extent in order to accept but only in this gesture is sanity.

In Sita's struggle and final acceptance there is thus this sense of defeat for the individual. But sacrifice, denial or defeat is unfortunately the lot of many a sensitive individual. There is an awareness in Desai's vision of a grim irony, the hard recognition of the unfairness in life where some are privileged without reason—the rich man, the outwardly beautiful woman. These undeserved privileges engender a smugness, a philistinism that distort all value system in life. But such is the force of society where these privileges count a great deal. And it is the sensitive individual who is in a minority that ultimately suffers. This theme underlies the story of Nirode and Arun in *Voices in the City* and of Sita and Raman in *Where shall we go this Summer*"?

Through this awareness of irony, the writer attempts to reach a tragic vision. But Desai appears to over-reach by making the more sensitive characters mere victims and caricatures of tragic figures. In her recent novel, *Fire on the Mountain*, the femininity and sensitivity of Nanda Kaul, Ila Das, and Raka only result in grotesqueness, a total incapacity to cope with themselves. They are victims of their own hyper-sensitivity. So Sita's compromise at the end of *Where shall we go this Summer*? is by contrast a very positive gesture.

In a review of *Fire on the Mountain* Mrinal Pande draws attention to the colonial spirit and the use of the English language that have left their peculiar mark on post-Independent India.[5] Desai's work especially has been influenced by these forces in Indian life and her novels are essentially textured out of this stuff. Although *Where shall we go this Summer*? impresses one as being a tour de force, it suffers less from the grotesqueries and incongruities that one finds in her later novel, *Fire on the Mountain*, and the langauge too is less "Anglo-Indian." Altogether, it is an interesting addition to Anita Desai's achievement as an Indian novellst writing in English.

NOTES

1. Anita Desai, *Where shall we go this Summer?*, Delhi Vikas Publishing House, 1975, p. 13.
2. *Ibid.*, p. 14.
3. Suresh Kohli, "The Fiction of Anita Desai," *The Statesman* (Sunday Magazine Section), 6th Nov. 1977, p. 3.
4. *Where shall we go this Summer?*.p.101.
5. Mrinal Pande, "Women without Men.", *The Times of India* (Sunday Magazine Section), 18th Dec., 1977, p. 1.

24

The Poetry of Kamala Das: Limits of Over-exposure

The publication of Kamala Das' third volume of poems, *The Old Playhouse and other Poems* in 1973, establishes both her weakness and strength as a poet. The weakness is demonstrated in the most obvious fact that many of the poems in the collection are stale—they have appeared in numerous places again and again. Is the poet not capable of growth, change, progression, variety—the vital factors that unmistkably announce the signs of life? Where is that fecundity, the creative dynamism that provides the work of a writer with the necessary tension, and substantiates his art? The very few poems that are new in the volume demonstrate another weakness—her penchant for dwelling on the theme of sensuality. In poem after poem Kamala Das is interested only in talking about her sexual exploits, her physical life, the moods of her body. This is, indeed, a valid enough theme for any poet. The greatest poetry of a Sylvia Plath or Anne Sexton, or Judith Wright, to name but a few contemporary women poets, deals with the theme uppermost in a woman's consciousness, namely, the power of her body. But in these superior women poets the body becomes a stepping stone, a metaphor, for the exploration of deeper subjects like the woman's longing for independence and freedom, the quest for an individual identity, the hunger for establishing a meaningful relation with a man, with the outside world. The primarily emotionally triggered poetic efforts are transformed into intellectually sustained works of art, transcending the narrow references to the poet's private grievances against a man or her marriage. Sylvia Plath's works like "Daddy" and "The Three Women," Anne Sexton's cluster of poems called "Live or Die," and Judith Wright's collection called "Woman to Man" demonstrate the poet's capacity to use her narrow but deep woman's world and experiences towards universalising her responses. The complaints against a man and marriage, or the happiness of womanly fulfilment in childbirth and housewifery are all there as the inevitable raw material but the poets invariably grow towards a new awareness and a deeping strength of their identity as woman and artists as they handle this material and progress from one creative effort to another.

This essential strength Kamala Das lacks. But she attempts to convert her weakness into her strength. She makes up for the lack of depth of experience by her flamboyant references to her sexual encounters, her more than daring treatment of her unorthodox private life. The references are so flamboyant as to make one suspect that they are imagined poses, fantasies of sexual neuroticism. The publication of her so-called autobiographical account, *My Story* in 1974, has only added to the suspicion. The salacious details of her sexual pranks are repetitious and formula-based in this account. After reading such a confession it is difficult to determine where the poseur ends and the artist begins even in her poetry. The flagrant eroticism loses its strength and becomes aweakness in her art as it is bound to become in life. As a result Kamala Das finally appears to be a poet of decadence, a poet who is a victim of the inadequacies of her life, failing to gain control even over her art. Her three collections of poems to date, namely, *Summer in Calcutta* (1965), *The Descendants* (1967), and *The Old Play house and Other Poems* (1973), establish this closed, vicious circle.

Summer in Calcutta began with highpromise. Here was a woman who would introduce a new angle, a new 'zing' to use the blurb of one of her works—perhaps a new vision, to poetry written in English by Indians. In 1964 and 1965 she was not only one of the first Indian English poets but was also the first of the new women poets to come into prominence.

Many of the poems in the collection have a genuine ring of originality and boldness thematically, although technically they are invariably lyrical and rather tenuous. The subjective, personal tone runs throughout the volume. The poet is so intensely obsessed with her self that the extreme attitude appears like a mockery of narcissism.

The very first poem, "The Dance of Eunuchs," serves as an exemplary contrast to some subsequent pieces in the volume. The bizarre dance of the body-conscious eunuchs is a concrete metaphor for the poet's own body-language packed into the later poems. What saves the· poem from grotesqueness is the underlying self-awareness and irony of the poet. This is as much as the body is worth—to undergo the pathetic acrobatics involving the limbs without engaging the mind. This is the dance of the man and woman both—celebrating at the end the season of drought. It is highly ironical that the eunuchs dance at a marriage or on the birth of a child. Are they celebrating fertility of the defeat of it? The paradoxical narture of the situation and the customary "Indianness" of the scene help to make the "Dance of Eunuchs" one of the Kamala Das' best poems.

Poems like "The Wild Bougainvillae" "My Grand-mother's House" and above all, "The Introduction" make one feel that her earleist work in still the best. The poet is discovering herself and the reader joins her quest in trying to know who she is. "The

Forest Fire" and "An Introduction" reveal her to be someone who is already old and tired and disappointed at the beginning of the quest. They predict a closed circle that she was to build to herself out of her poetry. They indicate a defeat for the poet not a triumph. In an "Introduction" one sees the confusion and lack of control that Kamala Das suffers from the subject of her own poetry. It begins with the oft-quoted lines—with the poet's declarations about being an,

> ...Indian, very brown, born in Malabar, I speak in
> three languages, write in two, dream in one...

In the course of the rapid series of statements the poet goes through the full gamut of her life and ends the poem in echoes of Upanishadic rhythm:

> ....I am sinner,
> I am saint, I am the beloved and the
> Betrayed. I have no joys which are not yours, no
> Aches which are not yours. I too call myself I.
> "An Introduction"

In spite of these bold assertions, one doesn't know more about the poet at the end than at the beginning. The egotistical references to her body, her love-life, sound too loud to be true and convincing. What the poet lacks is a deeper understanding about herself.

Poems in her next collection. *The Descendants,* carry the quest for self-awareness no further. The very first poem, "Suicide," reveals the poet's inner mood explicitly. There is a weariness and a disgust expressed about the vagaries of the experience of love and lust. There is also the torture the body feels similar to the tossed—about sea. But at the end the mood is of stagnation, a deadness. The poet does not have the courage to kill herself and returns with a feeling of deadness remaining within her—the sea has the soul but tosses back the body.

Consequent to the tone of the first piece "The Suicide"

many of the poems in the collection dwell on the poet's preoccupation with the theme of lust. "The Invitation," "The Captive," "The Doubt," "The Proud One," "The Convicts" form a cluster re-inforcing this theme without significantly deepening or enlarging it. The repetitiousness of the idea suggests an orgiastic indulgence in the rites of the body.

"Jaisurya," however, is a slight variation on the theme. In keeping with her tendency to treat her body as an elemental force, a part of the naturalistic order—"For a while I too was earth," she maintains—she continues to celebrate every movement of her female functioning. The poem focuses on her experience of childbirth. Using the cliche images of darkness and light to speak of the emergence of the child from the womb into the world—an obvious suggestion made in the name Jaisurya itself—she wallows in the feeling of mother-love in the course of the poem. This sudden switch to the glorification of the maternal instinct seems to be rather irreconcilable with the bold, sexy suggestions of lust she throws at one in poems like "Composition" and "The Looking Glass." The personae in the poems are surely mixed up. The personality of the poet appears to be too much at the mercy of the body's pulls—so much that she cannot project a proper dominant strain even to herself. As a result, the bewildered confused identity renders her incapable of gaining any kind of control over her moods or progress in her artistic treatment of these moods.

"Composition," the last poem in the collection comes as a culmination to the poet's confessional mood. The first poem, "The Suicide" had introduced the image of the sea in which the poet wiishes to be submerged. "Composition," works out the desire to the lyrical conclusion:

> Ultimately,
> I have come face to face with the sea.

The sea obviously has elemental associations—merging with the sea symbolises the merging of the poet's consciousness with the oblivion of peace.

The poem "Composition" has strong overtones of the American confessional poet. Sylvia Plath, both in theme and technique. Some of the lines are on echo of Plath's "Lady Lazarus.":

> I must
> most deliberately
> whip up a froth of desire,
> a passion to suit the occasion,
> I must let my mind striptease
> I must extrude
> autobiography
>
> —"Composition"

The strident, lyrical long-windedness in some of their poems is adapted to an autobiographical style by both poets. Resorting to shock-tactics and blatantly posing as women defying the dominance of men, both poets give concrete expression of a modern woman's predicament. But Kamala Das stops where Sylvia Plath begins. The Indian poet is enmeshed in the preoccupation of the problems of the flesh and its lust, the American poet casts aside the problems, cuts her body into pieces in poems like "Lady Lazarus" to arise in a spirit of independence and achieve greater mastery over herself, her art. The cloying, torrid sex episodes that Kamala Das speaks of in poems like "The Convicts" and "Conflagration" have no equivalent in Plath.

In pieces like Das's "Jaisurya" and Plath's "Nick and the Candlesticks," poems dealingwith their motherhood, one sees the essential difference between the two poets. Kamala Das mystifies the womb's experience, is more interested in the event as it affects her. Plath rationalises the baby's birth and wonders about its place in the world. Their egos work with characteristic centripetal and centrifugal forcefulness, respectively. Das delves into her body for the feeling of the experience. Plath into her mind for the meaning of it. Between them the two poets demonstrate the possibilities—and impossibilities—of the lyrical mode for the modern poet.

Even in some later poems published in *"The Illustrated Weekly of India"* (27th Nov. 77, p. 45), once again Das echoes Plath. Their quarrel with the father-husband-image is a recurring image in both poets. In "Colussus" and "The Beekeper's Daughter" Sylvia Plath dwells on the frustrations of the woman under a domineering, male presence. But she uses the Freudian obsession with strong, over—conscious awareness to wrest her own independence from this image, in life as in art. Kamala Das, on the other hand, is content to resign herself to the inevitable syndrome of the obedient Indian woman:

> If if have loved others, father,
> I swear I have loved you the most.
>
> (*The Illustrated Weekly of India*. 27 Nov., 77, p. 45)

The American poet, in contrast, declares:

> If I've kiilled one man, I've killed two—
> The vampire who said he was you
> And drank my blood for a year,
> Seven years, if you want to know.
> Daddy, daddy, you bastard, I'm through.
>
> "Daddy"

On the whole, *The Descendants* is a collection that does not add anything substantial to Kamala Das' effort. It is too slender in bulk and casual and moody in tone to contribute towards a solid and significant achievement.

The Old Playhouse and Other Poems is Das's last collection of poems to date. Of the thirty-three items, not many are new. The drying up of the creative fecundity of the poet is evident much too soon. The developmental strength that one looks for in a poet's successive works is missing in these new additions. The theme of lust is once again the preoccupation of love or the extension of a self-quest.

But a few poems like the titular "The Old Playhouse", and "After the illness" are outstanding. Haunting questions like "What lusted then/For him, was it perhaps the deeply hidden soul?" with which the latter poem ends point towards some glimmerings of a deepening awareness as a woman and a poet, but whether Kamal Das will probe those questions further in her subsequent poetry is a matter for conjecture.

The first poem, "The Old Playhouse" serves as a paradigm setting forth the undersurface thematic pattern of the whole volume, in the same way as "The Dance of Eunuchs" did for *Summer in Calcutta*. The poet draws attention to her role-playing techniques and represents her mind as an old playhouse. The tension in the poem is once again set up on the opposition of the man woman relationship. The complaint of the woman continues—against the inadequacies of love, the intolerable sexual tyrannies. The poem ends on a note of protest against these impositions with the assertion that love

> must seek at last
> An end, a pure total freedom, it must will the mirrors
> To shatter and the kind night to erase the water.
>
> "The Old Playhouse"

The telling metaphor of the poet as actor in the drama of sexual conflict is evocatively worked out. The ephemeral, elusive nature of this thing called love between man and woman, the longing to find it and the inevitable disappointment of that longing, are drawn out through this metaphor of relationships being no more than role-playing The poem beautifully sustains the tone of joyous-sad feeling that haunts a deep relationship between a man and a woman. In the end the lingering sadness prevails for the poet declares

There is
> No more singing, no more a dance, my mind is an old
> Playhouse with all its lights put out.
>
> "The Old Playhouse"

Few other poems in the collection match the first one. In "Gino" once again we find the poet bogged down in the torrid zone of lust. The poem lacks careful working of idea and metaphor and is a medley of sexual images thrown in together for the sake of effect which after all turns out to be a cheap one.

Two notable pieces in the volume are the lyrical prose pieces at the end, "The Swamp" and "Sunset, Blue Bird." The poet is in her element in these prose-poems, singing about herself and her love-lorn life. "The Swamp" is richly descriptive, and the poem is clearly a metaphor serving to reveal the inner landscape of the poet's mood. The tropical lush background of Malabar is sensuously related to her own feeling of love. The piece is strategically placed after the poem "The Stone Age," which once again dwells on her own passionate nature.

Deliberately the poet binds herself to this naturalistic order where the body functions only as a part of nature, giving in to the pulls of the elemental forces. She is at the mercy of the instinctive urges. No doubt there is a primitivistic strength and power in these natural urges, but is that enough to sustain the poet in her effort to know love, to know herself?

The lyric urge and the resultant preoccupation with the subjective feelings are inadequate equipment for a modern poet who has to deal with a world that is becoming increasingly complex in every aspect. As the poet herself has ironically indicated, they result in her being trapped in the Stone Age, in the swamp. Repeated references confined to the subjective world can only result in purposeless over-exposure. The poetic urges are sadly dissipated in this decadent state.

Her most recent autobiographical work, "My Story," has focused critical attention on the sensationalism that is a strong element in her work. In his perceptive work on Kamala Das Devindra Kohli brings out the parallelism between her poetry and "My Story" by frequent, apt comparisons. But in spite of his emphasising the point that they are similar, the reader is not left with the feeling that Kamala Das' stance as a bold, flamboyant lover is authentic. The autobiography appears to be a fantasy rather than a true story. The salacious details of her sexual exploits introduce a flagrant eroticism into her work, so flagrant that it detracts from artistic and aesthetic finish.

In a passage in one of her prose pieces Das observes:

> The women of our house have all been frigid. Although I fought against this hereditary incompetence by moving into the hot orbits of conspicuously coarse, earthy males the experiments wore me down and I admitted defeat. "Frigidity and the sepia-tainted photograph."
>
> *Opinion* 27th Nov. 73, p. 30.

Such professions of the self are relatively much better suited for poetic treatment than for prose, as she herself has demonstrated. "My Story" does not add much towards a better understandingof Kamala Das. On the contrary, it exposes some of the weaknesses of the poet who had started out with such high promise in *Summer in Calcutta*.

The lyric mode, whiich Kamala Das uses in her short, characteristically short poems, has an inherent limitation especially for purposes of the modern poet. The pressures and complexities of contemporary thought and feeling appear incongrous when fitted into the tenuous, lyric expression. Poets like Sylvia Plath and Anne Sexton, who have needed to be personal in their poetry, and who give expression to the tortures of the private psyche in their poems, have sought to extend the lyrical into the more complex confessional mode, where the variety of their experiences can be handledwith greater sophistication. The confessional mode includes the personal andthe autobiographical elements and is not merely subjective. There is greater play of conscious awareness, of the objective world, on the part of the poet, larger scope for technical variety resulting in a poetry of a richer texture. Kamala Das has failed to achieve this complexity, either because her experiences have lacked variety or because her artistic technique has not been so ambitious.

As a result Kamala Das' poetic achievement, when re-assessed at this point, shows a marked negative quality—a decadence of theme and technique. Constant self-exposure in itself does not become satisfying, lyrical or confessional poetry—it can only descend into a glaring, deadening exhibitionism. In life such self-exposure is suicidal, in art it is unpardonably boring.

25

The Poetry of G.S. Sharat Chandra

If one were to look for new voices and changing directions in the field of Indian-English poetry in the beginning of the eighties, one would be met with an empty prospect. Unfortunately, no recent Indian-English poet has yet produced a substantial body of work that can really stand on its own merit for close, extended, individual critical assessment and serve as a solid contribution to the development of Indian-English poetry today. Indo-English poetry of the contemporary period has to be treated collectively rather than individually to attain some significance.

The only exception, perhaps, is the achievement of Kamala Das, who despite her not so substantial output has a poetic style and personality that are unmistakably there in her poems. Her range is narrow as she has chosen to dwell mainly on the theme of a woman's love, but the narrowness is more than made up by the genuineness and depth of treatment in her best poems like "The Old Playhouse," "The Housebuilders," or "The Paper Moon." The instinct, the sixth sense of the poet and woman work remarkably in her primarily subjective poems like "The Wild Bougainvillaea" and set her apart from her other contemporary academician poets. Hers is a truly remarkable poetic voice. But woefully enough, she has failed to strengthen and develop that poetic style after a rich beginning. Whether the shortcoming was inherent in the poet or in her theme is a matter for useless speculation, for who can separate the dancer from the dance? The perversities, the vagaries of sexual love have at last undone the poet and the woman in Kamala Das but nevertheless triumphantly contributed to her striking poetic personality.

No doubt Indo-English poetry desperately needs new voices, and new directions at the present time. And it is heartening to hear these new voices whenever they come up, few and far between as they are.

To date G.S. Sharat Chandra has published three slender collections of poems that are noteworthy of critical attention, namely, *Bharata Natyam Dancer* (1968), *April in Nanjangud* (1971), and *Once or Twice* (1974). The fourth collection called *Offsprings of Servegna* (1975) is mainly a transcreational work based on the vacanas of Servegna, a medieval Kannada saintfigure.

For a new reader of Sharat Chandra's poetry there could not be a better introduction to the poet than in some clearly autobiographical poems in this first collection, *The Bharata Natyam Dancer*. By naturally using the familiar idiom of his background he tells us where he comes from—his "Matrudesh" is one where stark poverty and bleakness prevail:

I know a village where women
Are sold while they are children
I know a nation where death
Is a blessing to the dead and living.

"Matrudesh"

In another poem his memory dwells on Devi, the milkman's wife who coaxes her five-month old calf into a watery grave in the Cauvery river as it had been blinded by grazing on some poisonous herbs. In the course of a few unsentimental lines the poet brings out the strength and compassion of this village woman who is clearly a living symbol of the rural, natural background the poet knows and remembers. The picture of Devi as Kali, loaded with all the meaning of Indian village life stands out in both the poet's and the reader's mind. The title poem, "The Bharata Natyam Dancer," proves to be paradigmatic of some of the characteristics that one will repeatedly come across even in the later poems of Sharat Chandra—a clear sense of humour, a wry, ironical tone sometimes directed against others and sometimes against himself, with an underlying critical questioning about his background, his choices, his identity, his life. The poem is a direct dig against the Establishment, the purveyors of national art and culture and the "culture vultures." The poet is obviously not dwelling on the dancer, despite the title, but is concentrating on the ministerial audience. The poem misses a chance of developing the expected dialectic between culture and philistinism and merely becomes a one-sided, sardonic exposure of the crudity of the whole experience which is exploited for political purposes. The reaction in the poem is of an ordinary man, not of a poet, and the feeling of the artist is completely left out, to the reader's disappointment.

In many poems in the collection one meets with this disconcerting, characteristic style of the poet—of referring to bygone memories of people, fleeting visions of women known and left, of relationships never fully established, of thoughts never completely expressed. The poet is much too tentative in approach. "To X now a Model" speaks about a girl he knew and who is now no more than a painful memory to him, perhaps a loved one. "Pen Friends" is about letters that do not get written between mothers and sons. In a short poem called "Mom and Dad" the poet has a dream about mom pelting dad with icy pebbles and then bringing hima rain-coat once again hinting at Freudian failures of relationships. "Sort of," "On Flight," "Relatives," "Dawn," "Tell her to Return." "At a Summer Camp" also deal with flashes and visions of someone known, someone left, someone gone...

In these poems the poet is obviously discovering himself, his relationships to others. He is not sure of anything hence the flight, the fleeting touch, and the only thing that is permanent is the memory. The last significant lines in the collection are:

> You are best remembered
> As a face hung up in long red hair.
> Squeeze in the hand gently exchanged in the dark.
>
> "At a Summer Camp"

There are a few other poems in the volume which fit into no pattern, that are without significant themes or ideas, that seem to be no more than verbal exercises of a beginning poet. "On Record," "Echo?" "Magician," are examples of this type. "The Lute" once again speaks about the failed contact between the song and the lute, "2 Questions" of a gap between the word and the page and "The Black Pigeon" of a love-messenger that has not come back with the message.

In a series of poems like "The Visit," "Relatives," and "The Tourist" one cannot miss the introduction to the poet as someone who has left his India to live ina strange land. "Tourist" establishes the identity of the poet as a man who is characteristically moving from place to place, from person to person, from memory to memory, and that is the image that emerges at the end of the reading of this first collection. The poet is still trying his hand over a variety of topics and has not yet succeeded in working out anything firmly, indetail in any of these poem. They altogether present the texture of life as apprehended by an average man...Feelings, moods ideas are imagistically caught in some tentative lines in these early poems.

The next collection, *April in Nanjangud*, is a thin wedge of a book containing some maturer poems of Sharat Chandra. That the poems are characteristically diminutive may be deduced from the observation that there are as many as 57 items ina type of volume that the *London Times*, describes as a "wholemeal (pocket) sandwich," according to the blurb commenting on the

London Magazine editions of which this is one. Some of the poems in this volume are reprints from the earlier *Bharata Natyam Dancer*. The pieces cover a wide variety of ideas and observations of the poet.

The title poem "April in Nanjangud," is rather disappointing. It sets up expectations by the use of the word April, bringing to the reader's mind the famous references to April in Chaucer, T.S. Eliot, and the well known exclamation of even a minor poet inspired by the month to exclaim: "Oh! to be in England/Now that April's there!" but the expectations are just not fulfilled either thematically or technically. April is not spring in Nanjangud, it is drought. The poem refers to the heat, the dryness, the deserted road,and the dusty village. But it is puzzling as to how April already could have established itself as the season of drought inNanjangud. Seasonally, April is a month poised between winter and spring for the English poet, or Spring and summer for the Indian poet. The days in April, dry as they are, still hold promise of sweet showers to come and the drought season can make itself felt only much later, should these showers fail. The poet seems to be ignoring the ambiguous seasonal factor of April while speaking of the dryness and heat merely for effect. The poem does not develop even this theme of the heat and dust of a tropical landscape fully. It is a fleeting collection of a few images that suggest the feeling of summer merely. The title is much too impressive for the poem to bear and the poem itself lets down reader's expectations.

The tone of critical irony and sometimes humour can be found in many poems like "As the Mayor leaves for New Delhi" and "The Donkey." Poems suchas "Flying in the Wind," "Approaches," "Morning" are short addresses to women, or on the ephemeral, beautiful feeling of love. Once again, the poems are merest brusheson these topics and nothing is developed either individually or in the cluster. In short pieces such as "A Swim." "Roof," "Fish," "Chairs," what the poet seems to be doing is to suggest the feel of life, of movement or stillness. They are stray, disconnected observations of someone eager to feel the words that can bring out these simple moments of life vividly. The poet is fond of the word and the image primarily and the idea or the feeling or the emotional urge is of secondary consideration. There are a few poems like "The Watchman," "The Woman in My Icebox," "Mad Leader from Mars," "Bronze Men" which are difficult to understand and identify in the context of everyday experience and response. They appear to be exercises of the poet's verbal and imaginative skill rather than poems of true experience.

The best pieces in the volume are those that deal with the poet's knowledge of human relationships—for instance, "Two Distant People." and "Paths of Dream," or reminiscences of childhood as in "Consistently Ignored" and "The Black Deity." Such poems are anchored in deeper feelings of the poet's consciousness and are not mere surface verbal exercises, obviously. On the whole, *April in Nanjangud* is interesting in its variety for any reader. The poems make for a satisfactory, casual reading of poems by an Indian-English poet.

But one has to note that the collection is still lacking in a feeling or sincere poetic urgency or thematic pressures. The poet is skimming on surfaces of emotion and expression and does not seem to be fully drawn into the task of writing at hand. His verbal virtuosity is noteworthy but one wishes that it could be employed towards a more engaging, involved purposeful expression of personality. Many of the poems are about the submerged discontent of a stranger in a strange land. The discontent never surface into rage.

Besides writing his own poems Sharat Chandra has translated some poems from medieval Kannada into English. This has resulted in a volume called *The Offsprings of Servegna* (Writer's Workshop, Calcutta; 1975). In the Kannada version they are more like axioms, aphorisms, and proverbs but the poet here translates them into haikulike verses, that he calls "Worthy poems," a phrase he derives from the refrain that runs through the original saying. A number of these poems were published first in the *London Magazine.* The poet calls them offssprings rather than translations, for some of the pieces are his own but written under the "influence ofthe spirit of Servegna." The aphoristic statements form small clusters of verse, which together make up a pattern of wise, age-old pronouncements on the lessons life teaches us.

The whole collection is too slender for one to make any significant critical comment. Individually and even collectively the poems are no more than suggestive phrases and cryptic observations. But even the exercise of translating these might have helped the poet to discipline his own style, for one notices that Sharat Chandra's own poems in the volume are short and cryptic. The poetic achievement in this volume is obviously of a secondary nature, only providing him with the inclusive experience of being translator as well and does not really do justice either to the bulk and weightiness of the original work or towards increasing the dimensions of the poet's themes or techniques. Without depute the poems have a quaint ring and the freshness of something different that deservedly found a place in a journal like the *London Magazine,* but one is tantalisingly left wishing for more translations, more vigorous compilation of the original composer, a better dynamic exchange of idea and techniques between the saint-poet and the translator. Only in one poem, "The Inequities of Love" is the reader rewarded thus.

One of the more recent publications of Sharat Chandra's own poems. *Once or Twice* (Hippopotamus Press, England; 1974), contains some of his better poems. The best ones are those in memory of his father—poems that are tender and simple, telling us as much of the absent father as of the present poet. The thoughful tone with which he considers his old parent's illness, death, and his own return from abroad to witness these amidst the relatives he has left behind, all told in disconnected phrases and lines, comes through touchingly. This cluster introduces a growing, serious preoccupation that is to be found in some other poems here like, "Once or Twice," "For All Aliens" and "Mount Pleasant,U.S.A."—the poet's concern with his senseof displacement, his feeling of alienation as someone living in the far-off United States. These are short poems dealing with the business of living in a foreign country. The poet employs a strategy of peopling an interior landscape with memories of people he knew, in order to perpetuate the past. But the parting has been too long and the distance has been too wide for these emotional spurts to have any intensity. Nostalgia is a duty for poets in Sharat Chandra's position and after a time it ceases to be a virtue.

In a recent interview, A.K. Ramanujan draws attention to his own similar predicament and says: that "...one's being an exile, an expatriate takes on a new meaning." (*The Humanities Review* (New Delhi), vol. 3,no.1, June 1981,p.11). But the word for poets like Ramanujan and Sharat Chandra is more appropriately "immigrant" rather than "exile" or "expatriate." Changing countries for better prospects does not make one an exile or expatriate. Even if they call themselves self-exiled, the reasons for staying or going away are vital factors in the development of the poet's consciousness. Merely remembering the past ina distant country in order to fend off a bleak future can become nothing more than a poetic ploy to fill moments of boredom and vacuity.

Perhaps the only hope for poets like these is to face the reasons that have prompted the choice, consciously or unconsciously, understand the falseness of the position, and reconcile themselves to whatever loss of country, culture, and context their choice might have entailed. Merely looking to the relationships of the past is a sure sign of sentimentality that will end in sterility. A predominantly Western-educated poet, as all Indian poets writing in English irrevocably are, cannot double back on his Tamil or Kannada ever again. It is a way of no return. An attempt to do so will only result is a two-fold spuriousness, an attitude of pretentiousness. A post-Western consciousness deliberately re-seeking its Tamil or Kannada or Telugu inheritance does so to its own detriment. The answer is only confrontation, inclusion, adaptation, assimilation of whatever is in the poet's purview. What results may be synthetic but it will be genuinely synthetic without pretentions. This is Sharat Chandra's strength, that he has this power of assimilation.

In a short poem called "Reasons for Staying" Sharat Chandra expresses it all honestly:

> I am talking to the kitchen table
> full of roses.
> The language is my own,
> I tell them
> I own them.
>
> There are roses because I say so,
> the vase is mine
> so is the kitchen
> I like them red
> I pay for the water
>
> "Reasons for Staying"

The poet is unsentimental and clear-eyed enough to realize that he is alone with his language amidst the materiality of the context, but has the assertiveness to confront the situation and make these objects his own. It is this bold attempt at adaptation that is a refreshing sign in a poet like Sharat Chandra. He does not use the word exile or expatriate but writes a challenging poem called "Aliens." Repeatedly he resorts to the tone of self-irony and self-mockery while speaking about his feeling of alienation. This is a redeeming intellectual attitude in a poet. "Aliens" is one of his best poems not only because it contains a serious theme but also because the poet takes the trouble of developing such a theme at a greater length than he has hitherto been capable of. These are new directions in his poetic effort and one hopes the poet will develop on these, otherwise what M.K. Naik says of Ramanujan may become equally true of Sharat Chandra, that the poet shows "... an inability or disinclination (one hopes it is the latter and not the former) to have a bold, all-out confrontation with experience opting instead for sporadic skirmishes, minor engagements and hit and run tacties." (*Humanities Review*, *op. cit*., p. 18).

"Bangla (Waterpipe) Desh," the last poem in *Once or Twice* is also noteworthy for its length and ironic tone. The poet describes the horror of the Bangladesh war, but towards the end the irony is too open and topical and the lack of subtlety is also responsible for the loss of poignancy:

> Here comes the ambassadors—
> The ambassador of the U.S.A. controls
> The umbilical cord of the poor.
> Bow to him with highest priority.
> Show the ambassadors in which tunnel you're best hunted
> And they'll show you where the food packages are hidden...
>
> "Bangla (Waterpipe) Desh"

This slender volume is Sharat Chandra's best poetic effort to date. One only hopes that in this end is his beginning and that he will build further upon this maturing of themes and techniques. Let it not be a farewell gesture of "Driving into Winter," as the poet expresses beautifully in one of his hitherto unpublished poems that should make us read the poet, but let it be a gesture of driving forward, rootless as the movement may be, that should reach us to him.

26

History as Metafiction—The Ayodhya Theme in Shashi Deshpande's *Small Remedies*

Just as we often think about the state of Indian society in terms of "before Independence" and "after Independence", perhaps we should now also consider it as "before Ayodhya" and "after Ayodhya". The day, 6 December 1992, has in present times become much more than a date. The events of that day have gone far beyond the political limits of their meaning. The deepest impact of the actions and events of that day are to be ultimately seen in the personal dimension. How did that incident of the destruction of an old structure of brick, mortar and mud—a destrucion which took only a few hours to be completed—make itself felt in the minds of the people of the entire country? Not a day passes without some reference or the other being made to the Ayodhya issue in the daily news-reports, and media.

In recent times we have seen several film directors in our country imaginatively recreating in memorable films, mostly with sad undersones, the evils of communal warfare and the misery and suffering that the ensuing violence unleashes on the innocent victims. Mani Ratnam's "Bombay" Gulzar's "Maachis", Mahesh Bhatt's "Zakhm," and Khalid Mohamed's "Fiza", come to mind as examples. Perhaps the most significant literary treatment of the Ayodhya incident has now appeared in Shashi Deshpande's recent novel, *Small Remedies*. One must not forget to also mention here a short story in Kannada titled, "Ondu Thundu Godae" ("A Bit of Wall"), by the well-known writer, Bolwar Mahamad Kunhi. Kunhi's extended short story is extraordinary in that he treats the explosive Ayodhya theme in a humorous, personal vein. He recounts the story of how the old woman, roti-Phatumma, wanted to build her own house by acquiring from someone what she believed was a bit of the wall from the broken pieces of the Babri Masjid. Roti-Phatumma was determined on using this bit of wall as part of the construction for her own new house. With a tongue-in-cheek wit Kunhi balances admirably the serious, comic, and poignant aspects of the story.

The movies depict the horror and brutal cruelty through searing images and violent action whereas Deshpande in *Small Remedies* has internalised these same aspects and brought out the intensity of suffering through words and language. There is at first, in the style of the novelist, a sign of withdrawal from and avoidance of the violence and terror that was unleashed by the demolition at Ayodhya. Whereas the art of imagery in the films vivifies the terror, anger, and the misery of suffering in a raw and open manner, verbal art, on the other hand, reaches inward into the passions and emotions that were at the root of this terror. While the impact of the visuals is immediate and momentary,the impact of the words and language is indirect but longlasting. The controlled formalism and the enmeshed, multi-layered narrataive technique of *Small Remedies* lays bare the innermost psychological consequences of the violence of death and destrucion slowly but surely.

Although the manipulation of time and memory contributes to the intricate structure of *Small Remedies* which includes flashbacks, interior monologues, dreams, nightmares, surrealistic visions and epiphanies, it must also be pointed out here that such a style slows down the dynamics of action in the story. The novel is somewhat wanting in narrative energy. But then, grief is hardly an emotion to be dramatised or enacted energetically. It can only be suffered and ultimately accepted as shown in the rounded ending of *Small Remedies.*

The Ayodhya episode is only present at the still centre of the novel; it is only the princess's pea in a thickly padded mattress, so to speak, the small seed inside the core. But the theme of the novel is contained in this seed. How far did Ayodhya, and the consequent Bombay riots and the serial blasts have their impact on two women and their families? Madhu Saptarishi, the narrator of the novel, considers the events as they affected the life of Savitribai Indorekar, a reputed musician, and also as they affected her own life. Savitribai has lost her daughter, her love-child, Munni, and Madhu has lost her eighteen-year old son, Aditya an only child, in the bombing of a bus in Bombay on 12 March 1993.

Basically *Small Remedies* is about the grief of these two women. In fact grief is the one word which occurs most often in the novel, almost on every third page. To cope with the trauma of her grief for her dead son, Madhu undertakes to write the biography of Bai. The common bond linking Madhu with Bai are several. They were first of all neighbours in the small town of Neemgaon. They were mothers who had lost their youthful children through violent deaths. They were creative artists—one is a writer and the other is a musician. And they are now biographer and subject.

Although the novel purportedly appears to be a biography of Bai it eventually develops into an autobiography of Madhu. Even as a biography it is about a fictitious character. The novel is also a documentary, although an indirect one, of the historical event of the razing of the Babri Masjid to the ground in Ayodhya on 6 December 1992. In the middle of *Small Remedies,* Madhu, while speaking about her being a woman and how she can never be not noticed, says exasperatedly, "It's becoming increasingly clear to me that I cannot keep myself out of this book of Bai's that I cannot be the invisible narrator... Like fiction writers, like historians, the teller of a story needs to construct a plausible narrative biography that Bai expects..." In another context she compares the biographer to the six blind men who are trying to describe an elephant. Like the blind men the biographer must collect bits and pieces of information about a person from several people and then write them all into a connected biography.

Obviously Deshpande problematises the genre of the novel in *Small Remedies*. This is done to show how difficult it is for someone to write about a person's life, to pack into words the fact, the truths, about the person. Madhu is the writer of Bai's biography. She is at the same time writing her own life. There are so many similarities between the researcher and the life she is researching. The plot structure in *Small Remedies* is one of echoes and reflections as a result of this interaction. In a self reflexive manner Madhu tries to find the meaning of her own life in the light of the lives of Savitribai and her aunt Leela. Like Margaret Atwood's *Alias Grace* and Carol Shields' *Small Ceremonies*, Shashi Deshpande's *Small Remedies*, which is comparable to the novel of these Canadian writers, can best be described as "historiographic metafiction" in the words of the Canadian critic Linda Hutcheon.

As it happens there is not much of a life remaining in Savitribai after she has had a heart attack and a paralytic stroke. Madhu sees her after a gap of twenty long years and the Bai that she encounters now at close quarters is an old woman devastated by illness. She has become a selfish, sick woman totally dependent on others. Madhu is disappointed in her effort to learn from Bai as to how she has accepted the violent death of her daughter. But Bai has now rejected both her lover, Ghulam Saab, and their love child, Munni. Perhaps the deterioration of her life as a musician followed as a resuslt of these cruel rejections.

A number of images in the novel seem to suggest that

being human is to suffer a disease; to love is to suffer an illness. There are many references to doctors, illnesses, and maladies in *Small Remedies*, as the title itself indicates. There are also several deaths in the novel, many of them violent. Joe's heart attacks and death; Leela's cancer and her death; Madhu's mother's TB and her death; and later her father's; the suicide of the young man who is a visitor in Madhu's father's house, come to mind. Above all there are the deaths of Aditya and Shailaja in the bus disaster. Madhu herself who is in a spell of deep grief as a result of the violent death of Aditya seems to hover between a borderline state of life and death as indicated at the very beginning of the novel. The well-known feminist critic, Julia Kristeva, while speaking about the Nazi Holocaust, points out that it was in the survivors, especially the women and children, that the true meaning of death could be understood. The public political event invades the personal domain and lets loose a "malady of death". Kristeva believes that historically speaking, it is the political power that acted as the criminal and that deserves to be punished.

In *Small Remedies*, at the end we find that when the consequences of a political event reach out to turn into a personal disaster, it is the individual voice and action that must take on the political power as enemy No. 1 and confront it. When anti-social elements try to break up the musical prayer meeting at the temple of Bhavani where Hasina is to sing Madhu attacks their cowardliness in an article that she publishes in a newspaper. Wiser counsel prevails in the end and Hasina, the grand-daughter of Ghulam Saab, sings the vachanas of Akka soulfully at the feet of the goddess Bhavani. The healing power of music dispels Madhu's grief and mitigates the after-taste of violence and destruction. At last she breaks herself free from her grief-stricken silence and talks to Hari about Aditya's death. Her catharsis comes as a result of this confession and acknowledgement and she sets herself free to go back to her husband, Som, and to riot-torn Bombay to pick up her life from the debris.

27

Fantasy Beckons!

The overwhelming success of J.K. Rowling's recent book, *Harry Potter and the Goblet of Fire,* is truly fantastic. This children's fantasy, running into a whopping 644 pages, is said to have broken all publishing records when it went on sale. The U.S. first printing was 3.8 million copies and the U.K. 1.5. 345,435 copies were advance ordered on amazon.com, the Intenet book dealers. 200000 copies went on sale in Australia, 37000 copies were sold on the fist day in Britain alone.

Mind-boggling!

And to think that gloomy prophets had predicted certain death for books and the reading habit in an age of TV and computers! I remember how recently at a seminar on multi-media software for children when a thirteen year old boy, the son of one of the professors who had produced the software and the only youngster amidst the participants was asked which CD Rom on Mathematics he liked best, he replied, "None of them. I prefer books to all this stuff because I can carry my book wherever I like!"

It is interesting how Potter's world of magic and wizardry has cast its spell on not only the kids of the cyber age but also on their parents. Obviously fantasizing is an integral part of the human mind. Escape, subversion, wish fulfillment are all part of the politics of fantasy, and these feelings are there in the young and the old alike.

C.S. Lewis, the critic of English Renaissance literature points out that ghosts, wizards, giants, talking animals and gods are as old as the human imagination. But he laments, in the last three centuries with the complex development of the Novel and the rise of the realistic aesthetic, the elements of fantasy have been relegated to the stories of children and even there this kind of literature has been seriously questioned.

This is not entirely true, one feels. We can see that even in the predominantly realistic novel of the twentieth century fantasy is pervasively used. This mixture of realism and fantasy has resulted in the style of magic realism, a style which is used to great advantage by writers like Gabriel Garcia Marquez and Toni Morrison. Marquez's *Love in the Time of Cholera* is charged with the elements of love-fantasy. Fermina Daza and Florentino Ariza can come together as lovers only when they are old, decrepit, on the verge of death. But they can accept these harsh truths when they sail away in the ship. "New Fidelity" flying the cholera-flag, and continuing to fantasise about their earlier youthful romance. Morrison's novel, *Beloved,* deals with the tragic history of slave trade in North America. When Sethe, the black mother, kills her infant daughter. Beloved to save her from being sold as a slave, there is only a terrible story to follow. But Morrison employs a surrealistic style and unfolds the narrative in dreamlike sequences of fantasia. A harsh, horrible theme is thus made acceptable and readable through this stylistic device of fantasy.

Although Indian writing in English does not boast of pure, full scale fantasies like Rabelais' *Decameron* or Cervantes's *Don Quixote,* still the mostly realistic narratives of Indian writers are interspersed with fantastical episodes. G.V. Desani's *All about H. Hatterr*, published in the late forties of the twentieth century is perhaps the only unique example of a fantasy-novel that one can find in our writing. Even sustained works of magic realism are rare, except perhaps for Rushde's *Midnight's Children*.

J.R.R. Tolkien, the master craftsman of fantastical tales like *The Lord of the Rings* and *The Hobbit* describes fantasy as the highest power of the creative imagination. He coins the word "Sub-creation" to express this power. By means of it a fantasist creates a whole, imaginative world, a world with its own climate, geography, peoples and languages. It is a power not unlike the power of divine creation; it signifies man is made in the image of god, he maintains.

Escape from modern society through fantasizing about idealized landscapes untouched by industrialization and squalor, spinning yarns of science-fiction these are some of the devices of current fantasy-writing.

Obviously here we see the attempt of the writers to liberate themselves from the ugliness and impasse of the modern world. I remember even some years ago when I was making up the study list for the sophomore literature class in Wisconsin, when I asked for suggestions of titles from the students, more than half the class wanted a Tolkien book rather than the James Joyce or W.B. Yeats one on the list. And more recently on the Harvard campus the biggest attendance of audience I had seen was not for Norman Mailer's or Gore Vidal's lectures, not even for Seamus Heaney's reading of his own poems, but it was for the currently released animated movie of Walt Disney, "The Beauty and the Beast!" What do we conclude by all this? The more technological the society the greater the fascination for fantasy or science fiction and the pull towards alternative worlds?

In Indian English writing we do not have full-scale science-fiction novels yet, like Isaac Asimov's *Fantastic Voyage II*. Manjula Padmanabhan's science-fiction short stories are perhaps the first of their kind in our writing. Her narrative, "Cold Soup and Hot Death" a combination of fantasy, science-fiction, and satire is a chilling account of the sophisticated planning of their own sati by an American wife and her Rajasthani nobleman husband. Her Onassis-award winning play, *The Harvest*, is a fine example of fantasy edged by a cutting tone of satire. The playwright creates a weird, unrealistic world where human organ buying and selling is carried on as nonchalantly as buying and selling of any consumer product. A rich American woman has picked out the young Indian man, who being poor, is ready to sell his organs to be transplanted into her during her old age, and so she takes care of him by remote control, she living in America and he in Bombay! Welfed organs to be harvested when the time is ripe!.

Recently Kiran Desai's *Hullabaloo in the Guava Orchard* has entertained readers with its device of fantasy. The hilarious account of the mutual antics of the Tree Baba or Monkey Baba and his devotees is an effective spoof on modern socicty's blind belief in whatever seems even remotely spiritualistic. A young writer like Kiran gets away with her scathing exposure of the ridiculousness of a world where religious and spiritual nothings are revered as great holiness, by cleverly employing the doubly subversive device of fantasy and humour.

Among the earlier writers R.K. Narayan's books provide some episodes of fantasy. These are only interventions in otherwise realistic novels. The young boy, Swami in *Swami and Friends*, lives in a world of his own, he escapes from the harsh adult world whenever he wants to by just giving free rein to his imaginings. The escape route is his safety valve, for it helps him to preserve his child's world and at the same time build a bridge gradually, cautiously into the adult world. Swami fantasizes in order to transcend the limitations of the child's world and grow strong as an adult so that he can cope with the awesome reality.

As in this young boy's story, even in the writings of some

Indian women novelists fantasies of sexuality, freedom, power, alternate worlds in which women are autonomous, self-defining people, are commonly found as novelistic devices. Here fantasy acts as an intuitive challenge to perceived reality. Thus some of the women characters that noteworthy women writers have created are good examples of such people who have encaped to a world of fantasy in an effort to beat harsh reality. Maya in Anita Desai's novel *When Peacocks Called* and Dimple Das Gupta in Bharati Mukherjee's *Wife* come to mind in this context.

We perceive both Maya and Dimple as being "mad" but as far as they themselves are concerned their "madness" is an effective deflector of the unbearable reality and they create fantastic worlds for themselves under the grip of this so-called madness or hysteria. One's fantasy can create a dystopia or an utopia as escape route. Insanity, abnormality of response, may be a part of building up a world of escape. Dimple is capricious and she lives in a world of fantasy, the readers think, but to Dimple herself that is her real world. Life in New York in the closed confines of a tiny flat with potted plants in the window as only company, is life in a mad-house to this girl from busy Calcutta. So she resorts to living in a world of make-believe where the TV screen and the drawing room scene merge. She wears a petticoat and a pair of dark glasses as her day wear. The dark glasses perhaps aid in covering up reality and help her in imagining a world of fantasy into which she retreats whenever she likes. In other words Dimple subverts the actual reality effectively and defies and defeats her husband's sense of the real, rational world. It is a feminine way of resorting to abnormality and near-childishness and irresponsibility in order to defy the masculine world and the domineering demands of the husband. But unfortunately Dimple's fantasies get the better of her because of her helpless situation as an immigrant in an alien culture and alas! she goes over the brink and stabs and kills her husband with a kitchen knife in reflex action. She fantasizes that this will free her from all that her husband signified, namely, life amidst a strange culture that she cannot absorb, male domination, the constrictions of wife-bood, etc.

Desai's heroine Maya also acts in similar ways and pushes her husband to his death from the roof. The delusive fantasies of Dimple and Maya end terribly. They attempt to subvert the male-dominated world even if it means facing self-destruction. Desai and Mukherjee have created in their novels disturbing worlds resulting from fantasies of dystopia.

28

Whither Feminism?

New concepts like post-feminism, neofeminism, ecofeminism, power-feminism, womanism, femmenism, etc. being introduced into the discourse on feminism in the present context emphasize the increasing contemporary relevance of the ideology. Inspite of more than half a century having passed since writers like Simone de Beauvior, Betty Freidan, Luce Irigaray, among others stirred up the debate on recognising the importance of difference in identity and worth of women in social and emotional contexts, women are still finding themselves left far behind in their right to claim a position of equality and dignity in society.

Although a great deal of advance has been made in the process of emancipating women from the injustice, marginalization, and degradation that they suffer in the context of the patriarchal family system which is still prevalent in middleclass homes, sometimes the true positions of mother/wife/daughter even in urban educated families are pitiable. If the man in the family subjugates the woman then it follows instinctively that the woman will exericse her power to subjugate the child. The chain of domination and subjugation is inevitable if we passively allow the naturalistic and instinctual behaviour to dictate family relationships in the guise of love/affection/sentiment. Indisputably it is in the family system that gender reform should start.

It is not too much to expect today that the woman take things into her hand and shape the roles of the members of her family into a more harmonious equation. Many women at least in an urban context are quite self aware and they also serve as bread winners for the family. An educated woman should trouble herself to organize the family set-up with the help of her informed mind and a less educated woman can attempt it with the strength of her background tradition. This renewal of faith in her own natural capacity rather than being resigned to demoralizing social conditions is what critic Naomi Wolf hails as power feminism.

Many feel that the family system is sacrosanct and is not to be interfered with. But the old fashioned system which was based more on spiritual and economic foundations rather than on civil liberties certainly has to be over-hauled and reinvented if it has to survive in the modern world. The relations between the men and women, and parents and children within the family have to be re-established according to a just pattern of civil liberties. They have to be more democratic. The woman has to learn self-representation before trying to guide her children or her family. In order to achieve this self-representation she must know what her rights are and wrest these rights. These rights are connected to her womanliness - the right to choice of maternity, right to a culture dependent on feminine needs, and the dignity to be a civil individual within the family. Women want freedom not to do as they please but to choose to do the right thing by themselves.

There is so much that women can do to change the face of family relationships that now seem to be threatened by the onslaught from the outside social forces like swiftly changing economic conditions, increasing violence, erosion of civil behaviour, exploitation of caste/class, and destructive terrorism. Unless women themselves realize that it is undignified and self-destructive to continue in the intimidating, subjugating pattern that even now exists in the patriarchal family system, not much can be done by anyone towards their liberation. Many times, it is distressing to see that even educated women seem to be enjoying and thus perpetuating this unjust situation.

I happened to visit a friend's house recently. The family was celebrating the 90th birthday of the father. A photographer had been called, banquets had been arranged throughout the day for the immumerable guests lining up in the specially erected pandal in the garden, and the birthday man himself was smothered amidst scores of floral bouquets. This celebration had come after equally grand celebrations that had taken place when the father had completed 60 and 80 years, respectively. My friend observed remorsefully that no one had thought of cerebrating the 60th or 80th birthdays of her mother who had died two years before at the age of 84 after rearing eight children.

More often than not it is the women themselves who are responsible for their enslavement. Although economically and socially independent, many educated Indian women in bourgeo—is families submit to a repressive patriarchal system because of the safety and escape from individual responsibility that it affords.

Leading feminists like Germaine Greer and Gloria Steinem were aware that women were alienated because of natural differences from men. Acceptance and protection of the differences must be demanded. An individual identity for the woman must be rightfully granted to her irrespective of these differences which are natural.

The singer Madonna with her flaunting individuality and sexuality has become a super-icon of this type of liberated woman who celebrates her gender difference. She exploits her sexual power aggressively both in her professional and her personal lives. Although she sang her song "Like a Virgin" so soulfully, purely, she did so standing in her outlandish performing gear of sequinned tin breasts, hot pants, and heavy knee high cowboy boots. She played up her beautiful Madonna like face with eye shadow and blushing powders. She cashed in on her beauty and her sexuality and used her talent as a singer to the hilt, just as a boxer would use his muscles to encash its power. She showed how powerful her beauty was, how powerful her womanhood was, and this power was effectively reflected in the fabulous amount of money that her album brought her. Madonna herself marketed her womanhood to make her personality powerful, she did not let others exploit it. And there lies the differenec. She did not commodify her limbs as a man using her would, but she celebrated the attractive power of her body as a woman should. Yet she pays equal attention to her marriage with her lover Guy Ritchie, and takes care to spend quality time with her two children, Lourdes and Rocco. She has succeeded in becoming a reinvented Madonna of the twentieth century—virgain pure and creative in her singing and loving and strong in her maternal instincts.

In our own context we have actresses like Shabana Azmi and Hema Malini who have used their bodies and talents to acquire money/power in their careers but they have also emphasized their individual, liberated personalities by taking to activism and fighting for women's causes. Hema Malini as editor of the magazine, *New Woman* has given identity to this new persona of the Indian woman who is enlightened enough to articulate her being in whatever way comes to her homemaker career woman, writer, performer, as pure woman, etc.

Equality of opportunity would mean valorising and empowering all those jobs which are generally the domain of women, like nursing, teaching, home-making etc. both professionally and culturally. It is indeed ironical that institutional cooking as in restaurants and marriage parties is considered "professional" and is appropriated by men whereas cooking in the home continues to be regarded as un-technical and as "no work" and is attached to the woman! "No pay" for this work as well!

While Luce Irigaray argues that social change can take place when our laws reflect and recognize sexual difference between men and women, Collette Guillamin and Christine Delphy argue that historically the concept of difference especially has been used to keep women oppressed.

The earliest feminist, Simone de Beauvior believed that women were not the "second sex". She wanted no differentiation between the male and the female because she believed such discrimination was manufactured by social expediency. She believed she could not be called the "other" because this would imply the male to be the singular "One" from whom the "other/s" were derived. She argued for an "egalitarian feminism" based on a rehauling of the social system. The "unisex" syndrome of early feminism sprang from her argument.

But, on the other hand, Luce Irigaray believes in the acceptance of the differences which are natural and then the recognition of the other who could be either male or female. She believes in the two sexes, a natural duality and neither is first nor second—they are two, inclusive of their differences. And neither is to be alienated nor exploited if true democracy between individuals has to prevail. Irigaray celebrates the differences and places both male and female on the same plane. Her concept of feminism tries to balance the biological and the social dictates.

The French critic, Helene Cixous, takes still yet another position of recognizing the spirit of androgyny—a third space where male/female meet and merge. Both male/female possibilities exist in women and men where even the natural differences are given their place and then transcended. A man knitting/embroidering/changing diapers should not look any stranger than a woman piloting a plane or wielding a butcher's machete. In fact, in an article in the *Deccan Herald*

(13.02.2002). Dinesh Kumar makes an interesting argument for a "right touch to leadership" from "androgynous managers". He points to the improved gender relationships under such circumstances when he writes; "when my wife was due to deliver a baby, I dropped her at the nursing home and went to work. I returned in the evening to the clinic to be told that she had delivered a baby boy some time around mid-day. On the other hand, the same boy went through joint counselling sessions with his wife during the pregnancy period, was present during the delivery and participates fully in the growing up process of his daughter."

When Gloria Steinem, that highly visible icon of feminism recently married at the age of 66 the California businesman and pilot, David Bale, a man five years younger to her, one realizes that feminism is going places in the modern world. Shere Hite comments on this in the *Sunday Observer*, "Nothing's perfect but my recent research has shown that relationships between men and women have improved enormously. Gloria didn't marry before because the men she met simply did not understand or were not capable of taking in the whole of 'modern woman'."

Things have improved considerably for at least certain sections of our urban society. If not all women at least a majority of the women of middle class families now think of a career as a natural follow up after completing their education. The competitiveness among girls themselves pressurizes them into treading newer paths than their mothers did. The diversity of study courses at their disposal, computerization of many professional work fields, breaking up of the patriarchal family system, economic compulsions, peer pressure, and above all the confidence and support that they have derived from the world-wide feminist movements that have gone on in the background for more than half a century have empowered them. The self awareness about their rights and the courage to fight for these rights are also there to a certain extent.

What is now required is for the other half of the society, the men, to realize that just changing of laws is not enough but changing of minds should accompany it. The need of the hour is for femmenists. When directors of movies like "Fatal Attraction". "The Hand that Rocked the Cradle" or "Viraasat" insist on showing the working woman as all bad and the "family" woman as all good, the backlash against the feminist movement can hit hard. But the answers are in such movies as "Thelma and Louise" "Sleeping with the Enemy" "Fried GreenTomatoes at the Whistlestop Cafe." "Agnisakshi" or "Astitva" where the women learn to walk out of such horrible circumstances of "family".

After all, Marx has said it for all time in these words "No man who oppresses a woman can be free".

As Luce Irigaray maintains in an "Ethics of Sexual Difference", "A revolution in thought and ethics is needed. We need to re-interpret everything concerning the relations between subject and discourse, the subject and the world, the subject and the cosmic, the microcosmic and the macrocosmic. Everything, beginning with the way in which the subject has always been written in the masculine form, as man, even when it claimed to be universal or neutral."

Index

V

W

❑❑❑